OCT 0 8 2001	DATE		

Palestinians: From Peasants to Revolutionaries

Rosemary Sayigh

Palestinians: From Peasants to Revolutionaries

A people's history recorded by Rosemary Sayigh
from interviews with camp Palestinians in Lebanon.

Rosemary Sayigh

With an Introduction by
Noam Chomsky

Zed Press, 57 Caledonian Road, London N1 9DN.

Palestinians: From Peasants to Revolutionaries was first
published by Zed Press, 57 Caledonian Road, London
N1 9DN in April 1979.

ISBN   Hb 0 905762 24 X
        Pb 0 905762 25 8

Printed by Redwood Burn Ltd., Trowbridge, Wiltshire
Typeset by Bread 'n Roses
Designed by An Dekker
Cover Design by Mayblin/Shaw

Cover photo courtesy of Don McCullin

CONTENTS

DEDICATION AND ACKNOWLEDGEMENTS

This book is dedicated to the Palestinians whose experiences it aims to record, the Palestinians of the camps; also to Palestinians under Israeli occupation; and to the people of Tel al-Za'ter for whom no memorial can be adequate.

While recording interviews for this book, I met people of all ages, both sexes, and many different occupations: building labourers, laundry workers, traders and craftsmen, students, mothers of families. I can sincerely say that they are people with whom I should be happy to share a country. May this book convey something of their courage and goodheartedness.

Among the many who helped me I should like to record my particular gratitude to: Shereen Abdul-Razzak, Adnan abu-Hajer, Samir Ayoub, Nabil Badran, Badriyeh Habet, Bayan and Shafiq al-Hout, Hani Mundus, Rabah Mustafa, Sabah Nabulsi, Ahmad Saleh, Hala Sayegh, Bassem Sirhan, Hisham Sharabi, Michael Simpson; none of whom are responsible for errors or tendentious opinions. I should also like to record special gratitude to my family for tolerating my absenteeism.

Royalties from the sale of this book will be given to the Dar al-Sammood (for the orphans of Tel al-Za'ter), and to the Ghassan Kanafani Cultural Foundation.

Rosemary Sayigh
Beirut
November 1978

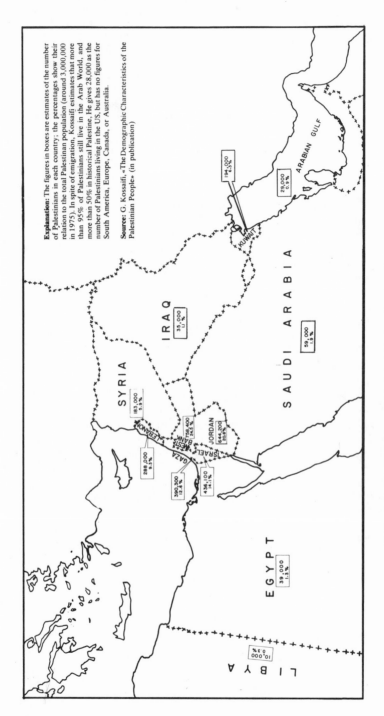

Explanation: The figures in boxes are estimates of the number of Palestinians in each country; the percentages show their relation to the total Palestinian population (around 3,000,000 in 1975). In spite of emigration, Kossaifi estimates that more than 95% of Palestinians still live in the Arab World, and more than 50% in historical Palestine. He gives 28,000 as the number of Palestinians living in the US, but has no figures for South America, Europe, Canada, or Australia.

Source: G. Kossaifi, «The Demographic Characteristics of the Palestinian People» (in publication)

THE PALESTINIAN DIASPORA (1975)

SYRIA

IRAQ

SAUDI ARABIA

EGYPT

LIBYA

JORDAN

LEBANON

ISRAEL

WEST BANK

GAZA

ARABIAN GULF

KUWAIT

183,000
5.9%

288,000
9.3%

390,300
12.6%

436,100
14.1%

758,400
24.5%

644,200
20.8%

35,000
1.1%

59,000
1.9%

194,000
6.3%

29,000
0.9%

39,000
1.3%

10,000
0.3%

INTRODUCTION
BY NOAM CHOMSKY

History is the property of the winners. That is true, generally, of nation, class and individual. The peasants whose voices are heard in Rosemary Sayigh's moving study refer to themselves as 'the donkeys of the earth'. Stories such as theirs rarely enter the chronicles of history. In the industrial societies there is little concern for their fate — with, of course, one notable exception: when some area is liberated from colonial rule, the deep sympathy for the downtrodden, so characteristic of Western sensibility, is suddenly aroused and there are no limits to the indignation over the suffering imposed on poor and innocent subjects of a harsh revolutionary regime. But, at other times, they are merely the donkeys of the earth, unknown to Western humanism.

If donkeys are compelled by the progress of civilization to graze in remote and unaccustomed pasture, or to be confined or set to hard labour, this cannot be considered a troubling moral issue. So we can perhaps understand the lack of concern in the West as the largely peasant society of Palestine, not to speak of the surrounding areas, has been destroyed over the past 30 years. The Puritan clergyman, Cotton Mather of colonial America, once wrote with regard to the decimation of the Indians by disease that 'the woods were almost cleared of these pernicious creatures, to make room for a better growth'. A related sentiment was expressed in more sophisticated modern terms by Chaim Weizmann, the first President of Israel, when the military operations of 1948 led to what he called 'a miraculous clearing of the land: the miraculous simplification of Israel's task'.

American and other Westerners have watched the successive waves of expulsion in silence. The flight of refugees from postwar Indochina, reduced to ruin, starvation and disease by the American war, is a major atrocity; but when, in March 1978 (to take a recent example of Israeli aggression), a quarter of a million Lebanese and Palestinians are driven from their villages and camps by a Western military force armed by the United States, the press and journals of opinion find space only to comment on questions of efficacy and tactics. Similarly, there was barely a whisper when the Jordan valley was cleared or when a million and a half Egyptians were driven from the Suez region (by the estimate of the Israeli Chief-of-Staff, Mordechai Gur) during the 'war of attrition' of 1970. Some

1

400,000 Palestinians, many already refugees, fled or were driven from their homes during the June war of 1967, and, as we know from U.N. Commander General Odd Bull and other sources, for many months afterwards. There were no protests from humanitarians in the West. On the contrary. In 1967, and even more dramatically in 1970, the U.S. alliance with Israel was solidified and aid rapidly increased, as Israel was perceived to be a guarantor of American interests in the region.

Nor was Western opinion appalled at the earlier flight and expulsion of refugees in 1948, under circumstances described vividly in the words of refugees in this book here, and few eyebrows have been raised as Israel since 1948 has ignored repeated calls in U.N. Declarations for resettlement or compensation. Only the 1947 Partition Resolution is sacrosanct; later U.N. General Assembly Resolutions are dismissed as insignificant scraps of paper.

The same is true in the case of the 'minor' expulsions, for example, in the region of Gaza and the North-eastern Sinai, where thousands of *bedouins*, many of them farmers for generations, have been expelled since 1950, with increasing severity in the past decade, to prepare the area for all-Jewish settlement. This has now gained some international attention only because the settlements in the Sinai may stand in the way of a political agreement of the sort favoured by the United States, which, for the present at least, offers nothing to the Palestinians beyond rhetorical pieties.

One of the refugees quoted in this book says that 'in twelve hours we had been changed from dignity to humiliation'. Sayigh's account of peasant life reminds us that the 'donkeys of the earth' before 1948 lived rich and full lives despite backwardness and poverty, that a vibrant and complex village society was destroyed as the land, carefully tended for countless generations, was miraculously cleared. This perception, too, is foreign to Western sensibility. Some of the most disgraceful rhetoric of the dismal Vietnam era was produced by liberal doves who explained the failure of American strategy there, as a 'reasonable strategy' for those 'who love life and fear "costs",' but inappropriate when directed against the peasants of Indochina who know no such feelings and who 'stoically accept the destruction of wealth and the loss of lives'; 'happiness, wealth, power — the very words in conjunction reveal a dimension of our experience beyond that of the Asian poor', who thus invite us, by their apathy, to carry our 'strategic logic to its conclusion, which is genocide', though we then balk, unwilling to 'destroy ourselves . . . by contradicting our own value system' (William Pfaff). To Western commentators, contemplating and explaining to us the mysterious workings of the Asian mind, it seems evident that these miserable peasants do not love life and cannot conceive of happiness. Perhaps such attitudes help explain the disregard for their suffering when the texture of their lives is unravelled as 'civilization' encroaches upon them.

The Jews of Europe suffered a disaster on a scale and of a character unknown in human history, following upon centuries of persecution and terror. Their growing national movement turned back to a homeland that had not been abandoned in memory of tradition. The author of the Balfour Declaration expressed widely-held sentiments in the industrial West when he wrote, in 1919, that 'Zionism, be it right or wrong, good or bad, is rooted in age-long tradition, in present needs, in future hopes, of far profounder import than the desires and prejudices of the 700,000 Arabs who now inhabit that ancient land.' Somehow the Palestinian peasants, mired in their prejudice, were never able to appreciate their moral responsibility to expiate the sins of Christian Europe. Whatever one may think of the conflicting claims to national and human rights in the former Palestine, it is difficult not to be appalled when Western politicians and intellectuals explain their backing for Israel's policies in terms of 'moral obligation', as if the sins of the Nazis and their predecessors, or of the Americans who closed the doors to refugees from Hitler's horrors, require the sacrifice of the Palestinians — on moral grounds. How easy it is to meet one's moral obligations by sacrificing someone else's life.

To see how little the plight and fate of the Palestinian peasant means to the Western mind, consider one of the incidents that is referred to several times in the text that follows — the Israeli occupation of the village of Hula on the Lebanese side of the Lebanon-Israel border in the fall of 1948. A young Lebanese who joined the Palestinian resistance explains that his family fled their village 'because the Zionists carried out a massacre in Hula, a village near ours, where they killed about 70 young men in a mosque'. Some information about this massacre has recently come to light in the Israeli press. A new Secretary-General was recently appointed to head the Jewish Agency, the executive of the World Zionist Organization, which is responsible for substantial development programmes within Israel and the occupied territories. The new Secretary-General, Shmuel Lahis, is none other than the man responsible for the Hula massacre. His commanding officer in the campaign of 1948 wrote a letter demanding that the appointment be cancelled, reporting the events that occurred. Hula was conquered without resistance. Many of the villagers fled, but about 100 who had surrendered remained. The men (over 50 in number, according to R. Barkan who investigated and reported the story for *Al-Hamishmar*, March 3 1978) were confined to a 'house' under the guard of Shmuel Lahis and another soldier, who 'killed all the captives who were in the house with a submachine gun and then blew up the house upon them to be their grave', so the commanding officer reports; the 'house' was in fact a mosque, according to the refugee just cited.

The aftermath of these events is revealing. Lahis was tried and sentenced to seven years in prison. An appeal court reduced the sentence to a year. Lahis awaited approval of the verdict by the Army Chief-of-

Staff under open detention, until the first anniversary of Israeli independence, when he received amnesty. Later, Lahis sought a lawyer's licence. The Israeli Legal Council, considering the matter, determined that what he had done 'was not an act which carries a stigma', so that he was registered as a lawyer in Israel. In fact, Lahis had already received, by then, a second amnesty which, according to the Israeli courts, 'denies the punishment and the charge as well'. The account in *Al-Hamishmar* ends: The villagers of Hula 'relied on their good contacts in the past with the people from over the border at [Kibbutz] Manara, and for that they paid with their lives.' Their murderer now holds one of the highest positions in the World Zionist Organization, with direct responsibility for policies affecting Jews and Arabs in Israel and under occupation.

All of this is unknown in the West, where events in Israel and world Zionism are closely followed and reported in detail. If it does become known, which is most unlikely, it will cause hardly a ripple. Recently I mentioned all these facts to a journalist who had spent 20 years reporting from Israel for a major journal and who continues, in the U.S., to write on affairs relating to Israel. He responded with a shrug, commenting that every war has its atrocities, which is true enough, but hardly to the point. If any of this does become known, it is unlikely to evoke comment from the moralists who write outraged denunciations of Palestinian terrorism.

Rosemary Sayigh's account carries us from the Palestinian society before what its members see as 'the Zionist invasion', through the 'disaster' of 1948, to the pain and torture of exile, and finally to the period when the Palestinian resistance created some form of new social structure within the camps and a hope for the future among those who now say not that they are the 'donkeys of the earth', but that 'everything in our lives is struggle'. It is striking to compare the reports of refugees in the Lebanese camps to those of Palestinians under Israeli military occupation, which we know from other sources. There are many points of similarity, among them the fact that, in effect, all have lived under what amounts to military government. Her study gives a revealing insight into the class character of Palestinian society as it has evolved through these tragedies, and also into the transition from the village loyalties of the peasant past to the emergence of a national movement.

What are the prospects for this national movement? What hope is there for a just peace that will satisfy the legitimate demands of Palestinians and Israeli Jews? It is difficult to offer an optimistic answer to these questions. Sayigh's study does not deal with them. Rather, it provides an invaluable record of the people who have been dispossessed as a result of Zionist successes, then persecuted in their own diaspora and reviled or disregarded in the West, but who have risen with new strength from every defeat.

Noam Chomsky
June 26 1978
Cambridge Massachusetts

PREFACE

Few people would now dispute that the greatest victims of the establishment of the state of Israel have been the Palestinians. As a people displaced from control of their resources by force, deprived of their national territory and identity, condemned to minority status in the countries of others, Palestinians claim the same right of concern from the world as other oppressed peoples, including the Jews. Yet their story has been suppressed, ignored, or distorted through the life-span of several generations, and only with the rise of the Resistance Movement after 1967 have a few solitary Palestinian voices — Mahmoud Darweesh, Fawaz Turki, Fawzi al-Asmar — begun to penetrate the wall of silence. Now it is time that the anonymous voices of the Palestinian masses should be added to these names.

This study aims to reconstruct some small part of the experience of Palestinians who were peasants until 1948, then became refugees, and who re-emerged after 1967 as militants and revolutionaries. The book is based on recorded interviews with camp Palestinians[1] in Lebanon, carried out between 1975 and 1978. About half the interviews took the form of uninterrupted life histories, others were responses to questions about particular aspects and historical phases of the Palestinian experience. The sample was what sociologists call a 'structured' one, chosen to avoid bias as between age groups, the sexes, educational and socio-economic level, and political tendency. In particular, an effort was made to find 'ordinary' Palestinians rather than leaders and spokesmen.

Palestinians: From Peasants to Revolutionaries is people's history, not official history. It is not concerned with great events or leading figures, but with the ordinary people's perceptions of these events, and with the ways they have transformed the lives of those classes of Palestinian — peasants, workers and the small bourgeoisie — who had no cushion between them and the Disaster of 1948. In all the many books on 'the Palestine problem', whether by Zionists or Arabs, the voices of the Palestinian people themselves have been missing. Yet the contemporary Middle Eastern scene is unintelligible without them.

An ethno-historical approach is essential because, from the beginning of the Mandate to its end, Palestinian society was predominantly a peasant one, though this was obscured by the fact that the national movement was led by aristocratic families, large landowners, and city merchants — the '*beys*' and '*effendis*' that provided such a useful target for Zionist propaganda. The first British census of 1921 found that 80% of the indigenous population depended on agriculture, while for the Muslim majority the figure was even higher, 90% (Christians, Jews, and other minorities being mainly urban). Palestine's small *bedouin*[2] component (semi-sedentarized) shared the same general conditions and poverty as the peasant class. And in spite of Jewish immigration, and the growth of industry and urbanization, by 1948 two-thirds of Palestine's Arab population was still rural. There is thus good reason to regard Palestinian society as a peasant society, and its struggle for liberation a peasant-based struggle.

During the whole period of the British occupation (1918-1948), the peasants contributed more than other classes to the national resistance movement; yet they never came close to leading it, or stamping it with their own class character, for reasons that students of peasant societies are familiar with. Of the six reasons that Eric Wolf[3] lists as deterrents to sustained peasant rebellion, perhaps it is the last, exclusion from knowledge, that most closely typifies the situation of the Palestinian peasantry. A *fellaheen* saying, reported by travellers in the mid-19th century, clearly shows their view of themselves in relation to other classes: 'City people are the lords of the world. Peasants are the donkeys of the world'.[4] Self-belittlement is common to most peasantries. But it is particularly deep-rooted in the Arab area, with its ancient cities as the centres of trade, power and Islamic doctrine.

The exclusion from knowledge and decision-making that perpetuated the subordination of Palestine's peasants was deepened under the British occupation. By 1948, only half the country's thousand small villages had schools, and these were only to 4th or 5th grade elementary school. After the Disaster the peasant refugees were to draw a direct relationship between their lack of education and their mass eviction. Moreover, educational inequalities in Palestine contributed crucially to differential life-chances in the dispersion. Palestinians with diplomas were able to find jobs easily in the newly developing Arab countries. Palestinians without education, capital or modern skills — in other words the mass of the peasant/worker/*bedouin* population -- were those who filled the camps. To the marginality of being peasants, was added a new marginality of being refugees.

Their economic transformation from being a class of small peasant-owners and sharecroppers to being a lumpen-proletarian on the fringe of cities, was followed rapidly by a further shift into services, with an emphasis on intellectual occupations, particularly teaching. But these radical economic changes have taken place from a basis of maintaining peasant values. As Bourdieu remarks of the Algerians under French occupation, adherence to tradition was for camp Palestinians in dispersion 'essentially a symbolic function; it played the role, objectively, of a language of refusal'.[5] At the same time the cohesiveness and collectivism of peasant social relations, formed in Palestine as a defence against class subordination, played a crucial role in their capacity to survive the crushing weight of the Disaster. It has been peasant culture and cohesion, not Western-inspired forms of organization, that have carried forward the idea and practice of resistance.

For more than half a century, the experience of the Palestinian masses has been one of constant pressure, crisis, threat and upheaval. Every kind of force has been brought to bear on them to give up their struggle, and to acquiesce in their re-distribution beyond Israel's borders. Yet resistance inside occupied Palestine and outside it, in spite of Israeli power, the 1970 massacres in Jordan, and the bloody two years' war in Lebanon, has not been snuffed out. This tenacity of resistance, continuing even in periods of confused leadership, is a clear mark of Third World peasant struggles, which always tend to become more radical as they encounter internal socio-political obstacles.

It is the position of the Palestinian masses at the heart of the 'Palestine problem' as victims, yet constantly deflected from active struggle to end this status of theirs, that makes them a recurrently militant factor in Arab politics. This is not merely because they are bound to resist, in one way or another, externally imposed solutions to their crisis, but also because their situation in the Arab world, as a 'dependent vanguard', makes them a particularly important focus of analysis of Arab political reality. The acute nature of their crisis forces them to penetrate this reality more profoundly than other Arabs, to diagnose it, to locate false turnings, and to re-think the assumptions of the modernizers and westernizers. Within the Palestinian Resistance Movement are the seeds of resistance to intellectual as well as political dependence.

The rise of the Resistance Movement, situating itself as an anti-imperialist, anti-colonialist liberation struggle like others in the Third World, did not fail to arouse new interest and support from radical groups outside the Arab world. Where an older generation of spokesmen had presented the 'Palestine problem' as a legal case, appealing to a fictitious system of international morality and using a legal and diplomatic language, the new militants spoke a language of defiance and struggle, rejecting altogether the bourgeois system of legality that had alienated Palestine from their parents. Older Palestinians had striven, through carefully correct speech and dress, to prove that they were as 'civilized' as Zionists; new Palestinians spoke to journalists in their shirt sleeves, in barely furnished offices. Yet, in spite of growing ties between the Resistance Movement and other anti-imperialist and anti-colonialist forces, residues of misunderstanding remain.

Some of these residues are best illustrated in the case of Jean-Paul Sartre, whose support of the Algerians is movingly expressed in his Introduction to Fanon's *The Wretched of the Earth*. Sartre's roots in resistance to fascism, and his long-standing ties with Jewish militants, have made him unable to see Israel clearly as a colonial state, or to see Palestinians as fighting a legitimate struggle. In America as in Europe, misperceptions of this kind have prevented campaigns and pressure groups in support of the Palestinians like those that built up around the Vietnam War.

The clearest vision, and most principled stands, have on the whole come from anti-Zionist Jews, though even they are not protected from the charge of anti-semitism. Names that spring immediately to mind are those of Elmer Berger, Moshe Menuhin, Nathan Weinstock, Hannah Arendt, Noam Chomsky, Ania Francos, Israel Shahak, Uri Davis and the Matzpen group. Their work has done more than anything else to strip from Israel the veil of sanctity that protected it from criticism.

Palestinians: From Peasants to Revolutionaries is written for two kinds of reader in particular: first those, whether in the Third World, the Communist countries, or the West, who support the Palestinian struggle in principle, but who know little of the specific social, political and cultural conditions within which the struggle unfolds. Second, all those with a specialist interest in the Arab area — journalists, students, teachers — who know the Palestine problem as an issue, but not as a concrete situation that three million people live daily.

Restriction of the book's focus to those Palestinians living in Lebanon is the result of the poverty of the single researcher, not of theoretical choice. Conditions in the different regions of the dispersion differ markedly. Lebanon has offered Palestinians a mixed bundle of hazards and advantages quite different from those of, say, Jordan. Some of the differences will be pointed out in this book, but there is still not enough information to give a complete overall view. From the perspective of the Palestinian masses, all parts of the *ghourba* are equally alien, and there is little tendency to see some regions as better or worse than others. For them, the total situation of land loss and dispersion is unacceptable, a constant pressure towards revolt. A peasant who has been dispossessed, his moral universe overturned, and then given access to knowledge through modern education, does not easily give up his struggle. His deeply rooted sense of possession, his obstinacy and patience, his long time horizon, combine to make him an enemy more formidable because his weakness is obvious, his strength concealed.

REFERENCES AND NOTES

1. The term 'camp Palestinian' is used throughout this book to mean those poorest classes — whether of peasant, *bedouin*, or city origin — who have spent a considerable period in, or on the edge of, refugee camps, or in low-income areas that resemble camps in all but name, in the various Arab countries bordering Palestine.

2. For all Arabic words see the Glossary.

3. E. Wolf, 'On Peasant Rebellions' in T. Shanin, (ed.), *Peasants and Peasants Societies*, (Penguin, London, 1971).

4. Another version of this ancient folk-saying gives the *bedouin*, not the city-dwellers, the status of 'lords'. The *bedouin* were as poor as the peasants, but enjoyed greater freedom from government oppression.

5. Quoted by E. Wolf, in his *Peasant Wars of the Twentieth Century*, (Faber, London, 1971).

1

THE PEASANT PAST

'Romantics to the contrary, it is not easy for a peasantry to engage in sustained rebellion. Peasants are especially handicapped in passing from passive recognition of wrongs to political participation as a means of setting them right.'
(E. Wolf[1])

'The (Palestinian) peasants are more prone to action and to revolt entailing self-sacrifice than other groups of society.'
(A.W.Kayyali[2])

'WE LIVED IN PARADISE'

'We lived in Paradise': this remark, so often heard from older Palestinians in the refugee camps, would be dismissed by many as mere sentimentality. It is true that these dispossessed peasants have recalled their homes in Palestine from a present so bleak that their poverty and class oppression there tend to be blurred. But there is truth in their view of peasant life as good, for, in spite of poverty, 'our land provided us with all our needs'. Village and clan solidarity formed a warm, strong, stable environment for the individual, a sense of rootedness and belonging. The proof of the strength of peasant social relations is that they survived in dispersion and helped Palestinians themselves to survive. They formed, too, an unbreakable umbilical cord that ties newborn Palestinians to the country that formed their forebears.

If the dominant image is one of Paradise Lost, probing into the people's recollections of village life brings up a wealth of concrete detail that gives depth and solidity to the picture. Anthropologists have often commented on the print-like memories of illiterate people. Where camp Palestinians are concerned there are two other social factors that reinforce group memory: the continuation of village groupings in the camps; and the daily gatherings of kinsfolk and neighbours in which conversation reverts back to Palestine, as a magnet needle points north. There is no detail of village life, from crops to quarrels, that people cannot remember in microscopic detail, in spite of — or perhaps because of — the completeness of their severance from their past.

Reconstructing this past through the views of contemporary camp Palestinians has several values. As folk history, it corrects the biases of the official historians. Most books on Palestine, even those not exclusively Zionist, have given little place to peasant conditions and culture. Even when writing of the uprising of 1936-39, essentially a peasant rebellion, there is a tendency either to skim over the peasants' role, or to view them as 'brigands', 'armed gangs', or 'wild young men'.[3] It is not surprising that camp Palestinians who have reflected on their past feel that their true history is well expressed by a self-educated labourer from Nahr al-Bared camp in Lebanon:

'The problem is that there is a break between Palestinian traditions and us. I am a Palestinian, yet if you want me to remember Palestinian traditions, it's very little. *Between my reality and the false history they've taught us there's no connection.*'

Yet the same man, who left Palestine at the age of seven, could remember vividly many details about his village:

'If you ask me about my village, I can remember the most important things, and even the small ones. I think the reason for this is deprivation. Second, our families would always talk about the past, and about their land, so that these things are impressed on the mind of the Palestinian child. He feels the difference between that life and this. He longs for that life to continue, and to make his own life a part of that country (Palestine).'

Re-creating Palestine through memory was not only a natural reaction to forcible separation, it was also a way — the only way — of passing on to children the homes that were their inheritance, even though they might be hawking Chiclets on the beaches of Beirut. At the same time there is a political element in this remembering, a denial of Zionist power to appropriate the peasants' environment and turn it into an armed fortress against them. Ex-peasant Palestinians know well that most of their villages have been erased or turned into Israeli settlements,[4] but this knowledge does not sever their ties with the land; instead it politicizes them. When the Palestinian quoted above says he 'longs to make his own life a part of that country', this, for him, involves political action: joining a Resistance group, defending his camp, organizing with fellow workers, working for the Return.

Militants in the camps tend to dismiss as unproductive the aimless mourning of the *jeel Falasteen*:[5] 'All their talk is about their own particular case, their land, their trees, their home, their position. . .' 'Old men, they used to speak about Palestine, their crops, their cows. Now they speak about the Revolution. But it is empty, useless.' At the same time, this remembering was a vital link with their country for young Palestinians born outside it. Something of the impact on them of their parents' tenacious holding-on to Palestine can be felt in this quotation from a 17-year old schoolgirl:

> 'Once at home — it was when Abu Ammar went to the U.N. — the conversation changed to the past, and how they used to live. And when they spoke, they wept, because of their attachment to their country. Whoever sits with them can understand more about Palestine than from going to meetings, because they lived the life. . . But what affected me most was their weeping, because their land was so dear to them.'

Darkening Crisis

The goodness of life before the Uprooting is only one side of the coin. Side by side with the image of Paradise Lost, stands a counter-image of darkening threat and crisis. It is very definitely not a Golden Age that is remembered, it is foreign occupation, oppression, violence, anxiety. Even though the villages kept much of their self-sufficiency, the effects of the Zionists' pressure on land and their boycott of Arab labour were felt from early on in the Mandate. It was the peasants who rioted in Jaffa in 1921 and in Jerusalem in 1929; it was the peasants who followed Sheikh Qassam[6] into the hills above Haifa in 1935, and who bore the brunt of the Great Rebellion of 1936-39. There are still old men in the camps who fought in that uprising, and everyone over the age of thirty-five can recall the crescendo of violence that preceded the Uprooting of 1948. Thus when people are not emphasizing the contrast between their present reality as refugees and their past as peasants in Palestine, there is no tendency to paint the past in unreal colours. On the contrary, they emphasize the continuity between the struggle in Palestine before the Disaster, and the struggle outside it afterwards. They have an image of Palestine as a continual target of invasion, as a precious land coveted by others; and linked to this image stands another of tenacious peasant struggle to hold on to their land, in spite of the superior force of the enemy, and the weaknesses of Palestinian/Arab leadership. It is in the historical continuity of this struggle that contemporary militants place themselves. And in this time-view, the present phase of dispersion is simply the most extreme of many forms of oppression that Palestinians have survived.

For even though the peasants were the backbone of Palestinian resistance to British occupation and Zionist immigration (just as their children have formed the fighting base of the Resistance movement today), they were also deeply embedded in a social structure and way of life that prevented them from understanding the full measure of the threat that faced them. They had lived under many occupations, but none had ever displaced them from their land. They knew the Zionists aimed to possess Palestine,[7] but they could not imagine a world in which such a thing could happen. Their belief in themselves, their ignorance of Zionist power (based on organization, not numbers), their old-fashioned concept of war,[8] their naive dependence on Arab promises of help: all these prevented them from fully understanding what was happening in the Forties, as Zionist preparations to take over the state mounted. Looking back at their peasant parents, today's Palestinians see them as goodhearted and patriotic, but politically unconscious. For the generations born outside Palestine, the *jeel al-nekba*,[9] political consciousness is the supreme good, the key to successful struggle. Sacrifice, steadfastness, faith — all the traditional peasant virtues — are still needed as the moral basis of struggle. But the lesson of the Disaster was that these qualities were not enough; they had to be guided by a correct political ideology, which could only be the product of consciousness. Only with consciousness would the defects of earlier uprisings be finally eliminated:

> 'They told us, "Palestinians you fought". It's true we fought, but how did we fight? Under what political line did we fight, under which leadership, and with what programmes? All these were missing.'[10]

Village Worlds and Consciousness

> 'The heart of rural society was the village. . . The majority of Palestinians were gathered into somewhat more than one thousand villages of varying size and fortune. After the extended family, the village was the most important unit in the fellah's life. Its functions were not only social and economic, but, in the broadest sense, political as well.'[11]

The division of the *fellaheen*[12] class into village units is the first determining factor to be grasped in understanding their social organization and consciousness. While the class category of *fellah* was commonly used, by the peasants themselves as well as other classes, to denote a hereditary occupation, place of residence, social status and way of life, it did not indicate more than an embryonic class consciousness. For, in identifying himself and his loyalties, the peasant would always refer to his village. A militant who has worked both among peasants in Egypt and amongst the sons of Palestinian peasants in the Resistance Movement, points out this fundamental difference between the two:

> 'At first I didn't notice any similarities between Palestinian and Egyptian peasants. Perhaps what surprised me most about Palestinians was their mobility; later I discovered that they are more attached than I thought to the land, to localities. I was faced by the problem of their regionalism: this one comes from Nablus, that one from 'Allar. They are deeply attached to their village, their first circle of belonging. The Egyptian peasant never says where he comes from unless he is asked repeatedly, and even then he never gives the name of his village, but the name of his province or its capital. But the Palestinian names his village first.'

The strength of village identification is clear from the way it has persisted in the camps. Quite small children usually know what village they come from, and village consciousness persists in spite of the fact that it has been overlaid by a Palestinian national consciousness, imbued by the Resistance movement.

While there are political and ecological factors that account for the difference between Egyptian and Palestinian peasants described above (particularly the weakness of central state power in Palestine, compared with its strength in Egypt), there are also factors internal to Palestinian peasant culture, particularly the population stability of villages. Their four or five constituent families remained the same for generation after generation. Few came and few left, except through birth and death. The occasional wealthy farmer who migrated to the city would keep his family home and plot in the village; and later in the Mandate, when pressure on land forced marginal peasants to seek work in the cities, they remained peasant commuters rather than becoming urbanites. Village officials, such as the *mukhtar* and the *imam*, were usually chosen from the local population — only teachers, because of the low level of schooling provided to the villages, were generally outsiders. In the absence of a landed feudal class, and the rarity of urban-to-rural migration, Palestinian villages were socially homogeneous, with relatively slight internal socio-economic differentiation. A village was 'a family of families', closely linked by a common history and continuous intermarriage.

The solidarity of the Palestinian village persisted because of the way it satisfied two sets of needs: those of the state for cheap administration, and those of the peasants for security. From the peasants' perspective, the stability and cohesiveness of village population fulfilled at least three vital functions: defence; continuous exploitation of the soil by families whose rights in land were based on custom, not legal documents; and a suitable milieu in which to carry on their distinctive cultural and social life. Here, for many reasons, the distinction between kin (*qaraeb*) and strangers (*gharaeb*) was crucial. Peasant culture, particularly the concept of family honour, depended for its maintenance on a community whose ancestors had lived together, and whose descendants would continue to live together for all foreseeable time. The key to the preservation of values lay in each family's need for the respect of its neighbours.

An illustration of village cohesiveness is given by Artas, a small village near Jerusalem, which was partially destroyed in a feud in the mid-nineteenth century, its families migrating to other villages in the vicinity. When several decades later they returned to rebuild Artas, all but one of the original families took part in the reconstruction. After the Uprooting the same 'grouping' instinct was a major factor in reconstituting large fragments of Palestinian villages in the camps. A man who had taken part in negotiating a camp site for his village told me that they decided to act collectively because this was the best way to secure their rights. From time immemorial Palestinian peasants had found solutions to their problems in village-based collective action.

The Village as Administrative Unit

Under both Ottoman and British rule the village-as-unit was maintained as the most economical way of taxing and controlling the peasantry. In the Ottoman system, to save the salaries of officials, tax collecting was farmed out to bidders at annual public auctions, usually to city merchants and money lenders. Villages were also expected to supply conscripts for the Turkish Army. These two forms of oppression were accepted by the peasants as part of their fate, and the medium of extracting both was the villages' own authority figures, its *shuyookh*, *wujaha'*, and *makhateer*. The economy of the system is clear from this description:

> 'The government gave the tax farmer a free hand to squeeze what he could from the peasants and, when needed and convenient, would give him the sanction of troops. In return . . . the tax farmer took over many of the police duties of the government.'[13]

Because of the rarity of visits by Turkish officials to the rural areas, and the absence of a local landed aristocracy,[14] class oppression of the peasantry in the Ottoman period was sporadic and diffuse rather than direct. Under the British, tax-farming was abolished and control of the villages became tighter through the proximity of the occupation army's encampments, the frequent visits of district officers, and pressure upon village *mukhtars* to play a stronger official role. As peasant resistance to the Mandate grew more militant, the law and practice of 'collective punishment' was introduced in an attempt to prevent villages from assisting the 'rebels': every house in a village suspected of sheltering the *mujahideen*, would be blown up.

In its relationship to authority, the village also strove to present a united front, patching up feuds to send a strong collective delegation to the *wali*,[15] or District Officer. The son of a former *mukhtar* expressed this fundamental rule of village politics when he said: 'We might have twenty men lying on the ground (from a local quarrel), but when the British came to investigate, we would face them as one man.'

Village Defence

The village revealed its defence function in its position and layout. The frequency of foreign invasion and *bedouin* raids, as well as the danger of malaria in the plains, made the peasants choose hill positions for their villages. From these strongpoints they would send out colonies (*khirbeh*) to the plains (where the soil was more fertile and the rainfall more plentiful) whenever strong central government made it reasonably safe to do so. Unlike many villages in the Mediterranean area, those of Palestine were not walled, but the clustering of their solid, stone-built houses in close formation, with walls almost a metre thick and flat rooftops from which lookout could be kept and stones hurled, made them a formidable obstacle to most attackers. Their invisible defence was their militancy. It was obligatory that every 'son of the village' should respond instantly to the call for defence or attack, without hesitation. Two strongly held peasant values upheld this kind of instant action: *rujuliyyeh* (courage, manliness) and *wajib* (duty, obligation). It was this spirit of collective militancy, called *faza'*,[16] that made whole villages descend on the cities to protest an injustice to one of their sons. A man of 42, from a village near Acre, remembers walking down as a child of five or six, with all the men of the village, to protest against the shooting by Jewish terrorists of one of their members in the police force.

Though this kind of spontaneous militancy would have offered a good basis to prolonged struggle if it had been integrated into a larger military/ political framework, its limitations without such a framework are obvious. The important thing was for the individual peasant to prove his manliness and his readiness to respond to the call of duty. The ultimate success or failure of the *faza'* was not seen as within the peasants' power to influence: it lay with the *wali* — chance, God — factors far beyond their control. Thus the spirit of *faza'* only operated within very narrow limits of accepted peasant class helplessness, effective in sustaining their self-respect, gaining them occasional small triumphs, but totally unable to alter the structural determinants of their oppression. In contrast to the petty wars that villages used to wage against each other over scarce resources (water, land, grazing rights), it is significant that Palestinian history records few general peasant uprisings against taxes, or against the more detested scourge of conscription, which took their most precious possession, their young men, and seldom returned them.[17]

It is not surprising that the population stability of Palestinian villages gave rise to each having its own particular reputation that has carried over into exile. Long after I had started doing fieldwork in a particular camp I discovered that those ex-villagers I was living amongst were notorious for shrewdness, aggressiveness and cunning: a reputation that they thoroughly enjoyed.

Other villages were specially known for their militancy; or for the quality of their fruit or vegetables; or for the beauty of their women. Most developed linguistic particularities, so that even today a camp Palestinian's speech gives away his village of origin. Other cultural products — embroidery styles, songs, folk sayings, dishes — are further evidence of village particularism, which was reinforced by in-village marriage, a custom so strong that it is still the marriage that camp families prefer. For girls, it had the great advantage that they did not have to leave their own family to live amongst 'strangers'. This had the result that the particular traditions of a village, and its ideal of solidarity, were passed on to children as much by mothers as by fathers.

In spite of their strong separate identities, Palestinian villages were not totally isolated from each other, but their links were formal and ceremonial rather than those of active solidarity. They would exchange visits at the time of feasts or in the case of the death of a notable, but their relations remained those of potential enemies (or allies), rivals who must be impressed or placated, rather than being rooted in a common consciousness of their shared class position. True, sectarian consciousness, so strong in neighbouring Lebanon and Syria, was largely suppressed in Mandate Palestine by the rapid development of nationalism. Yet the fact that most villages were predominantly either Muslim, or Christian, or Druze was certainly an added obstacle to their co-operation, particularly as British and Zionist policy emphasized their differences.

Apart from their poverty and low status, particularly their exclusion from knowledge, Palestinian peasants shared with each other values and customs that differentiated them from other classes within Palestine's indigenous population. In common with the *bedouin*, they believed in hospitality to strangers, generosity, loyalty to one's word and to people, the sanctity of an oath, the code of revenge and reconciliation, respect for elders and arbitrators — values not to be found among city people, or not to the same degree. Unlike the *bedouin*, however, they were anchored in the *beit* (home), in the land, in hard work:

> 'They believe in fate, in work, in the group. They are industrious and energetic, proud of their ability to "hit the rocks". They love their land in a very significant way — they touch it, smell it, know it piece by piece, stone by stone.'

Theirs could be called a culture of 'moral familism' in contrast to the 'amoral familism' that Banfield discovered in the villages of Southern Italy.

Recollections of al-Sha'b

Al-Sha'b was a village of about 1,700 inhabitants, in the district of Acre, famed for its olives. Z.K. who now teaches in Lebanon, studying history in his spare time, gave me a description of his village that deserves to be quoted in full as an authentic historical record:

> 'I was born in the city of Acre in 1936, after my father had left al-Sha'b to work in a match factory. He used also to sell *semneh* and oil which he brought from the village. One of the traditions of the village was that when the oldest child is born, especially if it is a boy, the grandparents take him to live with them. I used to love the life of the village and hated to go back to the city; in fact one of the ways they used to tease me was to say they were going to send me back, and I'd shout and weep and curse to show my anger. . .
>
> 'In the village I used to take the horse to drink, and listen to the old people talking, for my grandfather's house was in the centre of the village; it was the *mahwa*, the place where people gathered. Near it there was a *khan* where travellers stayed. I remember they came from Lebanon and Syria, especially from Berjah and Mnineen,

carrying goods to sell in the villages. Sometimes they used to stay in my grandfather's house as his guests. . .

'I remember that my grandfather's house was one of the largest. It had high arches, with storage space for oil and dried goods. There was a fireplace where we used to gather at night to hear stories that my aunt and grandparents would tell. The house had a large separate room for guests, the *mudafeh*, and opposite it there was a place for animals, cows and horses, and for cattlefeed and straw. The house had only one entrance, with a door that was closed with large iron bars. . .

'Outside the house was a raised area called *al-kussa*, where they would gather to discuss the news. I remember that one of the old men used to read aloud from the newspaper which reached the village in the afternoon. There was a bus which used to go three times a day to the city, otherwise people went by horse. They used to carry the village's products — eggs, chickens, figs, grapes — to Acre and Haifa.

'It was a custom of the village to celebrate happy events, such as weddings, jointly. All the people would gather, singing the *a'ataba* and *meyjana*, and dancing the *debkeh*. They'd perform the *sahja*, the ceremony of leading the bridegroom round the village, to the threshing floor, then to his house. He would be on horseback, and the men would walk behind him, singing. Then they'd bring the bride on horseback, with the women singing behind her, to the bridegroom's house. If the bridegroom's family was rich, they would give parties for forty days after the engagement. On the 40th day they'd slaughter and invite the village to supper.

'The house of the oldest member of the clan was the gathering place for all its members, especially at the time of the official feasts. He had to be ready to slaughter several sheep, and invite everyone in the family to eat. My grandfather would not tolerate any member of the family being absent. Usually when they gathered, especially at night in winter, they'd prepare special dishes: (*q*)*ursa* with *semneh* and sugar, *zalabi*, *bseesi*, macaroni, *arakeesh*, and many others. Their basic ingredients were simple — flour, oil, sugar — but they would decorate them like works of art. My grandfather used to cut the decorations himself, with the pruning knife he carried tucked in his leather belt, like all *fellaheen*.

'Another dish they loved was *musakhkhen*, made of bread covered with oil, onions, chicken and spices, which they cooked in a special oven called a *taboon*, made of dried mud. This was considered one of the best gifts that could be sent to people from the village who were living in the city, because they couldn't make it there.

'Everyone in the village grew their own vegetables. They grew beans, tomatoes, okra, under the olive trees or in empty spaces. The vegetables were never sold, they'd give them as gifts to kin or neighbours who hadn't land. Also they grew figs, watermelons, sesame, *fareeki*, all these were given as gifts, never sold. . .

'All the villagers used to go at the same time to harvest the olives, it was by the order of the *mukhtar*. All those who owned land with olives had to go, and any who didn't would be punished by the *mukhtar* or the Council. Representatives from each family sat on this Council to help the *mukhtar* to regulate village affairs. There were two *mukhtars*, one from the western quarter and one from the eastern.

'The *mukhtar* used to be chosen by the village, and officially appointed by the provincial governor. It was considered a position of leadership, but those who experienced it found that it cost a lot. I remember that one of my uncles was a *mukhtar*, and his son refused to inherit the position, on his father's advice. One of the *mukhtar*'s jobs was giving hospitality to missions, and even if his clan helped with expenses, it was still a heavy burden.

'Any stranger passing through the village would also be the guest of the *mukhtar*, or anyone with a guest-house. This was a large room, with mattresses always there, and a charcoal brazier with coffee pots which should always be hot. This was so that whenever a guest came he would find coffee ready, and would say that this guest-house is "living", its owner isn't so poor that he has to wait until the guest comes to make coffee. Usually there'd be more than one guest-house in each clan, not because of quarrels, but out of pride, to show that their homes were always open for hospitality.

'The largest crop of our village was olives, which were produced in great quantities. I remember that there were three mills for squeezing the olives and, when they were working, the dregs would flow in black channels down to Acre, and into the sea. Olives would be piled high in the guest-room of my grandfather's house, and when they took them to the mill, they'd grind them with a stone-mill, not one by one. All the village would harvest the olives, they even had to hire women to help. They used to come from Jweyya and Bint Jbeil in Lebanon. They'd take their wages in olives which they'd either sell or take to the mill for oil.

'The other important crop was sesame. It used to be harvested and put on the threshing floor in big circles until it was dry. Then it would be beaten so that the seeds would fall. They would be put in sacks and sold to merchants in Acre and Haifa. Other products were wheat and maize.

'As for schools, there was the Koranic school, where a *sheikh* taught religion. Only boys went to school, they used to refuse education to girls out of fear of scandals. There was also an official school from 1st to 7th elementary — boys used to come to it from nearby villages, from Mi'ar, Damoun, Kabool and Tamra. They used to teach Arabic, English, science, religion, history and agriculture. At the end of elementary, boys had to go on to Acre, Safed or Haifa to continue their education.

'One of the jobs available to villagers was to be employed by the government in the police. Many villagers took up this work, some reaching quite high positions. It was like a hereditary job — when the father was a policeman the sons would follow him.

'I remember discussions about relations between Arabs and Jews. My grandfather used to talk about the time before there were cars, when he had camels which were used to transport village produce to Haifa, Safed, Tiberias, and sometimes even to Aleppo. He had Jewish acquaintances in Tiberias to whom he used to sell goods. They used to talk, and the Jews would tell him "We are going to be the rulers of this country". My grandfather would get furious, cursing and shouting at them: "We will hit you with sticks and stones and kill you all, you sons of death!"

'I remember my grandfather, during the war of 1948, taking his stick and calling the youth of the village to attack the Jews, "Let's finish off these sons of death!" He thought that the Jews couldn't

> face the Arabs, because he was still mentally in the age of man-to-man fighting, not in the modern age when it's the best weapons that win. Most of the villagers thought like my grandfather, and they would try by any possible means to get hold of a weapon. Many sold a cow or a horse to buy a gun. They used to send missions to Syria and Lebanon to buy guns, especially old German guns, costing anywhere between £P40 to £P100, a lot for a poor peasant. . .'

This description brings out the profound sociability of Palestinian peasant life, and the importance of the celebrations that surrounded all important occasions with joy, in glowing contrast to the toil of everyday life. From the economist's viewpoint, these celebrations seemed wasteful — families would often go deep into debt to cover the week-long feasting that accompanied the marriage of sons. But from the peasants' perspective, celebration was a way of re-distributing surplus, since the richer the family, the more generous its entertaining was expected to be. Through these celebrations poorer peasant families were drawn into the warm circle of village life. Instead of saving, Palestinian peasants spent all that they had, and more, on obligatory gift giving and hospitality, knowing that in time of need they could call on the help of others.

Not just the recollections of survivors, but also the descriptions of anthropologists and travellers,[18] all confirm the sociability and love of life of Palestine's peasants, in tragic contrast to the fate that awaited them. Certainly there was poverty and hardship, for the villages were not Utopia; and there were internal forms of oppression in the influence of richer, larger families, as well as in the structure of the patriarchal family. But these were not severe, mainly because the compulsion in family and village to present a strong front to the outside world gave every voice the right to be heard, and just demands to be satisfied.

As a picture of village life in the last years of the Mandate, this quotation has a particular interest and pathos, coming as it does from a member of the *jeel al-nekba*, a 17-year old girl, based on listening to her grandmother:

> 'The last thing they were thinking of was to leave Palestine. Only a few young men who were educated realized at the end that their country was in danger. There was no consciousness. They lived daily — laughed, played, sang, went on outings. When young men and girls finished their work they would search for a wedding so as to enjoy themselves. All was pleasure. They didn't see the difficulties of life.'

Few awakenings from 'unconsciousness' have been harsher or more abrupt.

The Peasant Family

If the solidarity of 'sons of the village' was one effective defence mechanism against oppression, the solidarity of the peasant family was another. The family unit is the basis of all Arab societies, almost a counter-society in its strength. Amongst the peasants of Palestine, family solidarity was even more strongly developed than amongst other classes, to whom alternative sources of security were available. The absence of a strong state during the Ottoman period, the frequence of *bedouin* raids, the oppression of tax-collector and recruiting officer, the power of the mercantile class: these formed the structural setting within which the peasants' culture of 'moral familism' developed.

Several writers on the Palestinian peasantry have noted their profound domesticity; and the Palestinian anthropologist Tawfiq Canaan, in his study of the different forms of peasant household, quotes many folk sayings on the sanctity of the home, and on the network of superstitions and magic practices that surrounded it. He notes:

> 'The chief festive events in the life of the Palestinian peasant or townsman are three in number: marriage, the birth of male children, and the acquisition of a new house.'

The words most commonly used for house, *beit* or *dar*, are also synonyms for family. Founding a family was, and still is, a basic aim of life, a proof of adult status; and adults without children are pitied as incomplete. Even though a man remained subordinate to his father throughout the latter's whole lifetime, his subordination was lessened by the birth of his own first son.

Like other Arabs, Palestinian peasants were family oriented in feeling and organization, attaching supreme importance to the continuation of the male line ('The most fortunate family is that which is richest in male offspring'). But more than other Arabs, Palestinians enjoy domesticity for its own sake. Unlike Egyptian or Algerian peasants, who are described as spending most of their time outside the home, in male company, and whose houses are divided into public (male) and private (female) areas, Palestinians of peasant origin enjoy the sight and sound of their families. There is no sex segregation of house space, it being treated as an open social meeting ground between kin and neighbours, not as a private domestic preserve.

Of the many layers of kinship found among desert Arab tribes, Palestinian peasants took over only two: the male descent group, called the *hamuleh*; and the individual family/household, the *'a'ileh* (or *beit*, or *dar*). In keeping with its nature as a 'family of families', all relationships between people of the same village were translated into kinship terms, and the language of kinship dominated everyday life,[19] softening differences of power or wealth. Family genealogies were carefully remembered as they were the basis of each family's claim to 'founding member' status in the village. But even more important than the genealogies of each clan was the network of inter-relationships produced by their constant inter-marriage. This was in the forefront of discussion because it formed the basis of intra-village politics. How individuals or families would act in a given situation would depend on the way they evaluated the tug and pull of different relationships, interests and obligations.

The Family Collective

As in many other peasant economies, the family household was both production and consumption unit — a family collective. Its size, and the practice of pooling its labour and income, enabled it to survive in bad times, expand in good ones. Its economy was based primarily on its rights to family and communal village land, its labour power, and the social ties that could be converted into material aid when needed.

Although the nucleus of each household was a man and his wife, its composition indicated a much broader social and economic function than that of Western 'nuclear' families. Besides the couple's unmarried children, a Palestinian peasant family normally included their married sons, with their wives and children. This meant a large male and female labour group, more or less controlled by the father and the mother-in-law. It also meant that children were as much brought up by grandparents as by parents. And, in addition, the peasant household might include any, or all, of the following: widowed parents of the household head; widowed, divorced or unmarried female relatives of the household head; the children of sons who had died. Ideally, and in practice, the peasant family incorporated into itself all those who in other communities would have been isolates, left to fend for themselves. Such was the poverty of the villagers that very often all these people would sleep together in one room, though ideally extra rooms would be built round the courtyard for married sons.

The size and structure of the peasant family collective fitted Palestine's system of agricultural production and land tenure, both of which called for a year-round, medium-sized labour force. Because of the way village land was divided under the communal *masha'* form of tenure, family holdings were normally widely scattered.[20] Most areas sustained mixed, rather than single, crop farming, so that there was no season of the year without work to do. The fruit and olive trees that gave Palestinian peasants their slightly higher living standard than other Arab peasantries required year-round attention. Apart from the steel ploughshare, most farm implements were made by the peasants themselves. All these labour requirements meant that, unless the family's land was very small, the contribution of several adult sons was needed. Only as the pressure on land increased, and the average size of peasant family holdings diminished, did young men begin to look for work in the cities. Faced with the dilemma of too many mouths to feed and too little land, many families put their brightest sons through secondary school in the city, keeping the less promising ones to work on the land.

Women had as much to do as men in the family collectives, probably more. Besides normal domestic labour and childcare, it was they who dried and stored the foodstuffs on which the family would live in winter: grains, pulses, olives, olive oil, dried fruits. They tended the orchards that encircled the villages, looked after poultry, and often worked side by side in the fields with the men. Their strength can be felt in the way their children recollect them proudly as 'peasant-mothers', working unceasingly between home and field, carrying water and gathering firewood. In everyday language, woman and the home were symbolically linked: women were its basis not only through their childbearing function, but also through their economic contribution. And more than men, it was the women's job to maintain the network of social relations on which village and family solidarity depended. Their subordination in the patriarchal family, with its glorification of male heirs, was contradicted by the strong role played by women in everyday life. And though this was rare, women sometimes owned land and managed it themselves.[21]

The value of children to the peasant family was, and still is, basic. They are the key to its future, the guarantee to parents of a happy, respected old age, the ultimate reward for hard labour and the burden of parental responsibility. The pressure towards early marriage and large families goes beyond any simple economic explanation, such as that labour was the only factor of production that peasants could easily increase. Certainly a number of different factors contributed to the 'child-centred' culture of the peasant, especially high infant mortality,[22] conscription, and the need for a relatively large family labour force. But apart from these obvious ecological and economic factors, there is also the Palestinians' profound love of all fertility, natural or human, evident in a hundred small sayings of everyday life, for instance the custom of thanking a host with the words 'Farhattin, insha'allah'.[23] No event in the village was celebrated with greater joy and expense than a wedding.

Family Consciousness

Looking back at certain aspects of the solidarity of the clan (hamuleh), for instance the code of revenge,[24] most camp Palestinians today see them as 'backward'. Clan consciousness has given way to Palestinian national consciousness on the one hand, and a generalized family solidarity on the other. Honour killings[25] still occasionally occur in the camps, but it would be hard to find anyone to defend them as part of the Palestinian cultural heritage. Rather, they are looked at as a symptom of political frustration. When in 1973, after a serious confrontation with the Lebanese regime, there was a spate of five honour killings in Tell al-Za'ter camp, a deputation of women went to Abu Ammar to ask him to stop this kind of crime which had almost died out in the refugee period.

Other aspects of family solidarity are highly valued and consciously preserved, particularly the custom of giving help in time of sickness or unemployment — this, far more than U.N.R.W.A., has been the basis of camp Palestinians' economic survival. Many families and *haras* maintain collective funds, used mostly for education or medical expenses. Other traditional village forms of charity have persisted in the camps. For instance, the family I lived with during fieldwork had lost its chief male wage-earner, and every time a sheep was slaughtered in the quarter in fulfilment of a vow (for example, if a sick person recovers) our family would receive a portion, along with other needy families. Again, when a boy from the *hara* was hit by a passing car, one of his uncles instantly paid the large deposit required by most Beirut hospitals before they admit a patient.

The solidarity of the village and the solidarity of its families were not in contradiction, but reinforced each other. Quarrels and feuds were part of the stuff of village life and never seriously threatened economic co-operation or social cohesion. The tendency to feud, inherent in the scarcity of resources, and magnified by competition for honour and status, was balanced by the constant striving for reconciliation (*'atwi*). Conflict generated peace-creating mechanisms, the strongest of which was social pressure towards healing the breach. The minute a quarrel broke out — I have seen the same thing happening in the camps — a dozen people would start working to restore good relations. The indispensable visits to condole on the occasion of a death were often taken advantage of to reconcile feuding families. Intra-family conflict was controlled in a similar way, with women playing the main peace-keeping role.

The strict laws of peasant morality, particularly in regard to women, were enforced through the concepts of honour and reputation, which made each family the censor of the behaviour of its own members. The clustering and openness of village homes deprived them of privacy, just as the size of peasant families ensured that no one was ever alone. Fear of gossip was a sufficiently powerful source of control because of the consensus about values and the closed nature of the village world. There was no dissenting minority. Villagers might dispute about whether so-and-so had violated a particular point of the code; but they did not dispute the code itself. Loyalty to custom was one of the ways peasant families competed, and still compete, just as they compete now in loyalty to the Revolution.

It is a sign of the strength and resilience of the peasant family that it continues to exist in the camps, in spite of its severance from the land that was the material basis of the father's authority. The educational level and earning power of the young is now above that of their parents, but though the control of family elders over the young has been shaken, the family collective has survived. Most of the families I met during fieldwork were compound in structure, with married sons still living at home, and pooling expenditure. Adult offspring working abroad send back a large part of their earnings. When possible they form a family base in the country of work migration, not unlike the way Palestinian hill villages used to send out colonies to the plain.

Some of the tenacity of Palestinian peasant family cohesion can be felt in this observation by a camp organizer:

'Once I saw a child who died, a child from a village. People came from all over Lebanon for his funeral,[26] people from his family and his village, while perhaps if we had invited them to a political rally they wouldn't have come. Why is this? The answer is that there's no alternative for protection. It's only this belonging that gives them security.'

ECONOMIC SITUATION OF THE FELLAHEEN UNDER THE MANDATE

From time immemorial the peasants of Palestine had formed the tax and conscript basis of successive occupations: Roman, Byzantine, Arab, Ottoman, and now British. With the expulsion of the Turks in World War 1, and the occupation by the British, Palestine finally entered the trade circuit of the capitalist world, becoming fully exposed to the changes summed up in the word 'modernization'. Palestine's indigenous pre-capitalist economy continued to exist side by side with the separate Zionist economy[27] (with its unique mingling of socialist ideology and capitalist funding), and as in all cases of colonialism, the indigenous economy subsidized the invading one, besides providing the tax basis to finance its own occupation. Although the incipient Palestinian bourgeoisie suffered in its development from the more advanced organization and technical skill of Zionist enterprise and labour, it also benefited from increased trade, and from employment in the British administration.[28] It was the interests of the *fellaheen* that were more directly threatened by Zionist colonialism. This was because, while Zionist land purchase put an ever growing pressure on the supply of land, the Zionist boycott of Arab labour cut off alternative sources of income, whether in agriculture or industry. Thus the oppression of the peasant class changed under the Mandate from the type produced by Arab/Ottoman feudalism to a colonial type somewhat similar to that of Algeria or South Africa.

Basic Causes of Peasant Poverty

The causes of the poverty of the *fellaheen* of Palestine were similar to those of other Middle Eastern peasantries, and can be grouped into three main categories: i) difficult climatic and soil conditions; ii) class subordination; iii) absence of a positive state contribution.

Zionists exaggerated both the 'backwardness' of Palestine's peasants, as well as the potentialities of the land under their own management. For this reason it is useful to turn to geo-economic realities. Of Palestine's total

land area of 26,323,023 *dunums*,[29] almost half was (and is) too
mountainous or too arid to be cultivated except with lavish capital
investment. A good summary of Palestine's agricultural possibilities is
given by Ruedy:[30]

> 'While the inhabited portion possesses scattered valleys of
> exceptional fertility, the steepness, the high limestone base, the
> many rocky out-croppings, and the dependence upon unpredictable
> rainfall, give it an agricultural rating ranging from mediocre to
> incredibly poor.'

Ruedy adds, significantly:

> 'This poverty has been partially attenuated through exploitation of
> occasional springs and streams in the valley and *through centuries of
> painstaking terracing of hillsides.*'

Doreen Warriner also notes the shallowness and infertility of Palestine's
top soil: 'Its grain yields are the lowest of any Middle East country.'[31]

Cultivable land in Palestine was divided into two distinct types: *sahel*,
the coastal plain, and *jebel*, the hill country, and peasant exploitation of
these two very different areas depended on the overall political situation.
Cultivation of the rich alluvial plains gave a much higher yield, but the
fellaheen's access to it reflected their lack of power as a class. For while
their hill villages usually owned land in the plains, erecting temporary
dwellings for harvesting only, or the more permanent *khirbeh*, the richer
land attracted other cultivators. By the late 19th century the *sahel* had
begun to draw big city merchants, from as far away as Aleppo and Beirut,
because of the growing profitability of cash crops. And it was the sale of
some of these large non-Palestinian-owned latifundia to Jewish settlers that
caused the first peasant riots, even before the beginning of the Mandate.[32]

The second, much stronger pressure upon peasant exploitation of the
sahel came from the highly capitalized nature of Zionist agriculture, which
needed large, flat areas where machinery could be used. So, gradually, the
fellaheen were pushed back into the less fertile, less watered, more difficult
mountainous areas where their patient labour could eke a sufficient living
from soil that Arab capitalist and Zionist colonialist alike avoided. A
Palestinian economist noted in 1946:

> 'There is a quite marked conformity between the direction and
> stretch of Jewish owned land and the edge of the rich plains . . . it
> can be seen that the best land in Palestine, both for tree plantation
> and cereals, has fallen into Jewish hands, leaving for the Arabs the
> hilly and mountainous regions as well as most of the uncultivable
> land which is not State Domain.'[33]

In much the same way, though a hundred years earlier, French
colonists had settled upon the rich Algerian coastal plain and pushed the
indigenous peasantry back into the mountainous interior.

Village Self-sufficiency

Rain-fed cereals were Palestine's major agricultural product at the turn of the century, within a general agricultural system that Eric Wolf, in his study of world peasantries,[34] terms 'paleotechnic', characterized by the use of the scratch-plough and draught animals.[35] The possession of oxen was economically as important to a Palestinian peasant as ownership of land, since with oxen he could more easily enter into a profitable crop-sharing arrangement with a landowner, instead of becoming a mere *harrat*, or ploughman.[36]

Although Palestine had long been an exporter of high quality agricultural products (mainly grains, olive oil, soap, sesame and citrus fruit), the development of cash crops and market farming was restricted mainly to a few areas near the cities, at least until the World War II boom in the price of agricultural products towards the end of the Mandate. Cash crops were mainly financed and traded by city merchants through long-standing arrangements with particular villages, leaving the mass of peasants close to a subsistence economy. Rather than markets, the primary aim of peasant agriculture was subsistence and the payment of taxes and debts. The extent to which the bulk of peasant production stayed out of the markets can be gauged by the fact that, as late as 1930, only 20% of the total wheat crop and 14% of the barley crop were marketed.[37]

We have already seen in the description of *al-Sha'b* that fruit trees and vegetable patches were maintained by peasant families for their own consumption, and that there was little internal sale of these products. Accounts of village economies in the last years of the Mandate suggest that, in villages near cities, the transition to market farming was well under way, with the more entrepreneurial peasants turning into traders, like a man from al-Bassa who used his small passenger transport fleet to move fruit and vegetables from low-price to high-price areas. But the poor state of the roads and the lack of large, local markets slowed down this development. There were no state subsidized co-operatives, no cheap agricultural credit. The self-sufficiency of Palestinian villages, based on the wide range of foodstuffs they could produce and the only slight development of markets, did not change greatly under the Mandate.

The effects of this economic self-sufficiency upon Palestinian peasant consciousness and organization is suggested by this comparison between Egyptian and Palestinian peasants:

'The Egyptian village is not self-sufficient, it cannot live independently of the city, whereas the Palestinian village produced grain, fruits, vegetables and had certain artisan skills as well. The Egyptian village produces one crop, and depends on other areas to supply its basic needs. For instance, Upper Egypt, where they produce mainly sugar-cane, has to get its rice from other areas.

'This means that a Palestinian village could go on strike for six months, whereas an Egyptian village can't last more than one or two weeks. This deepened the sense of belonging in the Palestinian village, and its opposite in the Egyptian village.

In Palestine, two neighbouring villages could quarrel and cut their links. But an Egyptian village has to calculate, before quarrelling with a neighbouring village, whether it will be able to reach the town or not, because the town is indispensable to it.'[38]

For Palestinian peasants, the city had never been economically indispensable. They looked to the cities for leadership, as the crisis generated by Zionist immigration intensified; but until their final 'cleaning' from their land in 1948, the villagers still produced the bulk of their foodstuffs. During the summer of the war, many were the peasants — women and children as well as men — who crept back through the Israeli lines to retrieve the stocks of grain without which they could not live. Cash was a scarce commodity in the villages and banking had hardly begun to penetrate them.

Class Oppression: from Ottoman to British Rule

The absence of a positive state contribution to the rural areas of its Arab domain during the decline of the Ottoman Empire has been well described by Weulersse, a student of Marc Bloch, whose study of the peasants of Syria[39] gives one of the best accounts of the historical and structural determinants of Arab peasant poverty. The only weakness in Weulersse's account is that it excludes all but endogenous factors, such as absentee landlordism, the slightness of links between city and village, and the ancient contempt for the *fellaheen* generated by the Islamic empire's dependence on the *bedouin* for its military basis. It is to other writers[40] that we must turn for an idea of the decline of village handicrafts and prosperity during the early modern period, as a result of the penetration of modern capitalism.

But though the Ottoman state gave little to the peasants (not even a system of justice),[41] it took from them both taxes and conscripts. One writer estimates an annual loss in time of war of between 10 and 20,000 men, and camp Palestinians can still recall fathers and grandfathers who died in the Turkish Army. There can be little doubt that this form of oppression helped to create the pressure towards early marriage and maximum child production that makes the Palestinian birth rate one of the highest in the world.

Peasants had little chance to escape the payment of the state tax or tithe, especially as, if Granott is to be believed,[42] their own clan-leaders and *mukhtars* co-operated with the tax-farmers in extracting it from them. This description based on a 19th century traveller's gives a vivid picture of peasant poverty:

'From the stocks of wheat and barley which were left after the threshing, they first paid the taxes to the Government and the *waqf*. As a rule part of the produce was already long ago mortgaged to a

merchant from town from whom the *fellah* had borrowed money. . .
If the peasant had engaged a hired worker, a *harrat*, he also received
from the threshing what was due to him. Then the village priest, who
also acted as barber, now came for his payment. . . Also the
dervishes, the poor priests of the village, and the blind and leprous
all came in swarms to the threshing floor . . . and only rarely did
they go away empty handed. It was the lot of many a peasant, after
he had satisfied all the demands on his produce, whether justified or
not, to be left with the bare minimum required for feeding his
family and his beast until the next harvest.'[43]

A further deterioration in the peasants' situation came about when the
Ottoman government tax became payable in cash instead of grain. Severely
disadvantaged in negotiating the cash equivalent of the tithe, peasants were
delivered, bound hand and foot, to the moneylenders. Usually they were
forced to borrow from the same merchants who bought their crop and
advanced them seed, a situation of maximum vulnerability because it left
them no negotiating power, either in the price of the crop, or in the rate of
interest on loans. Interest rates varied between 30% and 200%.

The magnitude of the peasants' inherited debt burden at the time of the
Johnson-Crosbie investigation of 1930 is staggering. On the basis of data
collected from 12% of all villages, and 26% of all rural families, the
investigators calculated an average debt per family of £P27, and an average
yearly interest on debt of £P8. These figures must be set against an average
annual income for rural families of £P25 to £P30.

An even clearer picture of peasant indebtedness is provided by the
Johnson-Crosbie Report's breakdown of the 241 villages they investigated
into four categories: i) the majority (84) that were just able to meet cost
of living expenses; ii) those (70) that were able to meet cost of living
expenses plus taxes; iii) those (56) that were able to meet cost of living
plus taxes plus rent; and iv) the minority (31) that were able to meet all
these costs, plus interest on debt.

Most English histories of Palestine dwell on the evils of tax farming and
point to its abolition early in the Mandate as a sign of progress. But from
the peasant viewpoint British tax collection, though more honest, was
more oppressive. The tithe was a fixed percentage of the wheat crop only,
and though the tax farmers squeezed the peasants to the maximum, they
had no interest in making them bankrupt, or forcing them off the land.
The peasants' debts carried over from one year to the next, and from one
generation to the next, and carried no threat of eviction. Under the British,
however, all peasant property, not just their wheat crop, was taken as a
basis of tax evaluation, including fruit trees, houses, 'even our chickens'.
Not only was British assessment more thorough, but taxes were now
collected with the help of troops, whereas in Turkish times it was rare that
the provincial governor had enough troops at his disposal to terrorize the
villages.

The Mandate Government ordered a series of enquiries into the economic conditions of the villages, but it did very little to improve them. A man from Sa'sa (north of Safed) contrasts the actual poverty of his village under the British Mandate with its potential prosperity:

> 'I remember that in Sa'sa, which was famous for its olives, grapes and figs, the peasants produced thousands of kilos of figs each year. But there was no market. The British wouldn't encourage the selling of this good quality fruit, or help to pack it or export it. It was hard for the peasant to market his crop himself because the roads between the villages and the cities were bad. And after the peasant had harvested his wheat, the British would bring in cheap wheat by ship from Australia, and sell it in Haifa at ½ a piastre a kilo, knowing that the peasants could not sell at this price. It was British policy towards the peasants that they should always stay poor.'

Peasants were the class most directly oppressed by the tax system, Turkish or British, since, unlike the *bedouin*, they were tied to a single, identifiable locality; and unlike the city traders, they had no means to bribe. Their economic and social isolation from the city meant also their subordination to the city, as the centre of knowledge and the new money economy. Again unlike the *bedouin*, they were not linked to the ruling class by tribal leaders,[44] but only through more fragile patron/client links that could be manipulated for individual, but not group, interests.

The Changing Land Tenure System

Peasant poverty and peasant survival were also rooted in a system of land tenure that had begun to change under Westernizing pressure, and to the detriment of the *fellaheen*, in the middle of the 19th century. The Islamic jural view of land was that ultimately it belonged to the whole Muslim community (*al-'umma*), which in effect meant the state. But the collectivism of its ideal form naturally did not prevent the emergence of private, inheritable property. The renting out of state land (*miri*) was an important source of state revenue; *de facto* inheritance of this, as of other types of public land, for example the religious endowments called *waqf*, had the political effect of stabilizing the class structure, while maintaining the legal possibility of reversion to the state as a political weapon. The prebendal form[45] taken by feudal estates, in both the Arab and Ottoman empires, had the same characteristic of revocable private ownership, while at the peasant level, tenancy — the right to farm a given plot of land — passed from father to son in undisturbed succession until the mid-19th century. Neither the state, nor the large landholders, nor the tax farmers, had any interest in disturbing the peasant's tenancy, since it was the taxes and rent they produced that government and fief-holder wanted. The land itself had practically no market value. For the peasant it was unthinkable that 'for some whim of the government he could lose the land which is his livelihood'.[46]

What the Ottoman Land Reforms of 1856 and 1858 did was to lay the legal basis for fully private, disposable ownership of land. This was followed by the beginning of registration of land in the name of individuals. The significance of these measures from the point of view of the peasants can only be fully grasped if their class powerlessness is understood. Unlike large landholders and tribal leaders, they lacked the power needed to convert customary land use into legal land tenure. Indeed they did not grasp the meaning of the new laws, nor the concept 'ownership', so foreign was it to their own concept of 'rights'. In Palestine:

'. . . fearing that the tax collector and army recruiter would make effective use of the new registers, and hardly understanding the enormous importance of the new records and deeds to their own future, when the implementing regulations of the code began to be applied, they evaded massively and stubbornly.'[47]

Evasion took the form of registering land in the name of dead or fictitious persons; or, more dangerously, 'in the name of any important or influential man who could seem to offer some protection'[48] — *shuyookh*, notables, city merchants, even tax farmers. A.L.Tibawi[49] suggests that city merchants and money lenders purposely misrepresented the new land laws to the peasants, so as to persuade them to give them title. In the same way, *bedouin* tribal land was registered in the names of individual chiefs, and passed into their hold. The relationship of peasants to land thus legally alienated became that of tenants who could be evicted at will. Eviction, a commonplace in the history of European peasants, was a new, deeply threatening experience for Arab peasants. Not surprisingly, the first outbreaks of peasant violence in Palestine occurred with the first large land sales by absentee landlords to the Zionist immigrants.

With the local privatization of land began the polarization of landownership, throughout the Fertile Crescent area, into very large estates, usually run by agents for landlords who lived in cities, and very small plots that only supported peasant families through the survival of communal village land rights, and through wage labour. After describing the miserable poverty of Syrian peasants, mainly landless tenants on large estates, Weulersse remarks that the polarization of landownership was much less extreme in Palestine. There, the majority of peasants had some land, though of inadequate size.

In 1936, the British Government carried out an investigation of 322 villages, upon which the ownership breakdown in the Table below is based.

LAND OWNERSHIP IN PALESTINE — 1936

Size of holding (in dunums)	Owners as % of the population	Area owned as % of total cultivated land
Above 5000	0.01	19.2
1000-5000	0.20	8.2
100-1000	8.00	35.8
0-100	91.80	37.1

By combining the first two categories of landholding, we find that 27.4% of the land was owned by 0.21% of the population. An even clearer picture of peasant poverty is provided by the further breakdown of the last (0-100 *dunums*) category: 27.6% of the population owned plots of less than 40 *dunums*, while 21.9% owned plots of less than five *dunums* (four *dunums* = 1 acre).

What size of plot did a peasant family need to sustain itself without other sources of income? The Hope-Simpson Report of 1930 gave the following definitions of the minimum amount of land needed by a family of five: 130 *dunums* of unirrigated land; 100 *dunums* of rich land with livestock; 40 *dunums* of partially irrigated land with dairy farming; and 15 *dunums* of tree plantation.

From these figures it is clear that the majority of the *fellaheen* were eking out a living on plots of land far smaller than the minimum set by economists as viable. For, already by 1930, 30.7% of the rural population had no land at all, but worked on the land of others, while another third worked partly on self-owned plots of less than 5 *dunums*, and partly on the land of others.

Granott's examination of Palestine's large landowning class shows the biggest estate, that of the Shawwa family in Gaza, to have been 100,000 *dunums*, considerably less than the holdings of the Beirut Sursock family which had 240,000 *dunums* in the plain of Esdraelon alone.[50] Of the Palestinian families named — the Abdul Hadis, al-Hussainis, Tajis, Barghoothis, Jayoosis, al-Tabaris — none went beyond the 50 to 60,000 *dunum* range. These were certainly large estates, but not on the same scale as those of Syria, Iraq and Egypt. In Warriner's judgement, 'Palestine, by comparison with other Middle East countries, does not suffer from the evils of absenteeism on a large scale.'[51]

Peasant Resistance to Dispossession

Economic polarization within the peasant class as a result of the legal privatization of land was held back by the persistence of an ancient form of collective tenure called *masha'*, through which land held by village families was reapportioned at regular intervals, so that all qualities of land were equally distributed. Rights to grazing, wood, and — most important — water were also organized communally. Although the privatization of land ate into *masha'*, Granott estimated in 1945 that half of all Palestinian villages still had some communal land.

Economists regarded *masha'* as archaic, and as a factor contributing to peasant poverty. Along with the institution of equal inheritance,[52] it divided land into ever smaller strips, discouraging the adoption of modern agricultural methods such as the use of machinery, or pest and weed eradication. Granott cites an extreme case of a village with 781 hectares divided through inheritance into 23,696 strips of land. Warriner also cites a case of a parcel of 4.3 *dunums* (about 1 acre) being owned by 48 persons.

However, by attacking *masha'* and the Muslim inheritance code, the economists overlooked other basic causes of peasant poverty, such as class powerlessness, the burden of debt, and politically caused rigidity in the supply of land. They also overlooked the relationship of *masha'* to the two social units basic to the peasants' lives: the village and the clan. Ruedy gives a more balanced appraisal:

> 'From a social and psychological point of view . . . and as a reflection of the dependence of the individual upon the group for every security during a disorganized period of history, *masha'* represents an appropriate adaptation.'[53]

To put the matter in broader perspective, we should look beyond the culturally specific institution of *masha'*, and recognize that communal tenure and equal inheritance are a way of coping with poverty, through which both resources *and* poverty are fairly equally distributed throughout a peasantry, which thereby is enabled to stay on the land. Wolf well summarizes the alternatives that peasants face:

> '(They) can reduce the strength of selective pressures falling upon any one household by developing mechanisms for sharing resources in time of need. . . The opposite solution . . . is to let the selective pressures fall where they may, to maximise the success of the successful, and to eliminate those who cannot make the grade.'[54]

Not all Palestinian villages reacted to modernizing pressures in the same say. Granott noted that in villages where most land was privately owned, peasants were polarized into rich and poor, whereas villages with predominantly communal ownership tended towards equality. Religious affiliation and closeness to cities had something to do with this difference, Christian villages being much readier to adopt Western entrepreneurial values, along with class differentiation. There was also much difference between villages in their readiness to alienate village land to outsiders. The Five Village Study of 1944 found that in one village as much as 52.9% of village land was owned by non-residents, whereas in two other villages the figures were only 2.4% and 4%. The overall average was 20%.

The recollections of ex-peasants in the camps, of the landowning situation in Palestine under the Mandate, are remarkably consistent: 'Most people had a little land, though not enough.' It is clear from their descriptions that, though clan solidarity worked against the emergence of clearly differentiated classes in the villages, at least three categories of peasant family could be distinguished: i) those who owned more land than they could farm alone, and who would employ poorer relatives of other villagers; ii) those who owned plots of a size they could farm without outside labour, but which were not necessarily large enough to support them without other employment; iii) landless peasants, who often owned herds of goats and sheep, and/or worked the land of others. Even landless peasants, who often owned herds of goats and sheep, and/or worked the land of others. Even landless peasants usually owned their homes, and the land on which they stood, as well as having rights to grazing, water, etc., through their membership of the village. Thus, while there was rural-to-urban migration under the Mandate, not all landless peasants took part in this drift. A large number stayed in the villages, anchored by the peasant dream of acquiring land, and salvaged from bankruptcy by village collectivism.

But the peasant dream was threatened. The beginning of cash crops and market farming was bound to exacerbate the economic marginality of small peasant plots, forcing their eventual sale, even though Palestine's indigenous land tenure system, which has been well described as 'family feudalism', slowed down the process, both through splitting up large estates among family segments,[55] and through blocking the alienation of peasant family-owned land. It was difficult for a purely capitalist agriculture to emerge from the web of customary social relationships that bound rich and poor peasants together. Firestone's detailed study of crop-sharing arrangements in Mandate Palestine shows how the concept of 'partnership' gave even landless peasants a stake in land, especially if they could contribute plough-oxen and seed as well as their own labour.[56] Muslim law favoured partnership arrangements, and large landowners frequently sacrificed economic advantage in exchange for community status in their negotiations with the peasants who worked their land.

New Crafts and Skills

In assessing the situation of the poorest class of peasants whose plots were insufficient or who had no land at all, we have to remember not only village collectivism but also the possibilities of non-agricultural employment. Villages had always had small crafts and trades, and under the Mandate a substantial number of peasants found employment in the British-directed Police Force;[57] with the increase in British Army installations after the Great Rebellion, many also found work in army camps. Although the spread of modern education to the villages had been slow (held back, the peasants suspected, for political reasons), some 'sons of the village' were able to get administrative and clerical jobs in the city. The uneducated, like Z.K.'s father,[58] took sub-proletarian jobs in workshops and factories.

In the sample of 20 camp Palestinians interviewed in 1975, the father of only one had been in the *mallak*, or substantial landowning class, employing non-family labour; four fathers had been landless, working as hired labourers; two had been proletarians from Acre; and three had owned some land, but had combined farming with other occupations. This picture is probably fairly typical of peasant economics in the last decade of the Mandate, and helps to explain why, in spite of growing landlessness, Palestinian peasants continued to view themselves as a class of small owners. Most continued to farm small family plots under a wide variety of crop-sharing and rent arrangements, while supplementing family income in whatever ways Palestine's changing economy made possible. Here, we are struck by the contrast between the structural limitations to peasant employment and wage income set up by the Zionist boycott of Arab labour and the 'backwardness' of the indigenous economy, and the tenacity of peasant families in diversifying their sources of income. Their readiness to take up new crafts and skills and their unrelenting pressure on the authorities to provide schools for their children are indications of their search for income supplements that would enable their survival on dwindling plots of land. A man from Sa'sa' recalls the agitation for schools:

'I entered school when I was seven. We had one teacher, from Nablus, and though the schoolroom could hardly take 30 people, there used to be not less than 150 children. It went to the end of fourth elementary. Later they brought a second and a third teacher, but for secondary classes students had to go to the city. I remember how our families used to go every day to the *qaimaqam*[59] and his assistant to struggle for education for their children. They wanted to add classes to our school — four were not enough. They wanted English lessons. The villagers gathered as one hand in this struggle for schools, because the peasant nature is co-operative. So after a great while we got the fifth and sixth classes, and the school was enlarged, and the nucleus of a girls' school was set up.'

Peasant enthusiasm for education is a clear reflection of their understanding that their poverty and oppression as a class were tied to their exclusion from knowledge. Their hunger for schooling can be felt in every account of the period:

'My father was illiterate but he made every effort to give me education, although he was very poor. He built relations with the only teacher in the village and I entered the elementary school. At the end of elementary it was expected that I would go to secondary school in Tarshiha. I persuaded my father and four other students to bring us a private teacher in the summer to teach us English and the material of the fifth elementary, so that we could be admitted to secondary school. The four of us paid him three guineas, or 75p each, per month. Because my father was so poor I couldn't continue more than 37 days. So I studied the rest of the material alone, from the books of one of the other boys who was my cousin. We went to Tarsheeha and took the exam and we were all admitted.' (This man later became an outstanding organizer and political leader in the Resistance Movement, one of the few of peasant origin.)'

Not only parents, but children were drawn to the schools which, in spite of their poverty, were a new and exciting arrival in village life:

'When my father went to register me in the village school the teacher refused to take me because I was a year under age. My playmates were accepted, and I returned home weeping because the teacher refused to take me.'

Escaping from their villages under bombardment in 1948, it is striking
how many boys carried with them only their schoolbooks, and reaching
Lebanon, the first endeavour, after basic needs were covered, was to search
for means to continue children's interrupted education. Like their family
solidarity, and their roots in the land, hunger for education carried over
into dispersion, forming a continuity between Palestine and the *ghourba*.

The Shadow of Colonialist Expropriation

While the expansion of education in the villages would have lessened
the pressure on land, and increased peasant income by making skilled work
in cities available to them, there was a second, far more serious threat than
poverty to the peasants' relationship to their land. This was, of course,
Zionism. Granott's classic study of Palestinian land tenure emphasizes
endogenous factors that led to peasant poverty (large estates, tax-farming,
'uneconomic' agricultural methods, etc), but in line with Zionist policy he
says nothing of the pressure upon the supply of land created by Zionist
immigration. The fantasy of the founding fathers that Zionism could only
contribute to the prosperity of Palestine's indigenous population had to be
sustained by the man who directed Jewish land-purchasing policy, and
who knew better than anyone what its ultimate goals were.

In the perspective of the Uprooting, the two most significant trends in
the peasant/land relationship during the Mandate were decreases in the
average size of peasant family holdings, and increases in peasant
landlessness.

The average size of holdings decreased steadily throughout the Mandate:
75 *dunums* in 1930 (the Johnson-Crosbie Report); 45.3 *dunums* in 1936
(The Land Survey Department's Report based on 322 villages); 41.4
dunums in 1944 (the Five Village Study). Yet these figures do not give a
real indication of peasant poverty since these averages are inflated by the
size of large holdings. The government analysts who prepared the *Survey
of Palestine* submitted to the Anglo-American Committee of Inquiry in
1946, found that the median[60] size of holdings was in fact only 11.1
dunums in the earlier, larger study, and 21.3 *dunums* in the later one. In
the 1936 Report referred to earlier, the detailed breakdown of size of
holding shows that 21.9% of owners had plots of five *dunums* or less. In a
report prepared in 1946, Sayigh[61] compared the number of families living
on Arab-owned land with the number the land could support, and
calculated a 'congestion rate' of 229.7%.

As to landlessness, already by 1930 the Hope-Simpson Report
estimated that 29.4% of rural families were landless; Sayigh, writing in
1946, suggests a figure of 35%, more than one-third of the rural
population. When we remember that this figure does not include migrants
to cities, only landless peasants who had remained in the villages, we
realize that it probably underestimates the upheaval to which the peasant

class had been subjected by the Mandate. From the peasants' viewpoint, their situation now was far worse than it had been under the Ottomans. At that time, in spite of insecurity and oppression, any peasant with an ox and a plough could put new land under cultivation without fear that his right of use would be disputed. But with the beginning of the Mandate, Palestine was opened to the highest rate of immigration in the world[62] backed by the highest rate of colonial investment. Land prices rocketed as the result of this unprecedented demographic and financial pressure, and its supply became inelastic for all except big investors, like the Jewish Land Purchasing Agency and their middlemen.

Zionist Land Purchase

Peasant landlessness started before the Mandate with single sales of large areas of land by the Ottoman Administration and by non-Palestinian owners. These sales, many of which included whole villages, confronted the peasants with their first experience of legal eviction, something which had never been part of the *fellaheen* fate. It is striking that their immediate, spontaneous response was violent resistance[63] — a resistance which found, however, no echo in other segments of Palestinian society. Such large transactions — the most notorious being the sale in the early Twenties of 240,000 *dunums* in the fertile Vale of Esdraelon by the Beirut merchant family of Sursock — would have been impossible after the first few years of the Mandate owing to the rapid growth of nationalist sentiment. From then on, Zionist land acquisition was faced with obstacles that the founders of the movement had not anticipated.

Describing Jewish institutional land purchase up to 1936, Granott[64] gives the following breakdown of the sources of purchase by the three major Zionist buying agencies (see Table below).

JEWISH PURCHASES OF PALESTINIAN LAND UP TO 1936

Source of the Land Acquired	Total Land Acquired (in *dunums*)	(in %age)
Large absentee owners	358,974	52.6
Large resident owners	167,802	24.6
Government, churches and foreign companies	91,001	13.4
Fellaheen	64,201	9.4
Total Land Acquired	681,978	100.0

In spite of the energy and funds deployed by the Jewish Land Purchasing Agency and its sister organizations, the proportion of Jewish-owned land rose far more slowly than their population. By 1926, only 4% of all land (including state land) was Jewish-owned, and it took another eight years for this figure to reach 5%, and a further eleven to reach 6%.

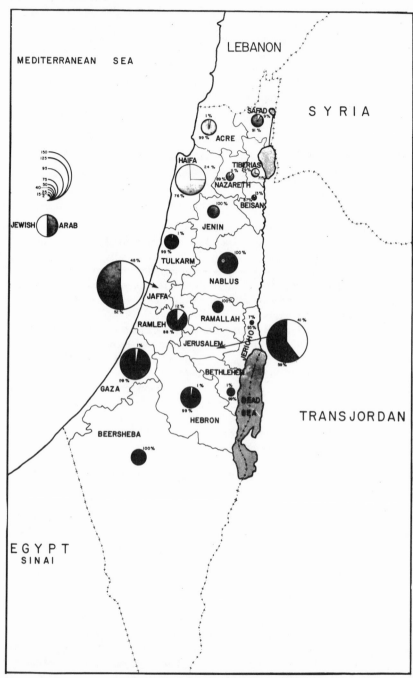

DISTRIBUTION OF ARAB AND JEWISH
POPULATION OF PALESTINE BY SUBDISTRICT (1931)

On the eve of the Disaster, it had not gone beyond 8.6%. Peasant resistance to land sales is abundantly clear in these figures.

If so little peasant-owned land was sold to the Zionists, how is it that Zionist acquisitions of land increased peasant landlessness and deepened their poverty? First, peasants were affected by the sale of land they did not own, but on which they lived and worked. The growth of Palestine's urban population from less than 20% at the beginning of the Mandate to 33% at the end (excluding the Jewish population), is one clear indication of a rural exodus that was not caused by the attraction of wage labour in the slums of Haifa, but by deterioration of conditions in the villages. Second, peasants were affected indirectly by the fact that land acquired by public Zionist bodies was permanently alienated.[65] Third, since only Jewish labour could be employed on Jewish land, or in Jewish commercial or industrial enterprises, the *fellaheen* were deprived of any possibility of supplementing their insufficient agricultural earnings through selling their labour in the colonialist sector.

The Hope-Simpson Inquiry of 1930, set up to investigate the causes of the Jaffa riots of 1929, clearly outlined the threat posed by Jewish land acquisition to the indigenous population:

> 'Actually the result of the purchase of land in Palestine by the Jewish National Fund has been that land has been extra-territorialized. It ceases to be land from which the Arab can gain any advantage either now or at any time in the future. Not only can he never hope to lease or cultivate it, but, by the stringent provisions of the lease of the Jewish National Fund, he is deprived for ever from employment on that land.'

If in the Twenties and Thirties Zionist land purchase constituted a threat to the peasants' economic situation, by the Forties the drive of their land purchasing policy had become primarily political and strategic, aimed at winning the confrontation that the Zionist movement's military arm had begun to plan. Granott, in his capacity as chairman of the Board of Directors of the Jewish National Fund (J.N.F.), describes how two apparently contradictory land purchase policies — concentration and dispersal — were followed simultaneously, with the double aim of strengthening existing settlements, and staking claims in areas that had previously been considered as purely Arab. In the last years of the Mandate the J.N.F. began to penetrate 'distant and undeveloped zones': Gaza, Beersheba, Beisan, Huleh. At the same time, build-up began in previously neglected frontier areas, particularly in Northern Galilee, to block the entry of arms and fighters from Syria and Lebanon. It was now that the peasants of Galilee, a district whose population had been 92% Arab in 1931, began to see new Jewish settlements appearing among them. In Granott's words:

> Land was bought in those parts where there was a danger of political change in favour of the Arabs, or of their being *wrenched from the body of the imminent state.*'[66]

The growing political power of the Zionist movement by 1945, and its readiness to break away from British tutelage, are clearly shown in the claim of the Jewish Land Convention, held that year in Tel Aviv, that the Jewish National Agency now controlled 1,765,000 *dunums* in Palestine. This was 215,000 *dunums* more than the amount shown in Mandate Government records, much of it in areas that had been banned in the Zoning Laws of 1940. These laws, prohibiting the sale of land to non-Arabs in certain areas, had seemed at the time an important concession to the Palestinian nationalist movement. But by the time they were introduced, the Zionist movement had succeeded in creating a Palestinian collaborating class — the *simsars*, or brokers — through whom they continued to acquire land in the banned zones, using stratagems such as faked mortgages and straw men.

Yet Zionists as percipient as Arlosoroff (one of the first to predict the necessity for 'revolutionary violence'[67]) realized that Herzl's dream of 'spiriting away' Palestine's indigenous population had no hope of realization. True, in their myopic refusal to recognize the existence of a long settled peasantry, Zionists attributed their failure to Britain's fears of antagonizing the Arabs. Yet undoubtedly it was the *fellaheen's* deep attachment to their land that prevented the Zionist movement from acquiring more than 8.6% of Palestine's total land area before 1948. It was, of course, not merely the peasants' emotional attachment to their land nor their nationalism that kept them stubbornly upon it, for despite these factors economic pressures could have forced them to sell against their will.[68] But what made it possible for the majority of the peasant class to stay on the land, in spite of deteriorating economic conditions, was the solidarity of family and village ties, and the strong element of collectivism in *fellaheen* culture. It was this tenacity of social and economic organization that made their eviction through military force inevitable. There was no other way.

In the face of the collapse of the national movement on the eve of the Disaster, the tenacious resistance of the peasants of Palestine to expropriation was negated by their society's political and military weakness. This weakness was very largely the product of the British occupation, and of Zionist colonialism's unusual resources; but it was also partly a product of Palestine's indigenous social structure and the type of leadership it threw up.

PALESTINIAN SOCIAL STRUCTURE UNDER THE MANDATE

Under the Mandate, the *fellaheen* formed the fragmented mass base of the type of social structure typically produced by white settler colonialism. At the apex of the pyramid was the metropolitan ruling class, in this case

British — a class of military men and administrators. Directly under them came two potential ruling groups, in competition for British patronage: the indigenous Palestinian aristocracy and the leadership of the Zionist movement. Each of these three leadership groups had different stances towards the peasantry that, at the beginning of the British occupation in 1918, made up at least 80% of the indigenous population.

Regionalism and Social Divisions

Prior to the arrival of the British, Palestine had been a small province in the Ottoman's Arab empire, split into *sanjaks*[69] which were often attached to different administrative centres. Thus, in the last period of Turkish rule, the districts of Acre and Nablus were administered from Beirut, while Jerusalem and the central provinces were ruled directly by the Ministry of the Interior in Istanbul. Among the legacies of Ottoman rule was what Wolf[70] describes in the Algerian case as 'the Turkish "checker-board" pattern of checks and balances, setting group against group to the ultimate benefit of the Turkish elite'. This pattern carried on into the Mandate, producing the vertical coalitions or factions that cut across classes, and aligned blocks of rival clans against each other, from the level of the leading Jerusalem families, through the lesser city clans and provincial gentry, down to the *bedouin* and village leaders. In formations like these, power and influence moved downwards from Government, through a series of patron/client ties, instead of rising upwards from an organized mass base.

In spite of the rapid growth of Palestinian Arab national consciousness in reaction to the British occupation and its patronage of Zionism, the political results of 400 years of Turkish domination were not easily transcended. The regionalism produced by poor communications and division into separate *sanjaks* helped block the spread of revolutionary resistance in the Thirties. For instance, the call of Sheikh Qassam to action in 1935 was not immediately followed in areas other then the hills round Haifa. Similarly, in the Great Rebellion, some parts of the country were far less active than others.

Regionalism was accompanied by other social divisions, a strong consciousness of small group membership, whether regional, sectarian, class or clan. Moreover centuries of insecurity and weak central government had strengthened the tendency towards small group autonomy. We have already seen how, at the peasant level, the village and extended family could provide for all their members' needs: defence, justice, economic subsistence, marriage, and all other forms of social and cultural exchange. Particularistic social divisions meant that the new political movements of the Mandate era retained within their structure the particular interests of the groups that composed them. In spite of the strength of national feeling, sectional interests were never transcended as they were to a greater degree in the Zionist movement.

Whereas the Zionist immigrants purposefully left their traditional social structure and culture behind them, turning themselves into 'new men' dedicated to the building of the Zionist state,[71] the Palestinians naturally carried with them into the Mandate all the social and cultural characteristics, the 'web of belonging', that had built up through their historical experience in Palestine. Whereas the class structure of Zionist settler society was relatively flat, composed mainly of middle and lower middle class elements, indigenous Palestinian society was pyramid-shaped. Zionist leadership was not 'ascriptive' like that of the Palestinians, but 'achieved', i.e. based on proved qualities of competence. And even though the immigrant settlers came from different cultures and spoke different languages, they were united in their sense of superiority to the 'natives'. In addition, Zionist leadership was relatively homogeneous, mostly coming from a single area of Russia.[72]

The Impact of British Rule

As the dominant class, the British Administration's view and treatment of the indigenous society was of capital importance in maintaining its divided nature. From the beginning the British refused to recognize the indigenous society as a people, or a nation, defining Palestinians in official documents as 'the non-Jewish communities'. They justified their refusal to accord Palestinian national leadership representative status by calling their society 'unstructured' (an absurd accusation to come from one of the most class-divided nations in the world), and by insisting on only dealing with sectional leaders. Implicit in this attitude was the intention to keep Palestinian society 'unstructured'. A second strategy was the encouragement of a collaborating 'opposition' party to counteract the growing anti-British feeling of the mainstream national movement led from 1929 by the Mufti, Hajj Amin Hussaini.[73]

It was to be a point of Zionist propaganda that the British government officials' social relations with the Palestinian aristocracy were better than with the Zionist leadership. But the political profit to the national movement from these social relations was far less than the Palestinian notables who enjoyed them believed; while, on the debit side, hobnobbing between the British ruling class and Arab aristocrats could be made to look bad to anti-imperialist, democratic public opinion in Europe and the US. By drawing close to the British, whether on the pretext of influencing them, learning from them, or spying out their intentions, the Palestinian traditional upper class and bourgeoisie only increased their distance from the mass of the Palestinian people. To large sections of the bourgeoisie, even those not in direct social contact with the British, it seemed the height of madness to challenge British power.

British Policy Towards the Peasants

In dealing with the *fellaheen*, the British Administration's purpose was to tax them more efficiently and to preserve their traditional forms of leadership. The government was concerned by peasant poverty and growing landlessness not only because these kept taxes low but, more seriously, because they threatened political disturbances that would be costly to suppress. The peasant initiated riots of 1921 in Jaffa and 1929 in Jerusalem were clear symptoms of popular resistance to the Mandate, but the recommendations of men like Haycraft and Shaw who investigated the causes of peasant violence had little long-term effect on Government policy. They urged restriction of Zionist immigration, but this was to contradict the logic of the Home Government's commitment to Zionism, which could only lead to a deepening of peasant poverty and the crushing of peasant resistance to British occupation and to Zionism.

The Palestinian Rebellion of 1936-39 was the most sustained phase of militant anti-imperialist struggle in the Arab world before the Algerian War of Independence. At its peak in 1938 it had mobilized an estimated 15,000 militants around a core of from 1,000 to 1,500 full-time fighters, forcing the British to increase their occupying army from one to two divisions (about 20,000 troops). As well as the British forces, the Palestinian guerrillas faced Zionist paramilitary organizations now well beyond the embryonic stage. It has been estimated[74] that 5,000 Palestinians were killed and 14,000 wounded through British action, excluding victims of Zionist attack. In one year alone, 1938, 5,679 Palestinians were jailed.

Older camp Palestinians well remember the Rebellion of 1936 which they see as the parent of the Armed Struggle Revolution of 1965. Some remember taking part in it, others who were children at the time remember feeling pride if 'sons' of their village were among the guerrillas. Methods of suppression included aerial bombardment, the mass dynamiting of villages suspected of helping the 'rebels', beating men with strips of prickly pear bush, and entering homes to ransack food stocks. A man who was a small child in 1939 remembers reprisals against his village:

'There's a picture stamped on my mind of all the people — men, women and children — gathered together on the threshing floor. Later when I asked about the incident, they told me that the British had collected all the people there and blown up the whole village. I think it was in 1939. They said that some people working with the Revolution had taken shelter in the village; also a bridge leading to it had been blown up. This was enough for the British to destroy all the houses. But the people went down to the city (Acre) to get help to rebuild.'

The quotation is interesting not only for what it tells about British methods of suppression (to be adopted more ruthlessly by the Israelis later), but also because of the collective reaction to stand firm that collective punishment aroused.

Relations Between Palestinian Peasants and Zionist Settlers

This subject is far too complex to be dealt with in a few paragraphs, but its main determinants can be simply stated: these were, on the one hand, Zionism's blind refusal to admit the existence of the Palestinian people in general, and the peasants in particular; and on the other, a white settler arrogance that made the elimination, or at least exploitation, of the peasants inevitable and natural.

One of the forms taken by the Zionist refusal to recognize the rootedness of the Palestinians was the myth that they were recent immigrants to Palestine.[75] This was particularly absurd in relation to the *fellaheen*, who were notorious for their attachment to their home villages: such a pronounced cultural trait could not have been produced if their immigration had been recent. A different layer in the Zionist attitude towards the *fellaheen* is revealed in the biblical phrase 'hewers of wood and drawers of water', so often used by Zionists, Christian and Jewish alike, to denote the role of the peasants as an ethnic proletariat in the Zionist utopia.

From the beginning, Zionist immigrants refused to understand the peasants' customary rights in land. Some of the earliest attacks on Jewish settlements, in the 1880s, came about because the settlers barred the peasants from grazing their herds on newly bought land. But relations between the first Jewish immigrants and the peasants were much better than those of the Second Aliyeh (1904-07) with its fatal decision to boycott Arab labour. An Arab peasantry could not form part of an exclusively Jewish state as the movement's leaders now conceived it; instead, Zionism created its own 'peasants' — Jewish settlers oriented towards agriculture through special indoctrination. That these would ultimately displace, or dominate, the Palestinian *fellaheen* seems to have been an idea expressed both by settlers and peasants from the early days of Zionist immigration. We have the anecdote of Z.K.'s grandfather,[76] probably dating as far back as the pre-Mandate period, to suggest that eventual Zionist domination was an explicit element in normal relations between settlers and peasants. An official of the Jewish Colonial Association reports peasants asking him, before the turn of the century: 'Is it true that the Jews want to retake this country?'[77] Peasant reactions were mixed: fear, anger, incredulity. Z.K.'s grandfather believed that the Arabs would never accept the alienation of Palestine, and it is possible that this faith in the impossibility of the Zionist dream had the effect of defusing peasant hostility.

Not only were the immigrants alien in their culture and way of life, but their consciousness as Zionists cut them off from normal social relations with the *fellaheen*. It did not require the difference of their Jewishness, nor any religious or racial fanaticism on the part of the peasants to make the latter feel that the immigrants posed a threat to them. Undoubtedly religion was one basis amongst others in the building of the Palestinian national resistance movement, and the concept of the *jihad* was never far from the minds of the nationalist orators. But this is no proof that religion played a strong role in peasant resistance. The fact that all early incidents of *fellaheen* violence were sparked off by evictions makes it clear that what they feared, and with reason, was the intrusion into their relationship with the land of a group with closer access to Government than themselves. Other non-Arab minorities to come to Palestine (protected by the Capitulations[78] or by foreign powers) had been traders. But the Zionists were the first to colonize the land, and even though the Ottoman Government did not formally encourage Zionist immigration, much state land was sold to the settlers between 1880 and 1918, probably through the corruption of local officials. With the British occupation formally pledged in the Balfour Declaration to encourage Zionist settlement, the peasant's rights in land suffered a new, much more threatening deterioration. Their class position gave them no access to Government except through tenuous patron/client ties with notables, or with provincial officials whom they had little reason to trust. In the absence of a strong national leadership that could protest effectively against their eviction, the peasants' only recourse was to sporadic violence.

Perception of the Zionist settlers as alien, and as 'the enemy', seems to have been widespread throughout the Palestinian population from the first years of the Mandate, or even earlier.[79] But it is significant that this early perception of the threat posed by Zionism did not generate a deep or implacable hostility. The attitude of the peasants towards the newcomers has always been far less rigid, less organized, and less ideological than the Zionists' attitudes towards them. The main outlines of these Zionist attitudes can be drawn in a few sentences: that the Palestinians do not exist;[80] that they were only 'custodians' of the land, never its owners; that they form a natural helot class for Israel's Spartans. Only a few minority voices express a different view. Like other white settlers, the average Zionist hardly saw (even today) the 'natives'; or he sees them through stereotypes such as 'dirty', 'lazy', or 'inefficient'.[81] In contrast, Palestinian peasant attitudes are more complex, revealing different ideological cross-currents as well as a clear evolution over time. The change in the terminology they used — from 'Jews' to 'Israelis' to 'Zionists' — is only one sign of a process of political learning set in motion by colonialist aggression and expropriation.

From the beginning, peasant attitudes towards the Zionist newcomers ranged through a wide gamut from spontaneous violence, nationalist rejection, suspicion, normal economic exchange, and even occasional friendship. It is typical that in the middle of the War of 1948, the parents of a wounded child should have taken him to be treated by a Jewish doctor in Acre. Even today, after three decades of misery and victimization, there is a striking absence in the camps of deep hostility towards Israelis. The Palestinian struggle is seen as rising out of moral obligation, not out of hatred; and it is without hatred that it is seen as continuing implacably 'until victory'.

Unlike Israelis, who are aften described as worshippers of pragmatism and mindless action, Palestinians of peasant origin are deeply reflective and one finds them persistently questioning their fate: What is the cause of their situation? What is the nature of the enemy? What are the Zionists' ultimate purposes? What is the basis of their success? What should be the basis of Palestinian resistance? Why was Palestine lost, and why had Arab action to restore Palestinian rights been so half-hearted? The links between Zionism, imperialism and Arab reaction are the clearest single lesson that Palestinians have drawn from their uprooting. In this view, Zionism is simply a tool to divide and subjugate the Arab world, and for Palestinians to struggle becomes in consequence an obligation of Arabism: hence the concept of the fighter as *fedai*, one who sacrifices himself, and as a *shaheed*, martyr, both ideas totally opposed to the Zionist 'man of steel' or Arab-fighter.

In the camps, it is rare to find the slightest reflection of Western-type 'anti-semitism'. Once, in a group discussion, when an old man made a passing reference to Hitler (attributing to him praise of the Palestinians for their courage), a younger man of the *jeel al-nekba* criticised him gently for mentioning the 'Nazi Hitler' without condemning him. He went on to say:

> 'Praise of Hitler was part of the wrong culture that was spread among us. Political understanding was missing, for example that way they talked about Nazis, as if it was something wonderful if Hitler made soap of the Jews. Why should we be happy? Because he attacked Jews, who were our enemies, they didn't see that he was a fascist, just as they didn't understand the connection between Israel and the imperialist capitalist system.'

Though it would be wrong to underestimate the Palestinian potentiality for sustained militancy, an anecdote told by a teacher from Sa'sa' well illustrates how their resistance has always been strongest at the emotional and symbolic level. The teacher remembered climbing as a boy to the peak of Mount Jermaq, the highest in Palestine, with a group from his village school:

> 'At the highest point we found a stone, on which the Jews had written in Hebrew, English and Arabic, "Palestine is ours". Our teacher translated it for us, but before he had finished we had read it in Arabic and scratched it out with our nails. We brought pieces of limestone and wrote, 'Palestine is Arab, it's for our people, not for the Jews.'

Relations Between the Indigenous Aristocracy and the Peasants

If the stance of the Zionist leadership towards the peasantry was a simple one of non-recognition, that of the indigenous ruling class was naturally more complex, made up of traditional attitudes of superiority, paternalism, neglect, and an embryonic nationalism. In the very early discussions of Zionist immigration that took place among the feudal and bourgeois Arab nationalist leaders of Damascus, Cairo, Beirut and Jerusalem, it was the Palestinian Muslim landowners who showed most concern at the threat posed by Zionism to the *fellaheen*[82] On the other hand, it is clear that all militant resistance, from the beginning of the Mandate to its end, was undertaken without real leadership or even participation by the indigenous ruling class.

A.W.Kayyali gives a neat description of the class-based division of labour within the Palestinian nationalist movement:

> '. . . the notables performed the role of diplomats; the educated middle classes that of the articulators of public opinion, and the peasants that of the actual fighters in the battle against the Zionist presence.'[83]

Barrington Moore's theory that the relationship between landed gentry and peasantries is crucial for the emergence of nationalism may help to explain the hesitant development of the Palestinian/Arab nationalist movement. Social distance between Arab landowners and peasants, deriving from the prebendal form of Byzantine/Arab/Turkish feudalism, had not been broken down by modern capitalist farming, such as began to develop in Northern Europe in the 17th century. Arab aristocrats, whatever their origins, lived in cities, and managed their estates through agents. It was unheard of for anyone of rank or wealth to live in the country. Even visiting it was rare.

> 'Living in the city, and for the city, the large landowner never manages his estates himself. . . He has no knowledge of the peasants who work on his land; he knows neither their name, their families, nor their character.'[84]

The only modification of Weulersse's picture of the Syrian landed gentry that is needed for it to apply to Palestine is that Palestine's leading families were not, on the whole, owners of vast estates. At the same time there existed in Palestine a class of rural gentry and rich farmers who lived on their estates and managed them. Some members of this class were active in the nationalist movement, but very few took up arms or fought with the peasant guerrillas.

Political Weakness of the National Leadership

In trying to understand the failure of the leaders of the Palestinian

nationalist movement to build a solid resistance to British occupation and
Zionist colonialism, commensurate with the early and rapid development
of nationalist consciousness, it is enlightening to grasp not merely the
distance of the aristocrats from the peasantry, but also their history as a
ruling group and the bases of their leadership. In the first place, in keeping
with Palestine's status as a province of Syria,[85] the Palestinian aristocracy
was a provincial aristocracy. One indication of this is the relatively minor
role played by Palestinians in the early Arab nationalist clubs, al-Fatat,
al-Ahd, the Decentralization Party, and the Beirut Reform Committee,[86]
even at meetings in which Zionist aims in Palestine were the subject of
discussion.

Though Arabic-speaking peoples lived in Palestine from before the time
of Christ, the ancestors of the leading families had mostly reached
Palestine with the Arab Conquest. Ottoman domination had demilitarized
them; unlike the notables of some other Arab cities, they had no tradition
of service in the Turkish Army. On the contrary, their roles were those of
provincial, not national or imperial gentry: bureaucratic, religious, judicial,
scholarly. Their status derived far more from lineage, and from traditional
symbolic functions such as guarding the holy places, than from great
wealth or political power.

While the leadership of the incipient Palestinian national movement was
not only confined to the *'ayan*, other elements were similarly upper class,
drawn mainly from the large landowners and merchants:

> 'Political power was largely concentrated at the upper tip of the
> socio-economic pyramid composed of small groups of heads of old
> and influential clans, other members of the landowning aristocracy,
> wealthy merchants and traders, and some professionals. Twenty-
> eight (or 87.5% of the 32 men who served as members of the Arab
> Higher Committee (A.H.C.)[87] from its founding in 1936 until 1948
> belonged to this upper segment of Palestinian society. Only four
> members . . . could be categorized as representatives of the
> bourgeoisie, and no A.H.C. member was ever selected from the
> peasants or the working class. . .
>
> 'The extent to which wealth and political power were
> concentrated in the cities is further demonstrated by the fact that
> 24 (or 85.7%) of the 28 elite members of the A.H.C. were born or
> had their family homes in key Palestinian cities. In fact . . . only four
> of the total group originated in rural areas, and only one from a
> tribal (pastoral) area.'[88]

The political style of Palestine's indigenous ruling class had been
formed by their co-option as intermediaries in the Ottoman administration,
as well as by their own class character as a non-militant gentry. Though
not without nationalist feeling, they were profoundly legalistic in their
attitude to political action. Faced with the threat of Zionism, their natural
resort was to diplomatic action: delegations to Istanbul or to London,
petitions, conferences, statements. In the face of every evidence of futility,
this leadership persisted in the only strategy it was capable of: attempts to

change the Mandate Government's commitment to Zionism through persuasion, argument, warnings, and, as an ultimate deterrent, hints of eventual violence.

Writing of the political style of the Arab notables, formed by their relationship to Ottoman power, Albert Hourani well describes the limitations of Palestine's indigenous leadership confronted with a 'struggle of destiny.'

> 'The political influence of the notables rests on two factors: on the one hand, they must have access to authority, and so be able to advise, to warn, and in general to speak for society, or some part of it; on the other, they must have some social power of their own, whatever its form and origin, which is not dependent on the ruler and gives them a position of accepted "natural" leadership. Around this independent power they can, if they are skilful, create a coalition of forces both urban and rural.'[89]

It was intrinsic to the methods of the Palestinian notables that they only threatened the Government with popular uprising, never made any concrete, sustained effort to raise the effectiveness of popular violence so that it could transcend the limitations of its spontaneity, and form a more than temporary threat to British domination. Rather, they allowed it to explode spontaneously, in the traditional manner, bringing in its train reprisals and suppression. All histories of the national movement make it clear that the leaders conceived their role as mobilizing the people to resist, not taking an active part themselves in the struggle.

When in March 1921 a Palestinian delegation led by Mayor Musa Kazem al-Hussaini visited Cairo, the Egyptian politician Ismail Sidki advised them to form a national party to work for independence. Musa Kazem's reply is revealing:

> '... that the intentions of the Palestinian delegation included complete independence, but they desired, if this were not possible, that the real power should be with the English and not with the Jews.'[90]

Protest followed protest as the British occupation proceeded from one anti-Palestinian action to the next, in fatal succession: the proclamation of the Balfour Declaration, the final separation of Palestine from Syria, the appointment of a Zionist Jew as first High Commissioner of Palestine. But when General Storrs, Military Governor of Jerusalem, threatened the Mayor and Council with loss of their jobs if their pressure for union with Syria continued, they dropped the unionist slogan. Kayyali comments:

> 'The efficiency of Storr's threats demonstrated the inadequacy of the traditional political notability to lead the populace in situations of conflict. When faced with a choice between a salaried government career and an uncertain future as popular political leaders, the elderly notables opted for the safer and more remunerative alternative.'[91]

The discrepancy between work and action that characterized the indigenous leadership also comes out in their reception of Herbert Samuel, the first High Commissioner. Before his arrival in May 1920, there had been rumours of plans to assassinate him. When he called a meeting of notables in October there were threats to boycott it. In the event, all the notables attended.

Not only did the indigenous ruling class have no experience of mass leadership, but the individual notable would never attempt such a course since it could only jeopardize his access to Government, and it was on this access that his influence and status depended. In spite of his reputation as an anti-British demagogue, the Mufti's tactics were essentially those of balancing a moderately nationalist stance against his acceptability to the Mandate Government as an instrument for defusing popular discontent. Over and over again, the Palestinian notables earned the praise of the British authorities for their help in controlling the 'mob'. In May 1921, the Mayors of Jerusalem, Tulkarm and Jaffa, the Muftis of Acre and Safed, and Qadi of Jerusalem, all received British decorations for their 'services in Palestine'.

It was symptomatic of the distance between the political and militant wings of the nationalist movement that when the first guerrilla leader, Sheikh Qassam, was killed soon after his call to armed struggle in 1935, none of the leading national figures attended his funeral. None of the military leaders of the 1936 Rebellion were from the ruling class.[92] Few anecdotes give a clearer picture of the incapacity of the Palestinian traditional leaders for serious struggle than the one told by a 'former intelligence officer' to the author of a study on the 1936 Rebellion.[93] A group of *bedouin* gathered in Beersheba telephoned to the Mufti asking what action they should take in support of the uprising that was beginning to spread through the country inthe wake of the killing of the District Commissioner for Galilee. The Mufti's reply to them was to do whatever they thought fit, and though this reply may have been due to knowledge that his telephone was tapped, all accounts of the Rebellion and the six months' strike that preceded it, make it clear that the people of Palestine led their leadership, not vice versa. Objectively, the role of the notables was to facilitate British domination. In yielding to the pressures of pro-British Arab politicians, like Nuri Said of Iraq and Emir Abdullah of Jordan, for an end to the Rebellion, the Arab Higher Committee threw away all the lessons of political organization that they could have learnt from the uprising, in spite of its ultimate repression. Instead, naively, they accepted the British White Paper of 1939 as a real gain, though every experience they had had of British rule should have taught them that concessions made by the Administration in Palestine would be negated by Zionist pressure on the Home Government. This verdict on the Palestinian leadership seems just:

'The upper classes could not think in terms of being obligated to the lower classes in the context of a total national struggle; they could only feel some obligation for the lower classes in as far as this did not conflict with their own vital interests.'[94]

Old and New Classes

It is possible, indeed probable, that a more energetic, more militant leadership could have built out of the Palestinian nationalist movement a force capable of delaying the Zionists' capture of the state in 1948, or at least limiting its area. Yet even a more effective leadership would have encountered serious difficulties in welding together the different segments of Palestinian society. There were sectarian differences between Muslim, Christian and Druze which, though largely suppressed by the growth of Arab consciousness during the Mandate, still existed at the level of the peasants. There were also the ancient class categories of peasant, nomad, and city-dweller, distinguished by marked differences of status, occupation and way of life. And on top of these traditional categories were new ones introduced by 'modernization'. The drift of landless peasants to the cities had begun to create an Arab proletariat, while the slow spread of modern education gave birth to an intelligentsia distinct from the traditional literati.

Hostility between peasants and *bedouin* had ancient origins. In times of drought, the *bedouin* were likely to raid the *fellaheen* for grain, or, alternatively, to guard client *fellaheen* against other *bedouin* in return for protection money. Although far less numerous in Palestine than in Syria, Jordan or Iraq, forming less than 5% of the Arab population, the *bedouin* were doubtless a factor in isolating villages, and preventing the accumulation of a peasant surplus.

The *bedouin* were just as poor as the peasants, if not poorer, but they enjoyed a higher status, partly through their historic connection with the Islamic empire, partly because, unlike the peasants, they were both mounted and armed. Their oppression by the state was always less than that of the peasants, and their tribal leaders often formed part of the ruling class. In Palestine, we find *bedouin* living peacefully among *fellaheen*, specializing in certain economic roles, such as raising cattle for ploughing, but there is little sign of their integration into the nationalist movement. In fact, it was not until the rise of the Resistance Movement after 1965, that a strong effort was made to break down social barriers between ex-peasants and ex-nomads in the camps. It is still a matter for comment if a worker of *bedu* origin is to be found in a camp clinic or a Resistance office.

Social distance between peasants and city-dwellers was as ancient as between peasants and *bedouin*. Cities were centres of state power, of trade and learning; they needed nothing from, and gave nothing to, the countryside:

'In the East . . . the city resembles a foreign body encapsulated within the countryside, imposed upon the rural regions which it dominates and exploits. . . The city consumes . . . without producing . . . it contributes none of the public and social services — law, education, technical equipment, health — which in the West justifies the city in the eyes of the countryside.'[95]

Because of peasant poverty there was little economic exchange to link rural and urban populations; cities traded with each other, and with more distant centres that produced or required luxury products.[96] Nineteenth century travellers to Palestine noticed that peasants were afraid to visit cities except in groups, and though by the end of the Mandate the *fellaheen* had got used to trading with the city, and to working and living in it, the class barrier continued in consciousness, particularly in the peasants' view that the city contained everything they lacked: goods, knowledge, closeness to sources of power. Surely their self-classification as 'the donkeys of the world' reflected the attitude of the city people, the *mudeniyeen*, towards them. And the fact that, today in the camps, the class labels *fellah* and *mudeni* are still used to categorize people, usually with the underlying assumption that to be *mudeni* is to be civilized, while to be *fellah* is to be primitive, suggests how deeply entrenched these class-based attitudes are.

Though wealthy peasants often migrated to cities, poverty restricted such migration to a very few. The traditional Muslim *kuttab* school was intended only to strengthen religious affiliation and did not provide a channel for clever peasant boys to enter government services (in the towns). In any case, the need of the Ottoman administration for clerical skills was so slight that it could easily be supplied by the city literati. But the peasants' understanding that their poverty and class subordination were linked to their lack of knowledge is clear from the energy with which, towards the end of the Mandate, they pressed for schools in the villages. We have seen that the spread of modern education to the rural areas was so slow under the Mandate that the *fellaheen* suspected a deliberate trick to keep them backward. Nevertheless, a trickle of peasant boys did manage to complete their education in the cities, and to find administrative and clerical work there. This small stratum of educated *fellaheen* was to play an exceptionally important role after the Uprooting; as teachers, as organizers, as social workers, they stayed close to the camp populations, unlike Palestine's urban population, who mainly used their educational and financial advantages for personal advancement.

While city Palestinians took part in the national movement, and in the General Strike of 1936, their participation in the Rebellion was much more limited. Essentially this was a peasant uprising with local peasant leaders and Arab volunteers from outside Palestine. The Arab Higher Committee initiated neither the Strike nor the Rebellion, both of which burst out spontaneously from mass discontent. A militant from Sa'sa' noted the different level of militancy between peasants and city people:

'If there was a British policy (towards the *fellaheen*) it was to make the peasant poorer, because they realized from 1917, 1927, 1935, that it was on the peasants' shoulders that the revolution would be carried, they are the ones who stick. Not that the people of the cities did not struggle, but the nature of city life is different. *The city dweller always has money in his pocket, unlike the peasant, who feels that if one crumb of soil, or stone goes from his land it is a catastrophe.*'

A small but telling anecdote told by an American journalist, Vincent Sheehan, who got caught in the Jerusalem riots of 1929, gives a measure of the distance between city Palestinians and the peasants:

'A man dressed as a city Arab noticed us standing there and thrust us almost by force into a doorway. "Stand there, stand there for God's sake" he said, "These fellaheen will kill you".[97]

It is clear here that the cosmopolitan urbanite feels much closer to the two foreigners than to the peasants who are his fellow countrymen. He distances himself from their violence. All through the history of Western penetration of the Arab world, we find notables and literati extending their protection to foreigners against the primitive resistance of the masses.

Palestinian cities grew under the Mandate, and began to lose their ancient corporate solidarity. To their original population of wealthy merchants, small traders and artisans, was now added a new proletarian element, made up mainly of landless peasants. Conflict between the upper classes who led the national movement, and the growing mass of wage labourers and small bourgeoisie was not slow in coming into the open. In 1925 the first workers' union was founded in Haifa, some of its first actions being against Palestinian industrialists. Not much later socialist and communist parties were formed, though these were cliques more than parties. Though the workers' movement had a great potential for reforming the structure and methods of the national movement, it had far too little time to consolidate itself and extend its reach to the more numerous peasant class, before the Zionists seized their historic moment to capture the state. It was inevitable that a Palestinian workers' movement would become part of the national struggle, rather than confine itself to purely economic goals; the Arab Palestinian Workers' League (A.P.W.L.), led by Sami Taha until his assassination in 1947, faced not only the powerful Histadrut, but also hostility from the Arab Higher Committee, while on its left, a communist inspired workers' league led by Michel Mitri accused the A.P.W.L. of being influenced by British trade unionism.

THE RISING TIDE OF ZIONISM

Recollections of a Labour Union Organizer

All these fissures and contradictions within the nationalist movement during the last years of the Mandate, the growing Zionist threat, the faltering of the national leadership (mostly in exile or in prison), are reflected in the memoirs of R.M. a man of peasant origin who became a union organizer in Haifa. His life history (of which this is a section) faithfully and poignantly records the feverish struggle of Palestinian patriots to stem the rising Zionist tide:

'I got more involved in nationalist work when I became employed in the Department of Public Works in Haifa. That's when I began to realize the difference in treatment between Jewish workers and Arab workers. Another factor was the increase of Zionist immigration. It was becoming obvious to me as I passed through Galilee, between my village and the city, that Zionist settlements were beginning to appear in places where before there had been no trace of them, for instance Nahariyeh. I realized that this land which had always belonged to Arabs was beginning to belong to Jews. . . Besides what I used to read about Zionist intentions, I began to feel them concretely.

'I joined the League of Workers in 1943 as an ordinary member, then was elected as a member of the administrative council of the union of the Public Works Department in Haifa, in which I was employed. . . Later I became the organizer and liaison officer in the Workers' League between a greater number of smaller unions, including the municipalities, the survey department, the port, the post office and transport. . . The Zionist working class movement was growing, and we used to organize Palestinian workers to face the Histadrut, which was supported by the Mandate. We struggled for equality in wages and in positions, and to limit the number and influence of Zionist employees in government departments.

'In the last years we began to think of building a political party based on the workers' movement and to combine union work with national struggle. As a preparation, we formed a number of co-operatives, outside the workers' union, including the tobacco farmers, fishermen, and others. . . We intended also to form a secret organization, but there wasn't time, for in 1947 came the Partition Plan, and what followed it, the Disaster and dispersion.

'The reason we did not form a political party was that, after studying the project, we realized that its leaders would not be from the working class, but from their friends, doctors, engineers, lawyers, who would make the party work for their interests, not for the workers. So we decided to postpone until we had enough working class leaders. But the time we had was too short to form the party correctly. . .

'The League was active in so many ways, organizing strikes, co-operatives, demonstrations. The most outstanding event in this period was the Haifa Oil Refinery strike where we hit Zionist workers and engineers who were trying to control the Refinery. Our workers in the British military camps used to write reports; in the

persecution *in Europe* were transformed into claims fixed upon *Palestine*, written into the Mandate Protocol, legitimated at Versailles, and given substance through immigration.

The Mandate also conferred a deceptive parity upon Zionists and Palestinians, as two oppressed peoples claiming statehood in Palestine, each subordinate to British occupation. In the final stage of the Mandate, Britain's real role as midwife of the Zionist state, and her professed role as neutral arbitrator, were both reversed by Zionist propaganda to that of 'imperialist oppressor of the Jewish nation in Palestine'. Zionism was able to pass itself off as a national liberation movement, and its real colonialist character was camouflaged.

Palestinian resistance was repressed by the British with ever-increasing severity, causing heavy losses of life and property, particularly among the peasant class. After 1939 the Palestinian population was totally disarmed, leaving it defenceless against Zionist force.

The Occupation contributed to the weakening of the indigenous economy and the impoverishment of the peasant class, by 'maintaining a fiscal structure which facilitated the extraction of surplus from the non-capitalist sector, and its partial transfer to the expanding capitalist sector'.[100]

The oppressive power of the British occupation was the principal cause of the Palestinian nationalist leadership's tendency to look outwards for Arab support, thus further weakening its links with the Palestinian masses. Arab government promises of support became the substitute for the internal mobilization that the national leadership could not achieve because of the British presence and its own limitations. The intervention of the Arab governments in the Palestine crisis was in fact in line with British and Zionist interests since it brought into play new channels for manipulation and control.

Finally, as in other British dominated colonies, British rule in Palestine reinforced the status of a traditional ruling class incapable of effective mass leadership, in fact utilizing them to hold their followings in check. The socio-cultural distance between the educated urban based middle class and the mainly illiterate peasants grew wider under the impact of 'modernization', a distance reflected in politics by the only slight participation of the middle class in the national struggle, and the dangerous underdevelopment of the rural areas. With the majority of the educated classes as non-militant and 'moderate' in their stance towards the British, resistance was deprived of organizational and ideological development, and remained coloured with religious fundamentalism. Freedom to express opinions (though not freedom to organize resistance) encouraged the proliferation of parties and tendencies that further fragmented the national movement.

The cumulative effect of Britain's occupation of Palestine was that in 1948, on the verge of war, the indigenous society was far weaker than it

had been in 1936, when the General Strike began. In spite of the
Palestinians' numerical superiority, and the steady growth in national
consciousness throughout the Mandate, the apparent power relationship
between the Zionists and the Palestinians on the eve of the war was the
reverse of the true one. The 'dismemberment' of the Palestinians was the
logical outcome of three decades of a systematically produced inequality
— military, political and social — between the two communities.

REFERENCES AND NOTES

1. Eric Wolf, 'On Peasant Rebellions', in T. Shanin (ed.), *Peasants and Peasant Societies*, (Penguin, Harmondsworth, 1971).

2. A.W.Kayyali, *Palestinian Arab Reactions to Zionism and the British Mandate 1917-1939*, (Ph.D. thesis, University of London, 1970).

3. Phrases used by Tom Bowden, 'The Politics of the Arab Rebellion in Palestine 1936-39, *Middle Eastern Studies*, May 1975.

4. See Israel Shahak, *Israeli League of Human and Civil Rights*, NEEBII, Beirut, undated, p.101 for a list of villages destroyed and tribes expelled.

5. Palestinians commonly name generations by relating them to historical periods; hence: *jeel Falasteen*, the generation formed in Palestine; *jeel al-nekba* the generation formed by the Disaster; *jeel al-thawra*, the generation formed by the Revolution of 1965.

6. Sheikh Izzideen Qassam, the first to organize armed struggle, killed by the British in 1935, in the hills above Haifa.

7. Early peasant consciousness of Zionist aims was reported by Albert Antebi, an official of the Jewish Colonial Association, before 1900. See also A.W.Kayyali, *op. cit.*

8. See Z.K.'s description of his grandfather, pp.17 and 18.

9. See Note 5 above.

10. A militant from Nahr al-Bared Camp in North Lebanon.

11. J. Ruedy, 'The Dynamics of Land Alienation' in I. Abu Lughod (ed.), *The Transformation of Palestine*, (Northwestern University, Evanston, 1971).

12. See Glossary for all Arabic words.

13. W. Polk, 'The Arabs and Palestine', in Plk, Asfour and Stamler, *Backdrop to Tragedy*, (Beacon Press, Boston, 1957).

14. In the Arab/Ottoman form of feudalism, land grants, or rights to draw rent from land, were made to officials of the state, who usually did not live on their lands or exercise any feudal function in relation to their peasant tenants.

15. In the Turkish administrative system, the largest division, the *wilayet*,

was directed by a *wali*, or Provincial Governor. Below this came the *sanjak*, directed by a *mutasarrif*; then the *caza*, directed by a *qaimaqam*; then the *nahie*, controlled by a *mudir* (who was elected from the local population). The lowest administrative level was the village, with its *moukhtar*.

16. *Faza'* is derived from the verb meaning to rush. Also, see Glossary of Arabic words.

17. E.A.Finn, *Palestine Peasantry* (Marshall, London, 1923), describes village conscripts being driven in a manacled chain to the port. The notes on which the book is based were made between 1845 and 1863, when the writer's husband was British Consul in Jerusalem.

18. For good studies of peasant culture see H. Granqvist's series on birth, childhood, marriage and death, based on the village of Artas, (published by Soderstrom, Helsingfors, between 1947 and 1962). Less scholarly accounts were written by E.A.Finn; by E. Grant, *The Peasantry of Palestine*, (Lippincott, Philadelphia, 1921), and G.R.Lees, *Village Life in Palestine*, (Longmans, London, 1905).

19. Villagers normally address each other in kinship terms; and Grant relates that two villages ended a period of feud in terms of a fictitious kin relationship between them.

20. Under *masha'* tenure, the various qualities of village land were all equally divided between village families, and re-apportioned periodically.

21. Z.K.'s grandmother was both richer in land than his grandfather, and the fourth largest landowner in al-Sha'b.

22. Until relatively recently the infant mortality rate among Palestinians has been estimated at 50%.

23. The literal meaning of this phrase is 'May they be happy in marrying', meaning the host's children.

24. The code of revenge is called the *khameesa* (meaning fifth), because it designated the five kinds of relatives responsible for paying the *diyya* (penalty money for a murder), or for avenging it.

25. The practice, general throughout the Eastern Mediterranean area, of killing an unmarried girl who has been gossiped about, usually carried out by a brother. Increasingly rare among Palestinians.

26. The speaker expresses surprise because large attendance at a funeral is usually reserved for adults.

27. For a critical analysis of Mandate Palestine's economic and fiscal system, see T. Asad, 'Anthropological Texts and Ideological Problems' in *Review of Middle Eastern Studies No. 1*, (Ithaca Press, London, 1975).

28. It was estimated by a Palestinian economist that 20% of the Arab urban population was employed by central or local government.

29. 10 *dunums* = 1 hectare = 2½ acres.

30. Ruedy, *op. cit.*, p.124.

31. D. Warriner, *Land and Poverty in the Middle East*, (Royal Institute of International Affairs, London, 1948), p.62.

32. The earliest examples of peasant violence are reported in the 1880s: attacks on surveyors who came to mark out land sold over the heads of peasant tenants, or on Jewish settlements that barred peasants from exercising traditional grazing rights.

33. Y.A.Sayigh, *The Scarcity of the Land: The Fact and the Problem*, an unpublished report prepared by the Arab Office for the Anglo-American Committee of Inquiry, 1946.

34. E. Wolf, *Peasants*, (Prentice Hall, New York, 1966).

35. The technology of Palestinian agricultural production remained relatively unchanged throughout the Mandate.

36. See Y. Firestone, 'Crop-Sharing Economics in Mandatory Palestine', Parts 1 and 2 in *Middle Eastern Studies*, Vol. II, Nos. 1, 2, for details of partnership agreements between landowners and peasant farmers in Mandate Palestine.

37. Johnson-Crosbie Report, 1930.

38. The source of this quote is a Resistance Movement organizer familiar with conditions in Upper Egypt.

39. J. Weulersse, *Paysans de Syrie et du Proche-Orient*, (Colin, Paris, 1946).

40. I.M.Smilianskaya, 'From Subsistence to Market Economies, 1850s' in C. Issawi (ed.), *The Economic History of the Middle East, 1800-1914*, (Chicago University Press, Chicago, 1966).

41. E.A.Finn, *op. cit.*, describes *fellaheen* distrust of corrupt city courts. They had their own code of justice, arbitrated by community elders.

42. A. Granott, *The Land System in Palestine: History and Structure*, (Eyre and Spottiswoode, London, 1952).

43. *Ibid.*, p.62.

44. For a preliminary study of Arab class structure, see James Bill, 'Class Analysis and the Dialectics of Modernization in the Middle East', *International Journal of Middle East Studies*, October 1972.

45. Max Weber coined the term 'prebendal' to distinguish a centralized state type of feudalism from the 'patrimonial' European type.

46. From E. Wolf on Algeria, in *Peasant Wars of the Twentieth Century*, (Faber, London, 1971).

47. Ruedy, *op. cit.*, p.124.

48. Polk, *op. cit.*, p.61.

49. A.L.Tibawi, *A Modern History of Syria*, (Macmillan, London, 1969), p.176.

50. See Palestine Research Centre (P.R.C.), *Village Statistics 1945*, (Palestine Research Centre, Beirut, 1970).

51. Warriner, *op. cit.*, p.64.

52. Wolf, in his study of world peasantries, divides inheritance systems into two: partible and impartible. The second produces two classes

of inheritors and non-inheritors. The first, which equalizes ownership, tends to be associated with strong central state systems because it maximizes taxpaying units. (E. Wolf, *op. cit.*).

53. Ruedy, *op. cit.*

54. Wolf, *op. cit.*, p.78.

55. Large estates, whether feudal or mercantile, were normally held by family agglomerates, not by individuals, and could only be consolidated into single holdings in rare cases where there were few heirs, or there were sales within families.

56. Firestone, *op. cit.*, notes that in Arab crop-sharing arrangements 'the crop follows the seed, not the land'. Landownership gave prestige, but not overwhelming economic advantages.

57. In a sample of 20 camp Palestinians interviewed in 1975, one respondent and the fathers of six others had worked in the Police Force in Palestine.

58. See p.17.

59. See Note 15 above.

60. The median is that size of holding which has as many holdings larger than it, as there are smaller. It is thus a much clearer indicator of the size of most peasant holdings than the average, or mean.

61. Y.A.Sayigh, *op. cit.*, p.20.

62. Between 1922 and 1945 the Jewish population of Palestine increased from 83,790 to 554,329. Of this increase, 28% was natural and 72% due to immigration (A. Zahlan and E. Hagopian, 'Palestine's Arab Population', *Journal for Palestine Studies*, Summer 1974.) The early immigration rate fluctuated widely. An early 'high' was 34,000 in 1925, reduced thereafter to a mere 3 or 4,000 until the beginning of Nazi persecution of the Jews in the Thirties.

63. A.W.Kayyali, *op. cit.*

64. Quoted by P.R.C., *op. cit.*, p.26.

65. Clause 3 of the Constitution of the Jewish Agency stated: 'Land is to be acquired as Jewish property ... and ... shall be held as the inalienable property of the Jewish people'.

66. A. Granott, 'The Strategy of Land Acquisition' in W. Khalidi (ed.), *From Haven to Conquest*, (Institute of Palestine Studies, Beirut, 1971).

67. C. Arlosoroff, Director of the Political Department of the Jewish National Agency Executive, advised Dr. Weizman in 1932 that Zionist goals in Palestine could not be achieved 'without a transition period during which the Jewish minority would exercise organized revolutionary rule'. See A.W.Khalidi, *op. cit.*, p.245.

68. A.W.Kayyali, *ibid.*, cites instances where peasant land was sold to Zionists by the Ottoman Government and by usurers because of taxes owed by the Arab landowner.

69. See Note 15 above.

70. E. Wolf, in *Peasant Wars of the Twentieth Century*, *op. cit.*, p.218.

71. D. Hirst, *The Gun and the Olive Branch*, (Faber, London, 1977), p.35, gives this quote from Joseph Trumpeldor, founder of the Zion Mule Corps in World War 1: 'We must raise a generation of men who have no interests and no habits. . . Bars of iron, elastic but of iron. Metal that can be forged to whatever is needed for the national machine.'

72. Uri Davis, *Israel: Utopia Incorporated?*, (Zed Press, London, 1977), p.8, cites a study of Zionist leaders by Tamarin and Rosenzweig which found that most came from within a circle of 600 kilometres around Pinsk.

73. Hajj Amin Hussaini, elected Grand Mufti of Jerusalem in 1929, was a natural leader of the nationalist movement, through his position as
he head of the Muslim majority and through the financial independence given him by control of *waqf*.

74. Appendix IV, A.W.Khalidi (ed.), *op. cit.*

75. An Israeli Ministry of Education guideline to teachers states: 'It is important that our youth should know that when we returned to this country we did not find any other nation here and certainly no nation which had lived here for hundreds of years. Such Arabs as we did find here arrived only a few decades before us in the 1830s and 1840s as refugees from the oppression of Muhammad Ali in Egypt.' Hirst, *op. cit.*, p.265. The only basis to this myth is that, when Muhammad Ali invaded Palestine in the 1830s, some of his soldiers settled there, in the villages of Beersheba and Gaza.

76. See p.19.

77. See Hirst, *op. cit.*, p.21.

78. The Capitulations were measures forced upon the declining Ottoman Empire by the European Powers, to gain legal immunity for their nationals so that they would not be subject to local laws and courts.

79. A.W.Kayyali, *op. cit.*, gives a detailed account of pre-Mandate Palestinian awareness of Zionist aims in Palestine.

80. The most notorious denial of the Palestinians' existence was that made by Golda Meir, when Prime Minister, in 1969. See Hirst, *op. cit.*, p.264.

81. For a modern example of Israeli anti-Arab prejudice, see I. Shahak, *op. cit.*, pp.161-2.

82. N. Mandel, 'Attempts at Arab-Zionist Entente, 1913-14', *Middle East Studies*, April 1965.

83. A.W.Kayyali, *op. cit.*, p.61.

84. Weulersse, *op. cit.*, p.126.

85. Prior to 1883 Palestine had formed part of the *wilayet* of Damascus, and was considered by many Arab and Palestinian nationalists as the southern province of Syria.

86. None of the leaders of these groups was Palestinian. Mandel

estimates Palestinian membership at around 12 out of a possible total of 126.

87. The Arab Higher Committee was formed in 1936, an attempt like the earlier Arab Executive to set up a counterpart to the Jewish National Agency, and to unify all trends within the national movement under one leadership.

88. Taysir Nashif, 'Palestinian Arab and Jewish Leadership in the Mandate Period', *Journal of Palestine Studies*, Summer 1977.

89. A. Hourani, 'Ottoman Reform and the Politics of the Notables', in W. Polk (ed.), *Beginning of Modernization in the Middle East: the Nineteenth Century*, (University of Chicago Press, Chicago, 1968).

90. A.W.Kayyali, *op. cit.*, p.139.

91. *Ibid.*, p.92.

92. Abdul Qader Hussaini, commander of the Jaysh al-Jihad al-Muqaddes in the 1948 War until his death in April defending Kastel, was the only member of the *'ayan* to become a military leader.

93. Tom Bowden, *op. cit.*

94. D. Waines, 'The Failure of the Nationalist Resistance' in I. Abu Lughod, *op. cit.*

95. Weulersse, *op. cit.* p.86.

96. See Ahmad al Kodsy, 'Nationalism and Class Struggles in the Arab World' in Kodsy and Lobel, *The Arab World*, (Monthly Review Press, New York and London, 1970), for a brief historical review of Arab class relations.

97. Quoted in Hirst, *op. cit.*, p.69.

98. Two examples: The pro-Arab recommendations of the Shaw Report, 1924, and the Hope-Simpson Report, 1930, were repudiated by Ramsay MacDonald under Zionist pressure. In the War of 1948, British Under-Secretary for Air, John Strachey, advised Richard Crossman, MP and ardent Zionist, that it would be permissible for the Haganah to blow up all bridges over the Jordan. Hirst, *op. cit.*, p.122.

99. One example: At the end of the General Strike, in 1936, the Government tried to wind up the Haganah, but the Army Command deterred it from pressing the attempt: Leonard Mosley 'Orde Wingate and Moshe Dayan, 1938' in W. Khalidi (ed.), *op. cit.*, p.375. See also Tom Bowden, *op. cit.*

100. Talal Asad, *op. cit.*, p.15.

2

THE UPROOTING

'My opinion is that if the Arab armies hadn't entered Palestine we wouldn't have left. In every Palestinian village they talked about what to do, that there was an enemy, that they must fight. But there was no planning. Every village was alone. If we had stayed we would have struggled, and had a successful revolution. The leaders in each village would have been a nucleus. But the leaders then, like Nuri Said and Abdullah, were bought, and Palestine lacked good leaders.' (Laundry worker, Bourj al-Barajneh Camp)

WHY DID THE PALESTINIANS FLEE?

An extraordinary controversy has surrounded the question of why the mass of Palestinian peasants fled from their villages during the War of 1948, taking refuge in parts of Palestine still under Arab control or crossing the borders into Lebanon, Syria and Jordan. Yet the reasons for their flight are so obvious that only deliberate mystification could have obscured them. The primary causes were: direct military attack on the villages; terrorism; lack of leadership; lack of arms; in short, chaos and fear. The myth that they left at the orders of the Arab leaders appears to have been invented in the Israeli Information Office in New York[1] many months after the end of the war, at a time when Israel still needed international goodwill; it was never substantiated by documentary evidence. Only in the case of one or two cities, for instance Haifa, could local Arab authorities be said to have 'ordered' flight by organizing evacuation. But in most of the country there was not even this slight degree of organization. There was no single Palestinian authority, no united Arab leadership, no policy either of mass resistance or mass evacuation. Especially in the countryside, there were no other sources of organization than the villages' own defence committees. Supplies, information, instructions: all were totally lacking. How could the peasants have been ordered to flee when the smaller villages did not even have a radio?

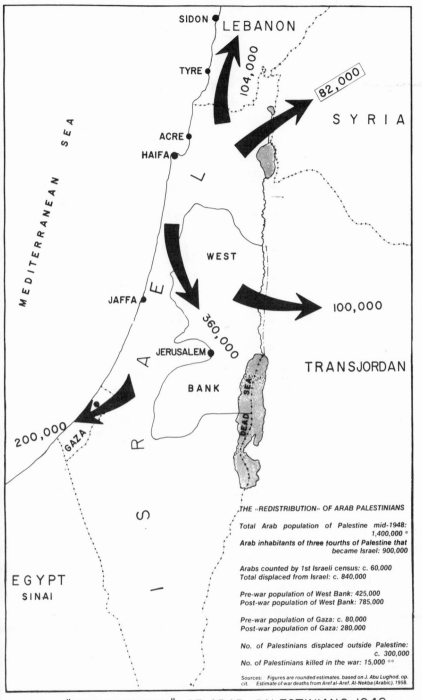

SIDON

LEBANON

TYRE

104,000

82,000

S Y R I A

ACRE

HAIFA

M E D I T E R R A N E A N   S E A

WEST

JAFFA

100,000

360,000

JERUSALEM

TRANSJORDAN

BANK

DEAD SEA

200,000

GAZA

I S R A E L

THE «REDISTRIBUTION» OF ARAB PALESTINIANS

Total Arab population of Palestine mid-1948:
1,400,000 *
Arab inhabitants of three fourths of Palestine that
became Israel: 900,000

Arabs counted by 1st Israeli census: c. 60,000
Total displaced from Israel: c. 840,000

Pre-war population of West Bank: 425,000
Post-war population of West Bank: 785,000

Pre-war population of Gaza: c. 80,000
Post-war population of Gaza: 280,000

No. of Palestinians displaced outside Palestine:
c. 300,000

No. of Palestinians killed in the war: 15,000 **

EGYPT

SINAI

Sources: Figures are rounded estimates. based on J. Abu Lughod. op.
cit.   Estimate of war deaths from Aref al-Aref. Al-Nekba (Arabic). 1958.

THE "REDISTRIBUTION" OF ARAB PALESTINIANS 1948

Arab Governments — the Broken Reed

In fact, there is evidence that what radio directives there were (issued by the Arab Higher Committee in Damascus early in the fighting)[2] ordered the Palestinians to stay put in their homes, and there can be little doubt that the danger of mass flight, which began in April 1948 with the first phase of the Zionists' attack plan, was clearly perceived by the 'leadership'. But the leaders could not call on the masses to stand firm when they themselves were outside Palestine.[3]

By mid 1948, the Arab Higher Committee was hardly even attempting to organize a resistance struggle, even though, in the last six months of the Mandate, it had managed to raise £P167,000 from the Palestinians to buy arms, and had canvassed the Arab governments zealously to obtain them. But their efforts were fruitless. Every Palestinian attempt to enlist concrete Arab support was met by evasion and bland complacency. The Syrian President told a leading Palestinian, 'our Army and its equipment are of the highest order and well able to deal with a few Jews'. The Iraqi Prime Minister told him that all that was needed were 'a few brooms' to drive the Jews into the sea. Saudis close to King Ibn Saud revealed both over-confidence and dependence on their foreign connections: 'once we get the green light from the British we can easily throw out the Jews.'[4] It is not surprising that many Palestinians concluded, after the Disaster, that the refusal of the regimes to give them adequate support *before* May 15, when the British finally withdrew from Palestine and the armies of Egypt, Jordan and Syria entered it, was caused by more than shortsightedness or stupidity. Many concluded that the Arab regimes, or individuals within them, were accomplices in an imperialist/Zionist conspiracy to remove them from their land.

The helplessness of the Palestinian leadership by April 1948, is made abundantly clear by the story of the *mukhtar* of the small village of al-Tabigha, in Eastern Galilee, one of the first areas to be attacked by the Zionists:

> 'Our tribe (*sic*) was very poorly armed. We had three hunting rifles. I had travelled to Syria on three different occasions to ask the Mufti for arms. The last time I went was a week before the village was captured. . . We were refused a meeting with the Mufti. We were asked to write down what arms we needed. We waited almost three hours . . . our papers were returned to us with a note written on the back saying, "Sorry, we have no arms".'[5]

In fact, long before this, control of the situation in Palestine (if it can be called control) had passed out of the hands of the Palestinian leadership and into those of the Arab regimes. It is significant that when in October 1947 the governments met in Aley (in Lebanon) to discuss the Palestine crisis, no Palestinian delegation was invited to attend. The legitimacy of the Arab Higher Committee was supported by some elements in the Arab

League, but opposed by King Abdullah of Jordan who had his own ambitions in Palestine.[6] Yet it was he who was nominated Supreme Commander of the Arab forces in Palestine by the Arab League in April.

Not only were the Arab regimes susceptible to Great Power pressure and divided by conflicting dynastic and regional motives, but there is every reason to doubt that they intended serious military intervention in Palestine. Early in 1948, the Political Committee of the Arab League advised members that massing Arab forces on the borders would convince the Great Powers to restrain the Zionists. Their military threat was political in purpose and it was with the greatest reluctance that the League finally took the decision to intervene, after Britain's announcement of its intention to complete withdrawal on May 15. Egypt's intervention remained doubtful until three days before D-Day and, in the field, each army followed the directives of its home government, pursuing limited objectives, without any overall strategy or co-ordination. Confusion in the direction of this most phoney of wars was compounded by the appointment within the Arab League of a Military Committee, nominally in charge of the Jaysh al-Inqadh,[7] or Arab Liberation Army (A.L.A.), a Damascus directed, Pan Arab force of irregulars led by a Lebanese professional soldier, Fawzi Qawukji.

None of the military forces present in Palestine during the year the War lasted had any clear policy towards the inhabitants of the country, whether of helping them to resist, or helping them to evacuate. This is clear from the memoirs of the war by men who fought in it, e.g. Fawzi Qawukji and Gamal Abdul Nasser,[8] as well as from the recollections of the peasant militants who tried to resist. By not joining forces with the latter, the professional soldiers in Palestine certainly contributed to their exodus. But that they ordered them to leave, or even gave them information that would encourage them to leave, goes against the norms of Arab behaviour. It is extremely unlikely that the regional commanders would have admitted to the villagers the true extent of Arab losses; usually they themselves did not know what was happening in other areas. Only in October, the last month of the War, is there clear evidence that A.L.A. commanders in Northern Galilee warned villagers that they were about to withdraw, giving them a chance to escape to Lebanon before the border was closed.[9]

Yet while the Arab forces present in Palestine never explicitly ordered a mass evacuation, there is a sense in which their presence, and the whole atmosphere of heated nationalism which accompanied Arab intervention in Palestine, helped to mystify the situation and to cloud Palestinians' understanding of what was really happening. False confidence in Arab promises to 'save' Palestine, inflated ideas of military strength, and inability to foresee the worst, all contributed something to the exodus (though not as much as did fear). There was no leader prescient or courageous enough to warn the Palestinians that, if they left their homes, it might be for ever. Hence the people stayed on in their villages, each village hoping that the War would not reach it; and when it became impossible to stay, they fled. Most had no time to think, as they fled under bombardment. But none had any idea of leaving Palestine for good, simply of finding a refuge near their village, until the battle was over; and for most of the early part of the War, flight was within Palestine itself. But even those who crossed the borders into Lebanon, Syria, or Jordan never imagined that they could be prevented from returning to their homes once the War was over, even if the Arab armies did not win. They say, 'We thought we were leaving for one or two weeks'; 'We locked our door and kept the key, expecting to return.' This certainty of return carried over into exile, helping to sustain morale in the first year of the loss of their country and their land, only gradually fading as it became clear that neither the United Nations nor the Arab regimes could procure for them this elementary justice against Israel's will.

For a long time after 1948 — for many until 1967 — faith in ultimate Arab victory continued to exercise a pacifying effect on the Palestinian masses, creating a mood of patient, loyal waiting rather than one of anger and action. From the beginning, the 'Arabization' of the Palestinian struggle had always carried the danger that the delusion it gave of strength would deflate the Palestinians' own capacity for struggle.

Yet even if the peasants had taken the decision not to flee, could they have faced organized Zionist violence on their own, as the structures of their society crumbled around them? Later they would say that it would have been better to have been massacred in thousands rather than to have left Palestine: it would have been difficult for the Zionists to have killed so many, and those who survived would have created a new, peasant based resistance. And, in fact, a minority did refuse to join the *hijra*,[10] staying on in the villages, preferring to live under Israeli domination rather than go into exile. But the terrorized majority, however they rationalized their decision, could not do anything but join the panic-stricken mass flight that a leading Zionist was to say 'miraculously simplified Israel's task'.[11]

ZIONIST MILITARY PREPAREDNESS

Entirely contrary to Arab expectations of easy victory in Palestine against 'a few Jews', was the prediction of the Commander of the British forces in Palestine, General D'Arcy, given in 1946 to an American journalist:

> 'We discussed with him what would happen if the British troops were withdrawn from Palestine. "If you were to withdraw British troops, the Haganah[12] would take over all Palestine tomorrow", General D'Arcy replied flatly. "But could the Haganah hold Palestine under such circumstances?" I asked. "Certainly", he said. "They could hold it against the entire Arab world".'[13]

The British Commander was one of the few people qualified to give an accurate estimate of the balance of military forces between the two contestants, for, unlike today, Zionist military capabilities in 1948 were a well kept secret, built up under the cover of the Jews' two thousand year old reputation for non-militancy. Until the mid Thirties, the Zionist movement had continued to depend principally on the British occupying forces for protection, while edging its way cautiously towards military preparedness. The building of the Haganah was skilfully carried out, partly with British help, partly in clandestinity, until it had reached a level of capability where the British occupation of Palestine was no longer a necessary protection, but had become instead an obstacle. The creation of Zionism's two principal terrorist organizations, the Irgun and the Stern, had two main objectives: to create an unacceptable level of losses within the British forces of occupation, so that public opinion in Britain would put pressure on the Home Government for withdrawal; and to create an atmosphere of panic amongst the Arab population.

While Herzl, himself a founder of Zionism, had foreseen early on that military power would be essential to achieving a Zionist state in Palestine ('Immigration is futile unless based on an assured supremacy'),[14] the strategy of the Jewish Agency during the early part of the Mandate was to press for full implementation of the Balfour Declaration as they understood it, i.e. for the creation of a Jewish state, without taking account of the opposition of those 'non-Jewish communities' which the Declaration had also promised to protect.[15] Conflict between Zionist and British interpretations of the Declaration was inevitable, leading to the emergence of a more militant Zionism led by men like Jabotinsky and Begin whose links with the official leadership were tenuous, but who exercised a growing influence on immigrant Jewish youth. Yet even as moderate a Zionist as Chaim Arlosoroff, who was deeply opposed to the Revisionists,[16] had already realized by 1932 that the established strategy of pressure on the British would not in itself lead to an Israeli state. Arlosoroff, who was Secretary-General of the Political Office of the Jewish National Agency, listed four reasons why this strategy was becoming obsolete: i) British policy was 'considerate to the sensibilities of the Arabs and Moslems', therefore would not help Zionism enough; ii) the number of Jews employed in government was insufficient;[17] iii) immigration quotas were insufficient; iv) land available for Zionist purchase was insufficient. Further, Arlosoroff foresaw the approaching termination of the Mandate, the growing independence of the Arab states, the possibility of their uniting and the likelihood of world war. All these considerations suggested that:

> 'Under the present circumstances Zionism cannot be realized without a transition period during which the Jewish minority would exercise organized revolutionary rule. It is impossible to attain a Jewish majority or numerical equality between the two peoples . . .

by means of systematic immigration and colonization, without a transition period of minority rule during which the state apparatus, the administration and the military establishment would be in the hands of the minority, in order to eliminate the danger of domination by the non-Jewish majority and suppress rebellion against us (it would be impossible to suppress such a rebellion unless the state machinery and military forces were in our hands). During this period a systematic policy of immigration, colonization and development would be practised.'[18]

The Zionist Goal: 'Transfer' the Palestinians

What was to happen, in terms of the Zionist leadership's strategy, to the indigenous population during and after 'organized revolutionary rule' by the Jewish minority? Although Zionist leaders had always emphasized their pacific intentions in their approaches to Palestinian and Arab leaders, the idea of the *transfer* of the Arab population was mooted early on in discussions with British sympathizers, and even earlier by militant Zionists. One of those who had fought in the Jewish Legion in World War I proposed 'the fantastic idea of resettling Palestinian Arabs back in the regions from which their forefathers had allegedly come to Palestine centuries ago'. In 1940 Joseph Weitz, an official in charge of colonization, wrote in his diary:

'Between ourselves it must be clear that there is no room for both peoples together in this country. . . We shall not achieve our goal of being an independent people with the Arabs in this small country. The only solution is a Palestine, at least Western Palestine (west of the Jordan river) without Arabs. . . And there is no other way than to transfer the Arabs from here to the neighbouring countries, to transfer all of them; not one village, not one tribe, should be left.'[19]

So reasonable did the Zionists' 'transfer' concept appear to some sectors of world opinion that it began to crop up regularly in proposals for solutions to the 'Palestine problem'. The Peel Partition Plan of 1937 urged an 'exchange of land and population'. Several British Colonial Secretaries, e.g. Winston Churchill and William Ormsby-Gore, had openly supported it. In 1944, the National Executive of the British Labour Party officially adopted the idea: 'Palestine surely is a case, on human grounds and to promote a stable settlement, for a transfer of population. Let the Arabs be encouraged to move out, as the Jews move in.' Exactly how Palestinian Arabs were to be 'encouraged' to leave their homes and land was not spelled out in this extraordinary piece of imperialist thinking disguised as a 'human' solution. Utopian fuzziness and pro-Jewish sentiment made it possible for even anti-imperialist sectors of Western public opinion to remain blind to the means used by the Zionists to achieve their goal of a Jewish majority and statehood in Palestine. Not only to Zionists, but to many others, the flight of the Palestinians appeared as a 'miraculous simplification'. That the 'miracle' had been carefully planned, and produced by military force, was an idea too disturbing to the liberals, too natural to the reactionaries, to be questioned by anyone.

Britain Helps the Haganah

The Arab Rebellion of 1936-39 had been useful to the Zionist movement in several ways: it had revealed the strength of Palestinian resistance to Zionism and British occupation; it had revealed the style and limitations of a peasants' war, and the absence of proper integration between the political and military wings of the national movement; but most of all, it had given the Zionists the chance to arm and train, at a time when the British were forcibly disarming the Palestinians. Although the Haganah had been ordered by the Administration to disband and give up their arms at the end of the six-months' General Strike that preceded the Rebellion, the British Army Command urged that the order not be enforced. At the same time, two new forces were set up: the 'Special Night Squads' trained by Orde Wingate; and a Jewish police force, the Notrim, which 'provided an excellent framework for training the Haganah'.[20] Increased from 1,240 in June 1936 to 2,863 by September, the Notrim were trained by Army officers, not police:

'The Army Command agreed to help train the Notrim, as police training was not sufficient. Thus hundreds of Haganah members received partial military training with the aid of the British Army, and the lessons were passed on in secret to thousands of others both inside and outside the ranks of the force which remained until the end of the British Mandate.'[21]

In 1938 the Notrim were reinforced by 3,000 special constables (Haganah members). In June, training in offensive methods began and mobile patrols (the Manin) were established. In 1939, ten companies of Jewish Settlement police, totalling 14,411, were formed, each company commanded by a British officer. In Tel Aviv there were 700 special constables, and in Haifa 1,000, all members of the Haganah. Through these and other paramilitary organizations almost all the Jewish population above the age of fourteen had received some degree of military training[22] by 1948, so that when war came the Zionist military command could count on a high level of mobilization from the civilian population. All the settlements also had their own trained militias.

The impact of Orde Wingate upon Zionism's military development was profound. It was under his influence, acting against directives from the British Army Command, that the Night Squads moved from their defensive function to attacks on Arab villages. It was Wingate who taught the advantages of surprise, of attacking at night and of avoiding conventional military methods. Patterns of Palestinian peasant action were carefully studied to enable attacks to succeed with minimal loss of Jewish life. Captured villagers were shot to make others reveal the places where arms were hidden.[23] All these characteristics were to become firmly rooted in Zionist militarism. Dayan, who was with him on the attack on an Arab village near the settlement of Hanita, said of Wingate:

> 'In some sense every leader of the Israeli Army even today is a disciple of Wingate. He gave us our technique, he was the inspiration of our tactics, he was our dynamic.'[24]

Wingate became chief trainer in a course for young Haganah officers, but was removed after a few months by the Army Command. After his departure from Palestine the 'Night Squads' were broken up, but:

> 'Wingate's work was not in vain. The Haganah's best officers were trained in the Special Night Squads, and Wingate's doctrines were taken over by the Israeli Defence Forces, which were established twelve days after the birth of the Jewish state.'[25]

Although it was not easy for the Zionist movement to procure arms independently of those which the British Army of occupation gave or allowed them, it was not as hard as for the Palestinian Arabs. The Notrim had arms legally, 'modern and of good quality, and supplied in growing quantities.'[26] But besides legal arms, there were two illegal sources of supply: smuggling from abroad; and manufacture in underground workshops. Arms were obtained from Belgium until 1935, then in 1938 a Polish source was established, underground at both ends. During the War of 1948 the first large consignment of Czech arms arrived (in March), followed by a steady flow from many sources after the establishment of the state on May 15. The Zionist movement was immeasurably helped in procuring arms by its international network, one branch of which, the Mossad, had the task of transporting immigrants from Europe to Palestine, while others specialized in locating arms suppliers. Besides procuring arms, the Zionist machine in Europe was able to block Arab attempts at arms purchase. As late as December 1947 a Czech arms deal with Syria was cancelled.[27]

Zionism Armed

Jewish underground workshops first began to produce arms in 1937, turning out hand grenades, rifle grenades, explosives and three inch mortars. One of their most successful inventions was the 'Little Davids', bombs containing 60lbs of TNT projected to a distance of 300 yards. The inaccuracy of the Davidka was of little disadvantage in use against densely populated areas. Another masterpiece was the barrel-bomb, filled with a mixture of explosives and petrol, which, when rolled downhill into villages or city quarters, produced 'an inferno of raging flames and endless explosions'.

The Anglo-American Committee of Inquiry's Report[28] in 1946 listed Zionist military forces (the Haganah) as consisting of a full-time strike force (the elite Palmach[29]), numbering 2,000 in peace time, with 4,000 on reserve; a field army of 16,000 trained in military operations (the Notrim); and a static reserve force of 40,000 part-time fighters, settlers and townspeople. In addition, the Zionists had been allowed to introduce one year's compulsory military service for school leavers, starting in 1945. The Report estimated the underground terrorist organizations at 3,000 to 5,000 for the Irgun and 200 to 300 for the Stern.

By the time serious fighting broke out in 1948, the Zionists could count on 36,000 front line troops; 32,000 second line troops; 15,410 settlement police; 32,000 Home Guards; and around 4,000 underground fighters (Stern plus Irgun). Out of a total Jewish population of 590,000, around 120,000, or more than one in five, were armed and trained to fight.

As for arms on the eve of war, a semi-official estimate gives the Zionists as possessing: 10,000 rifles, 450 light machine guns, 180 heavier machine guns, 96 three inch mortars, 67 two inch mortars, two 5mm field guns and an unknown quantity of smuggled and manufactured arms. After 15 May, 20 anti-aircraft guns arrived, along with a steady flow of light and heavy arms. The Jewish Defence Forces (J.D.F.)[30] had also improvized 800 armoured cars (mobility was one of the secrets of their success), as well as two Sherman and two Cromwell tanks. They also had 21 second-hand light Auster aircraft, which were effectively used to provision distant Jewish settlements and to bomb Arab villages. While the Arab forces throughout the war 'sat' on their positions, the J.D.F. used their land and air transport to erode these positions, and keep their own lines of communication open.

Plan Dalet

In what remained for many years the authoritative history of the 1948 War written by a military expert, Edgar O'Ballance makes passing reference to particular operations in the Zionists' overall attack plan, but nowhere does he mention Plan Dalet itself. This is a serious omission, since Plan Dalet marked a crucial change in the Haganah High Command's military and political objectives. The earlier plan which Plan Dalet superseded had aimed only:

> 'To gain control of the area allotted to the Jewish state and defend its borders, and those of the blocs of Jewish settlements and such Jewish populations as were outside those borders, against a regular or pararegular enemy operating from bases outside or inside the area of the Jewish state.'[31]

Plan Dalet aimed, in a series of 13 individually named operations, beginning on 1 April, to capture cities and villages in the part of Palestine which the Partition Plan of November 1947 had allotted to the Arabs, thus making impossible an Arab Palestinian state as proposed in that Plan and greatly enlarging the area of the proposed Jewish State, while emptying the whole Jewish occupied area of most of its Arab inhabitants. Lorch[32] says of this change that it was not 'a reversal of policy but a logical continuation'. In his study of the reasons why Palestinians in the Galilee area fled, Nafez Nazzal[33] states:

> 'Although Zionist historians dispute the contention that a number of these operations include provisions for the eviction of Arabs, the facts of the 1948 War, which resulted in the reluctant exile of the overwhelming majority of Palestinians from Jewish occupied areas, indicate that expulsion or incitement to leave was part of the policy put into practice.'

Using Zionist sources, the Palestinian scholar Walid Khalidi was able to piece together the different operations that made up Plan Dalet, all carried out before the British withdrew from Palestine and the Arab armies entered it:

1. Operation Nachshon, April 1: To carve out a corridor connecting Tel Aviv to Jerusalem and divide what would have been the Arab state under Partition into two;

2. Operation Harel, April 15: A continuation of Nachshon but centred on Arab villages near Latrun;

3. Operation Misparayim, April 21: To capture Haifa and rout its Arab population;

4. Operation Chametz, April 27: To destroy the Arab villages round Jaffa and so cut it off from contact with the rest of Palestine, facilitating its capture;

5. Operation Jevussi, April 27: To isolate Jerusalem by destroying the surrounding Arab villages;

6. Operation Yiftach, April 28: To rid Eastern Galilee of Arabs;

7. Operation Matateh, May 3: To destroy villages connecting Tiberias to Eastern Galilee;

8. Operation Maccabi, May 7: To destroy the Arab villages near Latrun, and penetrate into the Ramallah district;

9. Operation Gideon, May 11: To occupy Beisan and drive out the semi-sedentary *bedouin*;

10. Operation Barak, May 12: To destroy the Arab villages round Bureir on the way to the Negev;

11. Operation Ben Ami, May 14: To occupy Acre and clear Western Galilee of Arabs;

12. Operation Pitchfork, May 14: To occupy the Arab residential quarters in the New City of Jerusalem;

13. Operation Schfifon, May 14: To occupy the Old City of Jerusalem.[34]

Of these operations, not all succeeded: operations 1,2,5,8 and 13 were defeated while 10 was only partly successful. But the destruction of Arab villages in the successful operations was enough to ensure that a large part of Palestine's Arab population were already refugees before the withdrawal of the British Army of occupation. The three major Arab coastal cities, Jaffa, Haifa and Acre, had already been 'de-arabized', while the two main cities of Eastern Galilee, Tiberias and Safed, were taken on April 17/18 and May 9/10 respectively. With the city centres in Zionist hands, the villages had no hope of resisting for longer than their ammunition supplies lasted.

Terror as a Deliberate Zionist Strategy

Plan Dalet succeeded because it was carefully worked out and based on a detailed knowledge of the terrain of each village acquired by the Zionist scouts, the Gadna, whom the peasants had so often found camping on their land in the last years of the Mandate.[35] The psychology and customs of the peasants had been carefully studied, as well as the ties and relationships within and between villages. Terrorism was deliberately used not merely to create panic, but also to ensure that each man would be concerned primarily with the safety of his own family. Mass killing and rape were selectively used to build up an atmosphere in which men were forced to put the honour of their womenfolk and the lives of their children ahead of their patriotism. The Battle of Kabri[36] in March had mobilized men from many villages around, even though they had no modern communications system or transport. In April, men from several villages east of Jerusalem had joined Abdul Qader Hussaini's Jaysh al-Jihad al-Muqaddes[37] which was trying to retake the strategic village of Kastel. Some of them were probably from the small village of Deir Yasseen, only a few kilometres from Kastel.

The massacre of Deir Yasseen on April 8, in which at least 300 villagers were killed, attracted so much attention that it appeared an isolated atrocity, not closely connected with the general Zionist conduct of the War. At first the massacre was disowned by the Zionist leadership, and Ben Gurion sent a message of apology to King Abdullah, blaming the 'unofficial' terrorist groups. Yet a Palmach[38] unit had taken part in the assault, alongside the Irgun and Stern; and only three days after the massacre the Haganah and Irgun entered into an open alliance. Moreover there were other less publicized incidents of mass killing, carried out by ordinary units of the Haganah: Nasr al-Din near Tiberias; 'Ain al-Zeitouneh; al-Bi'na; al-Bassa; Safsaf; Hula, in Lebanon;[39] and doubtless others still unrecorded. Deir Yasseen was not an isolated, inexplicable atrocity in a war of defence against Arab invasion, as Zionist propaganda alleged, but part of a systematic campaign to terrorize the Palestinian peasants and force them to give up resistance.

Contemporary observers were puzzled that Deir Yasseen should be selected for attack, since it had always had peaceful relations with the Jewish settlements around it, and was even said to have driven away Arab fighters who wanted to shelter there. The only arms the village watchmen had were a few old Turkish and German hunting rifles. Most likely Deir Yasseen was chosen precisely because it could be taken with minimum casualties; and the purpose of the atrocities committed there was to put pressure on peasant militants fighting at Kastel to disperse and return temporarily to their villages. Kastel was finally lost to the Palmach on April 11, two days after the massacre, and Abdul Qader Hussaini, the leader of the Jaysh al-Jihad al-Muqaddes, was killed. With his death, the last hope of Palestinian resistance faded.

Survivors from the Deir Yasseen massacre (some of whom were driven in a triumphal procession round Jewish Jerusalem and then shot) gave chilling descriptions of individual atrocities to investigating Red Cross and British Mandate officials. The British investigator, Richard Catling, describes how difficult it was to persuade terrified and humiliated girls and women to describe what had been done to them, and to others who did not survive:

> 'I interviewed many of the womenfolk in order to glean some information on any atrocities committed in Deir Yasseen but the majority of those women are very shy and reluctant to relate their experiences especially in matters concerning sexual assault and they need great coaxing before they will divulge any information.[40] The recording of statements is hampered also by the hysterical state of the women who often break down . . . whilst the statement is being recorded. There is, however, no doubt that many sexual atrocities were committed by the attacking Jews. Many young schoolgirls were raped and later slaughtered. Old women were also molested. One story is current concerning a case in which a young girl was literally torn in two. Many infants were also butchered and killed.'[41]

An atrocity particularly calculated to horrify Arab peasants was the cutting open of the womb of a nine months' pregnant woman. This was the clearest of messages warning them that the Arab code of war, according to which women, children and old people were protected, no longer held good in Palestine. Men now had to choose: their country or their family. It was through such methods that a people with a thirty year tradition of resistance to British occupation and Zionist immigration were terrorized into flight.

While the Zionist organizations were anxious that the outside world should not know the details of what had happened at Deir Yasseen (and would have succeeded if it had not been for the courageous obstinacy of one Red Cross official),[42] they made sure that the news spread through the Palestinian population, both through the Jerusalem parade and the leaving of a few survivors. In the following months Zionist radio stations and loudspeaker vans were to make good use of the emotive words 'Deir Yasseen' to panic villages about to be attacked. Once an atmosphere of terror had been created, it was easy to exploit it to swell the exodus, with minimal losses to the attackers.

One of the ways that terror was used to avoid confrontation is described by Yigal Allon (a member of every Israeli Cabinet since 1961, and Deputy Prime Minister after 1967):

'We saw a need to clean the inner Galilee and to create a Jewish
territorial succession in the entire area of the Upper Galilee. . . We
therefore looked for means which did not force us into employing
force, in order to cause the tens of thousands of sulky (*sic*) Arabs
who remained in Galilee to flee. . . We tried to use a tactic which
took advantage of the impression created by the fall of Safed and
the (Arab) defeat in the area which was cleaned by Operation
Metateh — a tactic which worked miraculously well!

'I gathered all the Jewish *mukhtars*, who have contacts with Arabs
in different villages, and asked them to whisper in the ears of some
Arabs, that a great Jewish reinforcement has arrived in Galilee and
that it is going to burn all the villages of Huleh. They should suggest
to these Arabs, as their friends, to escape while there is still time.'[43]

O'Ballance's semi-official history of the 1948 War faithfully records the
Zionist myth that Palestinians left their homes at the orders of their
leaders, yet even he admits that the Zionist forces exercised some kind of
pressure to promote what he calls 'an unusual feature' of the 1948 War,
that is 'the complete and voluntary evacuation of the Arabs from their
towns and villages as the Jews advanced'. He notes in passing the expulsion
from villages and their destruction with dynamite, but emphasizes the use
of 'psychological' methods, blandly concluding:

'It was Jewish policy to *encourage* the Arabs to quit their homes,
and they used *psychological* warfare in *urging* (*sic*) them to do so.
Later, as the war wore on, they *ejected* those Arabs who clung to
their villages. This policy, which had such *amazing success*, had two
distinct advantages. First, it gave the Arab countries a vast refugee
problem to cope with, which their elementary economy and
administrative machinery were in no way capable of attacking, and
secondly, it ensured that the Jews had no fifth column in their
midst.'[44] (my italics)

PALESTINIAN AND ARAB FORCES

The Jaysh al-Jihad al-Muqaddes

The only purely Palestinian military force present in Palestine in 1948,
the Jaysh al-Jihad al-Muqaddes, had been formed by the Mufti (Hajj Amin
Hussaini) late in 1947, partly as a riposte to the Arab League sponsored
Jaysh al-Inqadh. The Mufti put at the head of the Jaysh al-Jihad his
nephew Abdul Qader who had accompanied him on his forced wanderings
in the last decade of the Mandate.[45] Abdul Qader may have had some
slight experience of war with the German Army, but he had never had any
formal military training. He was an honest patriot, almost the only
member of the ruling class ready to fight, and who possessed real qualities
of leadership. But he was prevented from returning to Palestine until
December 1947, too late to organize effective resistance. The Jaysh al-
Jihad is thought to have numbered not more than 5,000 men at most,

about the size of the Irgun and Stern combined, less than one-twentieth of the combined Jewish Defence Forces.

Lack of modern weapons was only one of the difficulties faced by the Jaysh al-Jihad. Finance was not totally lacking, since the Mufti received a subsidy from the Arab League as well as the contributions collected in Palestine by the National Fund. But procuring arms was much harder then finding money. No 'legal' sources were available, and the officials of the Arab governments were not courageous or nationalistic enough to risk British disapproval by supplying arms to the Palestinians. In fact, the Mufti's main source of supply was the *bedouin* of Libya and Egypt. In 1948, as in 1936, the Palestinians fought with weapons discarded in earlier wars, mostly rifles. Since even the transmission of messages between the Arab Higher Committee in Damascus and its personnel in Palestine was fraught with difficulty, it can be imagined how much harder it was to deliver arms to the fighters inside.[46]

The Jaysh al-Inqadh

The second Arab armed force present in Palestine before May 15, 1948 was the Pan Arab Jaysh al-Inqadh (or Arab Liberation Army) numbering between 3,000 and 4,000 men, of whom 1,500 were Palestinians. Its recruiting and training centre was Damascus, the only Arab capital considered by nationalists to be relatively free of British influence. Its leader, Fawzi al-Qawukji, had already begun to call for volunteers before the Military Committee of the Arab League decided to co-opt him, after it had been charged by an Arab League meeting to take the defence of Palestine in hand. The Mufti was opposed to Qawukji's appointment because he had connections with Iraq and the Hashemite dynasty. Nor were Qawukji's relations with the Military Committee that nominally controlled the Arab Liberation Army (A.L.A.) any better than with the Mufti's Arab Higher Committee; throughout the War he seldom replied to messages from Headquarters in Damascus; he, in turn, seldom received the arms he urgently requested. The confusions bred by this tragi-comedy of a war are well illustrated by the incident Qawukji describes in his memoirs[47] when he tried to cross the Syrian/Jordanian border at Deraa with the First Yarmouk Battalion in January 1948. His entry was supposed to have been cleared by Headquarters in Damascus, but Qawukji met unexpected Jordanian opposition, with the Governor of Irbed angrily asking him, 'How dare you cross without informing me in advance and giving us sufficient time to study the situation, especially as you know that we have a treaty with Britain which imposes certain obligations on us in cases like this?'[48] Headquarters advised him to force an entry, which he refused to do, eventually gaining permission to move openly through Jordan and cross the Allenby bridge 'not stealthily by night, and not piecemeal, but in broad daylight'. This open crossing of Allenby bridge was Qawukji's only triumph in Palestine.

Poorly trained both militarily and politically, lacking the formation necessary for mobilizing popular resistance, the A.L.A. cadres gave no help at all to the villagers they had supposedly entered Palestine to defend. Palestinians dubbed them the Jaysh al-Rikad (the 'Run Away Army') and years afterwards still remembered that force's invariable response to their requests for arms, directives, or military support: *'Maku awamer'* ('There are no orders').

Although supposedly an irregular force, the A.L.A. had ranks and a hierarchy of command similar to those of the Arab armies, and like them had a narrow professional elitist concept of war, taken over from the imperialist armies on whose pattern the new Arab armies were being formed. To them, anyone not in uniform was a 'civilian', intrinsically incapable of an active role in war. War was a serious business for professionals only — how could ignorant peasants fight? When the *mukhtar* of Lubiya went to the A.L.A. to ask for arms, he was refused because 'they have no men in uniform'.[49] Although the villagers themselves sometimes went to help A.L.A. units (e.g. at Sejera in Lower Galilee), there is only one recorded instance of the A.L.A. assisting them in return. The only members of the Jaysh al-Inqadh who fought with the peasants were deserters whose pay cheques were subsequently suspended. In the Battle of Kabri, a nearby A.L.A. unit refused to join the action until late afternoon, when women from the village were sent to shame them. And then, it is reported, they took from the people of Kabri all the weapons captured on the battlefield.[50]

When Saffuriyeh, a village in Lower Galilee, was bombed from the air and then shelled, the men took their families to a nearby wood and returned to defend their village:

> 'We counted on the A.L.A., stationed at Nazareth about six kilometres away, to come to our rescue . . . they did not. We were disorganized. . . We fought independently, every man for himself. There was no communication or co-ordination among us.'[51]

In all the cities, where the A.L.A. were stationed in some strength, there was less resistance to Jewish Defence Force attacks than in many villages. Acre fell overnight, enabling the J.D.F. to 'clean' all the villages of Western Galilee in little more than a week. When the J.D.F. attacked Safed on the night of May 9/10, the three top Arab commanders were not in the city, and rumours spread rapidly that the A.L.A. was withdrawing. The fall of Safed, considered an Arab stronghold, caused panic throughout the villages of Eastern Galilee.

Looking back at their experience of the A.L.A., Palestinian villagers accuse it not merely of passivity, but also in certain cases of collaborating with the enemy, or with the U.N. Truce Commission, in handing over villages without a fight. The inhabitants of Al-Birwa, who had succeeded in retaking their village after its first capture by the J.D.F., were persuaded by the commander of an A.L.A. unit stationed nearby to hand it over to them. One of the villagers recalled:

> 'We were certain that he was sincere and trusted the soldiers of the A.L.A. to protect the village. . . (We) were confident that our Arab brothers, who were well armed, would withstand a Jewish attack. But before long we saw them retreating from the village. We could not believe our eyes. . . They came to aid us and protect our village; instead, they handed over the village to the enemy.'

In the most detailed description yet written of a single Palestinian village during the year of the War, Elias Shoufani[52] shows how bad relations initially were between the inhabitants of Mi'ilya and the A.L.A. units quartered near them. The first contingent was Jordanian; and, arriving on a feast day, its soldiers entered the church to requisition people to help them unload their trucks, cook them food, bring water. Later, the Jordanians were replaced by Yemenis whose attitude to the villagers was not at first any less arrogant:

> 'It was immediately obvious from the Yemenis' behaviour that they were hostile to the local farmers, even despised them. From their headquarters in the school, they commandeered the village. They had no regard whatsoever for the property or work of those they had ostensibly come to liberate. A sort of *corvee* was imposed on the farmers. They were to dig trenches, bring firewood, supply water, and so forth. To supervise the working men, and because the soldiers had decided it was too tiring for them actively to patrol, the horses were conscripted.'[53]

However — and this is the main point of Shoufani's paper — relations between the village militia and the A.L.A. improved greatly during Mi'ilya's prolonged siege, particularly after the Haganah launched a strong attack in August, which was repulsed by the village militia fighting side by side with the A.L.A.:

> 'The battle welded the village, the militia, and the A.L.A. into an integrated body. Every soldier was at the front fighting. Every man in the village was busy lending a hand in the common effort. The militia fought hand in hand with the A.L.A. Other men transported ammunition and supplies to the front. Women carried food and water to the embattled men.
>
> 'When the villagers finally evacuated their homes some months later, the soldiers helped families carry out their children and belongings. By the end of the year's struggle the villagers and the Yemeni contingent had forged together a people's war of sorts against their common enemy.'[54]

Shoufani remarks that the A.L.A. soldiers had eventually even helped the farmers with their agricultural work. To the credit of the A.L.A. rank and file, Shoufani distinguishes between them and their leadership. Many of the ordinary soldiers only retreated after stubborn battles, with the greatest reluctance, and after hearing that their leaders had withdrawn. He recalls meeting Sergeant Salah on the day Mi'ilya fell:

'We were told that the commander-in-chief for the area, an Iraqi
called al-Azmah, had failed to notify Salah of the impending
withdrawal from the area of all A.L.A. forces. . . Today, twnty-four
years later, nowhere in the hills of Western Galilee, where Salah and
his fellow-fighters held out in repeated battles, is there a memorial
to these men.'[55]

The Jaysh al-Jihad al-Muqaddes and the Jaysh al-Inqadh were the only
Arab military forces present in Palestine before the British withdrawal on
May 14, by which time large areas of the country — the coastal plain,
Eastern and Western Galilee and all the cities except Old Jerusalem, Gaza,
and those of the West Bank — had already been 'cleaned' of most of their
Arab inhabitants. At this point the armies of five Arab states entered
Palestine, numbering altogether some 15,000 men (about one-eighth of the
number of the Jewish Defence Forces), their heaviest armour being 22
light tanks and 14 Spitfires. Estimates of the size and equipment of the
Arab armies published in the press were greatly inflated, probably as part
of the Arab regimes' policy of using threats so as to avoid actual
confrontation. None had battle experience, knowledge of the terrain, or
understanding of the enemy they were confronting. Their moves were
dictated by governments anxious for a negotiated settlement of the
'Palestine problem', and whose principal military purpose in Palestine was
to prevent one another from gaining an advantage. In 1948, as was to
happen more dramatically in 1967, the usefulness of an inflated Arab
military threat to the Zionists was to make the latter appear on the
defensive against an invasion, providing a screen behind which their
essentially aggressive action against the Palestinians passed practically
unnoticed.

WAR COMES TO THE VILLAGES

The indifference of the outside world to what had really happened in
Palestine during 1948, and the destruction of Palestinian national
institutions, meant that many years were to pass before survivors of that
War were able to record their experiences. If what happened to them had
happened to the Jews, or to Armenians, the whole 'civilized' world would
have been vibrating with horror and disapproval. But because this time the
persecutors were Jews, and the victims Arabs, no one wanted to know.
European observers on the scene minimized the scale of the Palestinian
tragedy; for example a report in *The Economist* of October 2 1948
estimated the number of refugees at 360,000 though they were at least
double that figure, and called for humanitarian aid rather than investigation
of the reasons behind the exodus. From the beginning, this was to be the
main Western reaction to the Palestinian refugee problem: extend material
aid to the survivors; ignore the political causes! *The Economist* article also

carries a brief eye-witness description of the state of expelled Palestinians in the first months of their destitution:

> 'Probably the most affecting sight in the hills is at Bir Zeit, north of Jerusalem, where about 14,000 destitutes are ranged on terrace upon terrace under the olive trees — a tree to a family — and are forced to consume the bark and burn the living wood that has meant a livelihood for generations. Here and at Nablus, where the organization is slightly more systematic, there is at present so little milk for babies that abortion seems the kindest way out.'[56]

Another chilling description of Palestinian suffering in the year of the Disaster is given by Count Bernadotte in his memoirs:

> 'I have made the acquaintance of a great many refugee camps; but I have never seen a more ghastly sight than that which met my eyes here, at Ramallah. The car was literally stormed by excited masses shouting with Oriental fervour that they wanted food and wanted to return to their homes. There were plenty of frightening faces in the sea of suffering humanity. I remember not least a group of scabby and helpless old men with tangled beards who thrust their emaciated faces into the car and held out scraps of bread that would certainly have been considered uneatable by ordinary people, but was their only food.'[57]

These are both descriptions by outsiders, vivid and moderately sympathetic, but lacking the essential element of subjectivity. What had been the concrete experiences of these thousands of expelled Palestinian peasants, *bedouin* and workers whom the world was henceforward to know, through U.N.R.W.A. brochures, as 'the Arab refugees'? Nobody thought of asking them until 1973, when a young Palestinian scholar, Nafez Nazzal, decided to focus his Ph.D. thesis on why the Palestinians had left their homes in 1948. To discover this he undertook widescale interviews among survivors of the 1948 War living in camps in Lebanon and Syria. Most of them had been agricultural in occupation, but they included policemen, teachers, shopkeepers, mechanics, *mukhtars*, bus-drivers, housewives, a doctor and a judge. From this wide coverage it is possible for the first time to build a first-hand picture of what happened when the War of 1948 came to the villages of Galilee.

Although each village had its own unique war history, Nazzal's inter-views reveal certain common themes: the village militias have old weapons, very little ammunition, and little training;[58] the early fall of the cities has a demoralizing effect; each village is isolated, cut off from news and organization; there is no national authority to give directives; the Arab military forces present in Palestine do not help to defend the villages; there are divisions within villages about whether it is better to resist, surrender, or take refuge.

Resistance must have appeared so hopeless without established channels of arms supplies that most village militias put up little more than a token fight before withdrawing to rejoin their families in nearby woods or villages.

But a minority of villages resisted stubbornly, particularly in the early part of the War, before demoralization had reached its lowest point. The inhabitants of al-Birwa and al-Sha'b both succeeded in retaking their villages after the first attack. Miyar is another village remembered for its resistance. Even allowing for an element of exaggeration, it is clear that the will to resist was there and could have been used by a leadership capable of rallying resistance.

Zionist Tactics

The form of attack used by the Jewish Defence Forces was rather uniform, though there is a clear difference between the early part of the War when Jewish military forces were overstretched and arms supplies still limited, and the final phase when it became possible for them to bomb villages from the air and use heavy artillery. In the early phase, in Western and Eastern Galilee, villages were attacked from two or three sides, leaving a road open north or east for flight. Attacks were usually launched one at a time, and villages not immediately affected often had the illusion that they would not be attacked at all. For instance the town of Nazareth, as late as July 16, was 'not worried' because it had 400 militia and relatively good arms. Even later, on October 29, most of the inhabitants of Mejd al-Kroom, 18 kilometres east of Acre, were still in their village, and only decided to evacuate when they saw the A.L.A. retreating.

Although the J.D.F. appeared amateur compared with European armies, they were infinitely more mobile and better armed than the villagers. In particular they had automatic weapons, which very few villages had, as well as mortars and a wide range of explosives. Although village militia resistance rarely lasted more than a few hours, casualties were heavy, and in certain cases (for instance al-Ghabsiyeh) shelling was directed at fleeing villagers.[59] After occupying a village, the J.D.F. would usually begin to dynamite its houses, for example in al-Zib:

> 'I slipped into the village about a month after it had fallen into Jewish hands, to bring a few things from my home. I talked to the elderly people who had remained;[60] they were all placed in Abu Saleh's house; they said that the Jewish soldiers had destroyed most of the al-Ramel area south of the village, and the eastern section.'[61]

Harry Levin, a Haganah reporter, described a Palmach attack on Kolonia (Qalunia), a village near Kastel, on April 12: 'When I left, sappers were blowing up houses. One after another. The solid stone buildings, some built in elaborate city style, exploded and crashed.'[62]

The ploy described by Allon of using Jewish or Druze *mukhtars* to warn other villages about to be attacked so that they would evacuate, was much used in the early part of the War, for instance at al-Birwa. Another device was disguise. In the case of al-Sumeiriyeh near Acre, one of the first villages in West Galilee to be attacked, an officer purporting to be from an

A.L.A. unit stationed in Acre promised that help would be sent in case of Jewish attack. As the J.D.F. attack began at dawn the next day, the families of al-Sumeiriyeh began to flee, leaving 35 armed men to defend the village:

> 'At sunrise . . . the villagers saw an armoured unit approaching from the south, along the road from Acre. Believing it to be the Arab force coming to their rescue (the men wore the red and white Arab headdress), Saleh Sa'id Ka'boush, positioned south of the village, began to fire in the air in welcome. But when he was fired upon and instantly killed, the villagers entrenched east of the village realized that the armoured unit was the enemy's and began to withdraw.'[63]

Even after the fall of a village, some inhabitants did not escape but tried to stay on. Their fate was varied. In certain cases, for example al-Bassa, Kabri, Safsaf, Mejd al-Kroom, al-Bi'na, mass killing was used to encourage complete evacuation. Sometimes only old people were allowed to stay, or removed to other villages. Mass deportation was the means of removing many villagers who managed to stay on as refugees in Druze villages after the end of the War. In rare cases, perhaps only in the case of Mi'ilya, inhabitants were allowed to return after leaving. Arrest, imprisonment and deportation were the lot of most individuals who attempted to stay,[64] or were caught trying to return to their homes.

Villagers' Reactions: Fight or Flight?

In many cases artillery attack began at night, without warning. Kweikat, a few kilometres east of Acre, had repelled at least one attempt at capture, but on the night of July 9/10 the J.D.F. surrounded the village and began to shell it:

> 'We were awakened by the loudest noise we had ever heard, shells exploding and artillery fire . . . the whole village was in panic. . . Most of the villagers began to flee with their pyjamas on. The wife of Qassim Ahmad Said fled carrying a pillow in her arms instead of her child.'[65]

Someone from the same village, now a middle-aged woman in Bourj al-Barajneh camp, gave me her recollections of the attack:

> 'It was the first night of Ramadan and we were sleeping on the roof. You know that we have *suhoor* at around 3 a.m. during Ramadan. Well, we had made tea, and my mother had just begun to lay the table. I remember that we had *bamieh*. That was when they started shelling the village. We left just as we were, some of us jumping from the roof, others from the stairs.'

In the panic of mass flight, it was common for families to become separated and children to get lost. A man from Nahr al-Bared camp recalled how this had happened to his infant daughter:

> 'When our village was attacked, the women and children and old

people left first. Because I had been in the police before 1948, I was one of those defending the village. When it was all over (i.e. the village fell) I came to the olive orchard, where the villagers were gathered, to look for my wife and children. I had a small daughter of three and a half, and in the fighting she had got separated from her mother. Some people said they'd seen her going up to a Druze village called Yerqa. I went on searching until morning without finding the girl. In the morning I went up to Yerqa. There were children playing in the square, and I saw my daughter standing there in front of a boy eating bread. She was hungry and she was asking the boy "Give me bread" and he was taking no notice of her. I came up behind her and clasped her in my arms, and I couldn't speak for tears. There she was, not with her father and mother, not in her house, not in anyone's house, alone and hungry. In twelve hours we had been changed from dignity to humiliation.'

Deeply torn between fear of losing their homes and fear for the lives of their children, families sometimes sent children ahead of them to Lebanon. R.H., as a boy of twelve, had been sent with an uncle to Bint Jbeil because he was the eldest in the family and his parents wanted to be sure he survived, in case they all perished. A woman originally from Kabri, a village which anticipated particularly fierce attack because of the successful ambush it had carried out in March[66] described to me how she had walked, a child of eight with a younger brother, all the way from Kabri to Tyre in Lebanon; somewhere on the way, she had dropped the blanket-roll her mother had given her. The terrible dilemma, whether to stay or to flee, split the old from the young, and sometimes even divided husbands and wives. Many were never to see each other again:

'My father, brother, wife and children stayed with me on the outskirts of the village of Farradiya, southwest of our village. My mother, sister, cousin and nephew remained in Safsaf. We stayed there until the Jews bombed the village of 'Ailaboon, forcing its people to flee north . . . there we learned that the Jews had also bombed Safsaf. My mother, sister, and other relatives were amongst those killed there.'[67]

Though old people were sometimes allowed to stay on in their villages, or in caves nearby, this was not always the case. A man in Bourj al-Barajneh told Nazzal of the last news he had had of his parents, given him by other old people who had stayed on with them in al-Bi'na, until December, when Jews put them in an open truck and drove them to Zububa, near Jenin:

'When they reached the border the Jews ordered them to cross the border to the Arab side. Many of the villagers were too sick to walk and were left behind in the rain. No one knows what happened to Nimr's parents.'[68]

Z.K., the man whose grandfather had wanted to attack the Jews with his stick, told me what had happened to his family after the fall of al-Sha'b:

'When we left the village, my paternal and maternal grandfather was taken by the Jews and thrown out to Jordan, he and two of his sons.

Two other of my uncles died on the way, near Jenin, but my grandfather, who was by now about 110 years old, went on to Aleppo where he had some relations with whom he stayed for a while, and then he joined us in Baalbeck (camp). It was very cold in Baalback for an old man, so we returned to Tyre. There, he decided to go back to Palestine. My father tried to convince him that he's an old man, and that he can't make it. That was in 1950. But he insisted on going, and without telling anyone he bought a donkey and hired a guide, and he got back to Palestine and reached our village. There he had a very difficult life since he was forbidden from staying, and had to hide in the fields in the daytime. My grandmother was in Mejd al-Kroom and couldn't reach him. After many attempts she managed to get to him. By then he was ill, and blind. Four or five years later he died.'

Another man who tried to stay on was R.M., later to become a Resistance Movement leader.[69] His account is interesting because it shows that there were attempts at local and regional organization as Palestine crumbled, though surely they were not capable of stemming the flood of refugees, nor aiding them once they had left their villages:

'In each village there was a local council, and out of all of them was formed a central committee. I was the vice-president of Sohmata's committee and became secretary of the central committee of Galilee. We started trying to organize civil affairs. We had to look to Lebanon to answer our needs because Acre was no longer available to us. The Zionists had occupied most of Palestine, and the A.L.A. had withdrawn to Aiteroun. Our struggle continued until October; that was when the Zionists attacked and took all of Galilee and our people were thrown out into Lebanon.

'I was one of the people who was against evacuation and because I believed this I stayed in my village until the people left. I suggested to them staying in the fields instead of the houses because of the danger of bombardment, and then go back and face our fate, even if it was to be killed. When the Zionists occupied our village, I was one of those arrested.

'One of the political errors of our leadership was that they didn't prevent evacuation. We should have stayed. I had a rifle and a Sten gun. My father told me, "The Zionists are coming, you know what they do to girls, take your two sisters and go to Lebanon." I said, "I prefer to shoot my sisters, and shoot you all, and keep the last bullet for myself. This would be better than leaving". Then they took our village and I was arrested, and they left. But our leadership was outside in Cairo, Damascus and Beirut. When the leaders are out they can't tell the people to stay.'

Along with others from his village, R.M. was arrested and imprisoned. He was moved from place to place inside Palestine and then, finally, thrown over the border at Mansoorah, with the words:

'You no longer have any place in Palestine. Go wherever you like. If you come back, you will be shot.'

That the mass of peasants were terrified not just of military attack, but also of rape, comes out clearly in R.M.'s account. The obligation of brothers to guard their sisters became a cause of conflict in many families, particularly when this obligation clashed with the young men's patriotism. One person, who was an adolescent girl at the time of the Uprooting, remembers a similar conflict in her own family:

> 'I had a brother in the army in Palestine. When we left he said, "I'm not leaving". He told my father: "I won't leave. This is my land and as long as I'm in my home no one can come and take it." My father talked to him about honour and his sisters — there was no political consciousness among the old generation — so my brother said: "If you are worried about such things, you can go into the fields." He insisted on staying, though there were bombardments and air-raids. Then a cousin who worked as a telephone operator with the A.L.A. got hit in an air-raid, and my brother was obliged to take him to Bint Jbeil. Then Sohmata fell, and all the villages around it. My father insisted that we should leave, like all the other people, so we went to the Druze village of Hurfeish. We didn't feel at home there. The Druzes kept threatening us that the Jews would come, so as to get rid of us. We wanted to go back to Sohmata, but we found no one to accompany us. So we took my brother's children with us and went to Rmeish. We had nothing but the clothes we stood up in. I remember that the children were thirsty and wanted to drink, and we had to drink from the same pools as the cattle.'

Refugees in Palestine

Not all villagers joined the streams of people flowing northwards to Lebanon and eastwards to the West Bank and Jordan. Though it is impossible to gauge this with any precision, it seems that the majority moved about within Palestine for as long as possible, seeking refuge with kin in safer villages, rather than leaving immediately for the neighbouring countries. One of Nazzal's informants, from al-Sumeiriyeh, took his family to Acre when the village fell; from Acre they went to al-Ghabisiyeh until it fell, then to the village of 'Amqa. From there, they went to Abu Sinan, until it surrendered, then to Tasheeha until its fall at the end of October. Only then did they cross over into Lebanon. A man who had been wounded in the Battle of Kabri told me:

> 'I was the last to leave our village (Saffouriyeh). I stayed in Nasra until the Jews took it, then I took refuge in Hmeimeh. I didn't want to go to Lebanon, because I knew Lebanon and Syria from 1936 when I used to go to buy guns there. From Hmeimeh I went back to Acre, from Acre back to Saffouriyeh, I and my wife, then from Saffouriyeh to Aloot. My brother advised me to go to Bint Jbeil but I said, "I don't want to see Lebanon". Then the Jews began to search all the houses, looking for men who had fought in '36 and '48. As I had been in hospital a long time, and many people had visited me, I began to fear for my life. It was only then that I decided to leave.'

In some cases, Druze villagers were generous and hospitable to the refugees, but more often it was their cool reception that gave fleeing villagers their first taste of what it would mean to be homeless and stateless. The man who went to the Druze village of Yerqa to look for his daughter met there a man whom he had once helped in prison:

'I said, "Hallo Muhanna". He saluted me, but he didn't say, "Tfaddal". I said, "Please, if you don't mind, a piece of bread for this child. I don't want any for myself." He said, "Wait here". Then he went to his house and brought a piece of bread, with five olives in it.'

While hovering as near as they dared to their villages, most attempted to infiltrate back to bring away food, blankets, or jewellery, abandoned in the first panic flight. This was usually not difficult, particularly in the early phase of the War, when the J.D.F. could only leave small units to occupy villages that had been captured:

'I took my family to Lebanon, but there was nothing for us to do there. I decided to return to the village (al-Khalisa) to dig up some money I had hidden in the courtyard. . . I had to return even though I knew it might cost me my life.'[70]

'I left my village without harvesting my grain. . . I returned to collect some of our tobacco and grain to keep my family from starving. . . At the village we found that the Jews had burned and destroyed our houses.'

'I returned to bring a few blankets, some pillows and food for my family. We left in such a hurry that I was unable to take anything with me.'[71]

The woman from Kweikat whose family had been about to eat *bamieh* on the night of the attack, spent a longer time than most as a refugee in her own country, Palestine:

'I was twelve when we left our village. We went to a village called Abu Sinan. We were a family, three girls, three boys, mother, father and grandfather, and we had nothing to eat. I used to take my younger brother and sister and creep back to get things from our home. My mother used to punish me for it, but I wasn't afraid of the Jews. I used to go in and get soap, flour, food to eat. One time when I was carrying a heavy sack of flour I trod on an electric wire which rang an alarm bell. That's when I fell and hurt my back. Another time the soldiers nearly caught us in our house, but we hid in a cupboard. It was our country, but we had become thieves in it!

'We used to get watermelon, okra, tomatoes and corn from our village. It was our land, we had sowed it, and we wanted to harvest it. Sometimes my mother and my aunt used to go at night — it was about eight or ten kilometres' walk. Once when they went, the guards saw them and shot my aunt through the head. You've seen her husband, Abu Saleh, and her daughter Amineh. What a hard life she's had!

'We didn't have money to rent from the Druzes. It was summer and we slept on the ground. When the winter came we rented a very small room, three metres by two. We stayed the whole winter in Abu Sinan and then, in March, the Israelis started pressing on the "refugees" — we were refugees in our own country! — to leave. They came at five o'clock at night, surrounded the village, and started

looking at ID cards. If anyone was a refugee they told him to fetch
his family and get into the trucks. We weren't allowed to take
anything with us. They filled nine big trucks, and then they took us
and threw us over the border, on the Merj al-Amer road.'

In at least one case, the peasants' determination to harvest their crops
spurred them into recapturing their village from the relatively small force
of J.D.F. that held it. Nazzal tells the story of al-Birwa in some detail:[72]

'The people of al-Birwa waited for about thirteen days (after the
first fall of their village on June 11). During this time they depended
upon the hospitality of the neighbouring villages. On the morning of
June 23, the villagers decided to recapture their village. It was almost
the end of the harvest time, and they wanted to harvest their fields
before the crop was ruined. The news of the plan spread throughout
the surrounding villages. My informants report that over two
hundred men and women assembled and made preparations to fight
for their village and their harvest. About ninety-six men were armed
with different makes of rifles, and they had thirty to forty-five
rounds of ammunition each. Officer Jassem, an Iraqi of the Arab
Liberation Army stationed at Tell al-Liyat, gave the villagers some
ammunition, but told them he could not join them because he had
no orders.'

Taken by surprise, the Jewish force withdrew to positions west of al-
Birwa, abandoning seven mechanical harvesters with which they had begun
to harvest the villagers' grain crop. How al-Birwa was subsequently handed
over to the A.L.A., who withdrew from it again almost immediately, has
already been described.[73]

The villagers of al-Birwa remained in the neighbourhood for some time
after the second fall of their village:

'Najib Sa'd's family stayed on in the outskirts of the village for
almost a week before deciding to go north to Lebanon. His wife
refused to go anywhere, hoping they would return to their home
soon. Haj 'Ali Fayyad stayed on a month (at al-Bi'na) after the
village had been occupied a second time, before deciding to leave to
Lebanon.'

Najib Sa'd told Nazzal of his attempt to slip back to the village to 'steal'
some of his belongings:

'We took refuge in Lebanon and life was not what we expected it to
be. Conditions were bad. We had nothing to live on. I became
desperate, and one night I decided to leave my family and go back to
the village to bring some money I had buried outside my house
before the Jews attacked. . . But I never reached my village. I was
caught by the Jews and put in jail. I did not stay long in jail. One day
the Jews filled a truck with prisoners, blindfolded us, and drove us
to the borders of Gaza. . . On our way, the Jews beat us and took
our watches and rings. When we arrived at our destination, they
assembled us, chose a man at random, and shot him in front of us.
They ordered us to run as fast as possible to the other side of the
border and not to look back. They were shooting in the air, and I
ran as I had never run before.'

Terror and Expulsion

There is no doubt that the J.D.F. used mass killing whenever they wished to clear a village or area completely of its inhabitants, some of whom, in spite of their fear of the Zionists, were even more afraid of abandoning their homes. In the case of a few villages, for example Kabri and al-Sha'b, J.D.F. behaviour was particularly vindictive because there were old accounts to settle. But in other cases, for example al-Bassa, which had always had peaceful relations with neighbouring Jewish settlements, terror was used strategically, to hold or destroy strongpoints, or to induce mass flight.

'Ain al-Zeitouneh in Eastern Galilee was one of the first villages to be attacked in Operation Yiftach. The Palmach's first assault was by rolling barrels filled with explosives and hand grenades down the hillside into the village. The village tried to surrender since its women and children had not been able to evacuate before the attack. But surrender made no difference. Thirty-seven of the village's young men were taken away and never seen again. Then the men and women of the village were separated into two groups, the women and children ordered to leave and the men told to follow them or be killed.[74]

The mainly Christian village of al-Bassa, near the Lebanese border, was not known for its militancy although it had taken part in the 1936-39 Uprising and had been bombed by the British. Many of its families had already taken refuge in Lebanon by May 14, leaving only about 40 armed men, some old people, and the usual minority who refused to leave:

> 'The people of al-Bassa did not expect any trouble from their Jewish neighbours at Ma'sub and Hanita; the Jews had assured the *mukhtars* of the village that they wished them no harm. They were in the habit of visiting the village from time to time and must have known that its people harboured no ill will towards Jews.'[75]

One of those who survived described what happened in al-Bassa after it was occupied by the J.D.F. on May 14:

> 'The day the village fell, Jewish soldiers ordered all those who remained in the village to gather in the church. They took a few young people . . . outside the church and shot them dead. Soon after, they ordered us to bury them. During the following day, we were transferred to al-Mazra'. . . There we met other elderly people gathered from the surrounding villages.[76]

People from al-Bassa who tried to 'infiltrate' back to retrieve their belongings were mostly killed by Jewish snipers entrenched at Jubeil, overlooking al-Bassa.

The village of Kabri, unlike al-Bassa, expected harsh treatment; therefore many of the villagers left before J.D.F. shelling started. A woman survivor, Amina Musa, told Nazzal her story:

> 'My husband and I left Kabri the day before it fell. We walked a few

hours to the east on the main Kabri-Tarshiha road. As it got dark, my husband suggested that we spend the night in the village orchard. . . At dawn while my husband was preparing for his morning prayer, our friend Rajeh passed us and urged us to proceed, urging that we run. My husband made his prayers, then we started to walk towards Tarshiha. It was not long before we were met by the Jews, who were coming from the north and the south towards Kabri. They stopped us and searched us. We had no weapons. They took my jewellery — gold earrings, a necklace and four bracelets . . . and forty pounds we had with us.'[77]

At that moment, the shelling of Kabri started, 'destroying everything'. The Jewish soldiers took the woman and her husband, along with a few other captured villagers, to an officer who interrogated them about where they came from. They told him they were from Sheikh Dawud, but an Arab collaborator told the officer that they were from Kabri. The men were then led away and subsequently shot, their wives abandoned on the Kabri-Tarshiha road. The next morning, Amina Musa found her husband's body and, with another woman's help, carried him to the cemetery and attempted to bury him in the correct position ('Until today I worry and pray that I buried him in the right way'). Six days later she left Kabri for Syria to look for a sister who had fled earlier.

Al-Bi'na was a village where refugees from many other villages had gathered. A survivor told Nazzal:

'The Jews grouped us with the other villagers, separating us from our women. We remained all day in the village courtyard . . . we were thirsty and hungry. Two villagers asked permission to bring water to the elderly and the children. The Jews took the men to get water, but they shot them instead. The Jews searched us, took what little money we had, our rings and our watches, and chose about 200 men at random and drove away with them in trucks towards Er-Rama. We do not know what happened to them. The rest of us were to proceed north to Lebanon. It was almost night. Al-Bi'na's *mukhtar* asked the Jews to permit us to stay overnight, promising to leave in the morning, rather than travel at night with our old men, women and children. The Jews rejected the *mukhtar's* request and gave us half an hour to leave. . . When the half hour passed the Jews began to shoot in the air, injuring my nine year old son in the knee. We walked a few hours until we reached Sajur. . . We were terrified, the road was full of people in every direction you looked . . . all in a hurry to get to Lebanon. . . I could not find the few loaves of bread I had brought with me to feed my children. They slept hungry that night.'[78]

In the case of Mejd al-Kroom, too, twelve men were picked at random and shot in front of the rest.

In the last phase of the War, the capture of Safsaf was crucial in completing the 'cleaning' of Northern and Central Galilee. After its 40 to 60 man militia had withdrawn, leaving many dead and wounded, the J.D.F. entered the village and shot 70 men in front of the rest of the

villagers who had remained behind. It was said that four girls were raped.
The effect of the massacre of Safsaf on the villages around was predictable.
A man from nearby Sa'sa' told me:

> 'My village, Sa'sa', didn't leave because of a battle. There was
> fighting around, there were air-raids and bombardments. But the
> reason we left was the news of the massacre of Safsaf, where fifty
> young men were killed. There were other massacres — Jish, Deir
> Yasseen — and there were stories of attacks on women's honour.
> Our villagers were especially concerned to protect their women, and
> because of this fear, many of the northern villages evacuated even
> before the war reached them.'

Sceptics might suggest that fears for the honour of women merely
provided a respectable reason for flight, compared with the outright fear
of death. This may be so since Palestinian peasants attach great importance
to courage. Yet such distinctions have no value since what really caused
the peasants' mass flight was the fact that they found themselves attacked
by organized violence on a scale far beyond their means to resist. If in
Palestine there had been a remote, inaccessible area that the peasants
could have withdrawn to, as the Chinese communists withdrew to Yunnan
or the Algerians to the Aures, there is no doubt that Palestinian peasant
fighters would never have crossed the borders into the neighbouring Arab
countries. But Palestine was so small that Zionist military forces could
easily control the three-quarters of it that they had succeeded in capturing
during the course of 1948. Deserted by their leadership, betrayed by the
negligence and shortsighted selfishness of the Arab regimes, what else
could the Palestinians do but flee? Villages that surrendered had no better
fate than villages that resisted. Only collaborators had their survival
guaranteed. Although Zionists continue to protest that Palestinians left
Palestine of their own accord,[79] without pressure, the testimony of
800,000 refugees refutes them.

It seems reasonable to summarize the effects of the War of 1948, during
which the state of Israel was established, by saying that the Zionist
movement succeeded, through organized violence, in transferring Jewish
dispersion and statelessness on to the Arabs of Palestine.

REFERENCES AND NOTES

1. The first known appearance of the 'Arab orders' theory of
Palestinian flight is a mimeographed pamphlet distributed by the
Israeli Information Office in New York, subsequently incorporated
in a memorandum presented by 19 prominent Americans to the U.N.
The mimeograph is thought to have been the work of Joseph

Schechtman, biographer of Jabotinsky.

2. Both W. Khalidi, 'What Made the Palestinians Leave?' *Middle East Forum* (Beirut, 1959; Arab Office of Information, London, 1963) and E. Childers, 'The Other Exodus' *The Spectator* (May 12, 1961) found BBC monitored records of Arab radio instructions to Palestinians to *stay* in their homes.

3. The only member of the Arab Higher Committee to stay in Palestine during the War was Dr. Hussain Fakhry Khalidi.

4. David Hirst, *The Gun and the Olive Branch* (Faber, London, 1977) p.135. Hirst also quotes Azzam Pasha, Secretary General of the Arab League, as declaring, 'If the Arabs do not win the war against the Jews in an outright offensive you may hang all their leaders and statesmen.'

5. Nafez Nazzal, *The Flight of the Palestinian Arabs from the Galilee, 1948* (Georgetown University, 1973), p.112-3. A version of the thesis is now being published by the Institute for Palestine Studies, Beirut, under the title, *1948: Palestinian Exodus from Galilee*.

6. E. Shoufani, 'The Fall of a Village', *Journal of Palestine Studies* (J.P.S.), (Summer 1972), tells how in the summer of 1948 King Abdullah sent an emissary to the villagers of Galilee offering to defend Galilee in return for their oath of allegiance. The Galileans refused.

7. The Jaysh al-Inqadh is sometimes translated as 'Arab Liberation Army', sometimes as 'Rescue Army'.

8. Fawzi Qawukji's memoirs of the War of 1948 can be found in the *Journal of Palestine Studies*, Nos. 4 and 5, (1972), Abdul Nasser's in No. 6, (1973), of the same journal.

9. Nazzal, *op. cit.* Survivors from Majd al-Kroom and Tarshiha told Nazzal that A.L.A. commanders had advised them to flee. In Safsaf, on the contrary, the A.L.A. was reported as preventing some villagers from leaving before the final Jewish attack.

10. The word *hijra*, most commonly used by camp Palestinians for the flight from Palestine, means literally, migration. Possibly an evocation of the Prophet Muhammad's *hijra* to Medina; or a way of euphemizing a painful reality.

11. Said by Chaim Weizmann, first President of Israel.

12. The Haganah was in a sense the official Zionist army. It grew out of the Hashomer, the armed guards of early Zionist settlements. Illegal for much of the Mandate, it was regarded as too law-abiding by the Revisionist wing of the Zionist Movement that gave birth to the terrorist Irgun and Stern.

13. Quoted by Hirst, *op. cit.*, p.134.

14. 'To his diaries, not published until twenty-six years after his death in 1904, Herzl confided his beliefs which, in his public utterances he had been careful to omit: that military power was an essential

component of his strategy and that, ideally, the Zionists should acquire the land of their choice by armed conquest.' Hirst, *op. cit.*, p.18.

15. The crucial paragraph in Balfour's letter to Lord Rothschild read: 'His Majesty's Government view with favour the establishment in Palestine of a national home for the Jewish people, and will use their best endeavours to facilitate the achievement of this object, it being clearly understood that nothing shall be done which may prejudice the civil and religious rights of the existing non-Jewish communities in Palestine...'

16. The Revisionist wing of the Zionist Movement was founded by Vladimir Jabotinsky in 1921, giving birth in 1937 to the Irgun. The Revisionists expressed a maximalist position in contrast to the 'moderation' of the official Zionist leadership. Their platform was: 1) Monism, the single ideal of the Jewish state; 2) Legyon, military training; 3) Gujis, national service; 4) Hadar, 'the transformation of the ghetto Jew ... into an aristocrat'. J. Bowyer Bell, *Terror out of Zion*, (St. Martin's Press, New York, 1977), p.19.

17. One part of the struggle of the Arab Palestinian Workers' League was to demand parity between Jews and Arabs, in status, number, and salary in government employment.

18. C. Arolosoroff, 'The Stages of Zionism and National Minority Rule' (a letter to Dr. Weizmann, June 1932) in W. Khalidi, *From Haven to Conquest*, (Institute for Palestine Studies, Beirut, 1971).

19. Quoted by Hirst, *op. cit.*, p.130.

20. D. Ben-Gurion, 'Britain's Contribution to Arming the Haganah' in Khalidi, *op. cit.*, p.371.

21. *Ibid.*, p.373.

22. See Uri Avnery's description of his recruitment to the Irgun at the age of 14: *Israel Without Zionists*, (Macmillan, New York, 1968).

23. See L. Mosley, 'Orde Wingate and Moshe Dayan, 1938' in Khalidi, *op. cit.*, p.375, for a revealing description of an attack led by Wingate against an Arab village near Hanita.

24. *Ibid.*, p.382.

25. D. Ben-Gurion, 'Our Friend; What Wingate did for us' in Khalidi, *op. cit.*, p.382.

26. *Ibid.*

27. Nazzal, *op. cit.*, p.3.

28. Anglo-American Committee of Inquiry Report, 1946.

29. The Palmach was an elite corps of special mobile squads formed from the Haganah in 1937. See E. O'Ballance, *The Arab-Israeli War of 1948*, (Faber, London, 1956), for details of the arms and manpower of Zionist and Arab military forces. O'Ballance took a professional soldier's attitude to the War, and thus misunderstood completely the role of the Zionist terrorist groups, dismissing them

as 'of limited usefulness'.

30. The Haganah, Notrim, and other legal Zionist forces were grouped together under the general title of Jewish Defence Forces, to become the Israeli Defence Forces a few days after the establishment of the new state.

31. Lt. Col. N. Lorch, 'Plan Dalet', excerpted from his *Israel's War of Independence 1947-1949*, (Hartmore House, Conn., 1968), in Khalidi, *op. cit.*, p.755.

32. *Ibid.*, p.756.

33. Nazzal, 'The Zionist Occupation of Western Galilee, 1948', *Journal of Palestine Studies*, No. 11 (1974).

34. Khalidi, *op. cit.*, Appendix VIII, p.856.

35. Based on H. Sacher, *Establishment of a State*, (William Clowes and Son, 1952), p.217. Hirst, *op. cit.* p.139, says: 'By 1947 (the Zionists) had mapped and catalogued information about every village, its strategic character and the quality of its inhabitants in Palestine.' Many Palestinians who could recall the last years of the Mandate, remembered Jewish scouts camping on their land.

36. In March 1948, the people of Kabri had ambushed a Jewish convoy provisioning a nearby settlement. Villagers from all around had joined in the fighting, which ended in the destruction of the convoy. See Nazzal, 'The Zionist Occupation of Western Galilee, 1948', *op. cit.*, for villagers' recollections of the battle.

37. See the Political Glossary.

38. See Note 29 above.

39. The massacre in 1949 of 70 young men in a mosque in Hula, near the border between Lebanon and Israel, caused a mass exodus from nearby villages such as Meys al-Jebel. See N. Chomsky's Introduction to this book, p.3.

40. The whole problem of women's 'honour' makes it doubly difficult for Arab girls to describe experiences of rape, which may make marriage and normal life impossible for them.

41. Assistant Inspector Richard Catling, cited in Lapierre and Collins, *O Jerusalem*, (Simon and Schuster, New York, 1972), p.276.

42. Irgun officials tried to force de Reynier to sign a false statement about Deir Yasseen by threatening his life. His book, *A Jerusalem un Drapeau Flottait sur la Ligne de Feu*, (La Baconniere, Neuchatel, 1950), was unobtainable for many years, but was reprinted in 1969 under a new title *1948: A Jerusalem*.

43. Yigal Allon, *The Book of the Palmach*, Vol. 2, p.286, cited in Khalidi, *op. cit.*, p.42.

44. O'Ballance, *op. cit.*, p.64.

45. The Mufti escaped from Palestine into Lebanon in 1938. From there he went to Baghdad, until the British hinted to the Iraqi government that his presence was unwelcome. The same thing happened when he

went to Iran, then to Turkey. Eventually he reached Germany where he spent most of World War II.

46. Lapierre and Collins, *op. cit.*, describe Abdul Qader Hussaini returning from Damascus in early April with three Bren guns he had bought in the *souk*, and 50 rifles given him by the Syrian President. With these he was supposed to take back Kastel from the Palmach.

47. Fawzi Qawukji, *op. cit.*

48. *Ibid.*, p.28.

49. Nazzal, thesis, *op. cit.*, p.187.

50. Nazzal, *Journal of Palestine Studies*, No. 11, pp.68-9. In recognition of their victory the people of Kabri received a gift of 11 rifles and some ammunition from A.L.A. Headquarters in Damascus.

51. Nazzal, thesis, *op. cit.*, p.177.

52. E. Shoufani, *op. cit.*

53. *Ibid.*, p.111.

54. *Ibid.*, p.112.

55. *Ibid.*, p.109.

56. 'The Arab Refugees', *The Economist*, (Oct. 2, 1948), p.540.

57. F. Bernadotte, *To Jerusalem*, (Hodder and Stoughton, London, 1951), p.200.

58. Nazzal gives details of the arms possessed by each village he investigated. For example al-Zib, with a population of 1,910, had a militia of between 70 and 75 men armed with about 60 assorted rifles, three or four Bren guns and one machine gun, with 50 to 70 rounds of ammunition per man. Most villages had much less than this.

59. Based on survivors' accounts, Nazzal gives the names of people killed in most of the villages he investigated.

60. Older villagers often preferred to die rather than leave their homes. Some were unable to walk, others were 'afraid of dying in a strange land' (Nazzal, thesis, *op. cit.*, p.203).

61. Nazzal, *Journal of Palestine Studies*, No. 11, p.65.

62. Quoted by B. Bishuti, *The Role of Zionist Terror in the Creation of Israel*, (Palestine Research Centre, Beirut, 1969).

63. Nazzal, *op. cit.*, p.63.

64. See for instance the case of R.M., Chap. 2, p.86.

65. Nazzal, thesis, *op. cit.*, p.171.

66. See Note 36 above.

67. Nazzal, thesis, *op. cit.*, p.121.

68. *Ibid.*, p.201.

69. For earlier recollections of R.M. see Chap. 1, p.54.

70. Nazzal, thesis, *op. cit.*, p.127.

71. *Ibid.*, p.128.

72. Nazzal wrote two descriptions of the episode of al-Birwa, a short one in his J.P.S. paper, and a much more detailed one in Arabic,

published in *Shu'oon Falastiniyyeh*, (Palestine Research Centre, Beirut, May 1973).

73. See Chap. 2, p.79.
74. Nazzal, thesis, *op. cit.*, p.37.
75. Nazzal, *J.P.S.* article cited above, p.66.
76. *Ibid.*, p.67.
77. *Ibid.*, p.70.
78. Nazzal, thesis, *op. cit.*, p.200.
79. This myth dies harder. A recent article by an ex-Haganah member, Paul Gutman, in *Commentary*, (October 1975), has a new version: the villagers left *before* Jewish attack, not at the orders of their leaders, but because the Palestinian notables had fled and the villagers always imitated the notables. Patriotism apart, the mass of villagers would not have left their homes unless they were forced to, for economic reasons.

3

THE NEW REALITY, 1948-1965

> During the 1948-49 War there occurred the massive separation of Arab labour from their directly controlled means of production. . . *The political and economic cost of this landlessness was transferred by military means to the neighbouring Arab countries and the UN.'* (T. Asad[1])

THE GREAT DISPERSION

With Israel's startling military victory, the displacement of the Palestinian masses that had been going on at a slow pace since the beginning of the Mandate leapt into a new dimension. Before 1948, Palestinian rights to land and nationhood had been supported, however precariously, by their presence in the country as a majority of the population, and by their resistance to Zionist colonialism. After 1948, Israeli military and political power became the dominant factor in the area. The new Zionist State's ruthless success in solving its need for land cleared of Palestinians, by continuing to displace them into the surrounding Arab area, was matched by the Arab governments' inability to prevent or reverse this displacement.

The bleak reality that faced Palestinians by the end of 1948 was that there no longer existed a Palestinian political entity. The Mufti attempted to declare a state in Gaza,[2] but he was too discredited to be able to rally resistance, especially in this poorest and most cut-off district. The carving up of Palestine into Arab spheres of influence, that had preceded the 1948 defeat and largely contributed to it, now reached its climax with King Abdullah's annexation of the West Bank, legitimized by a congress of hand-picked 'notables' at the Congress of Ariha (Jerash).[3] Gaza fell under lighter Egyptian jurisdiction.

Stricken by their incalculable losses,[4] stunned by the failure of the Arab armies, the Palestinians found themselves transformed from a 69% majority in their own country into a series of minorities scattered through several states, separated both from one another, and from Israeli-held

Palestine. They had been 'redistributed', rendering the consolidation of the Zionist State infinitely easier than it would have been if they had remained.

Demography of the Diaspora

Geopolitically, Palestinians now fell into three broad groupings: Firstly, in the three-quarters of Palestine controlled by Israel in 1948-49, around 60,000[5] Palestinian Arabs remained out of the 900,000 who would have been there if there had been no war. Of these, around 40,000 were refugees in the sense that they had lost their homes, or source of livelihood, or both. In terms of identity, they became Israel's 'Arab minority', and were issued with special ID cards denoting their non-Jewish status. They were almost entirely villagers, and more than half of them (65%) lived in Galilee. Most of the *bedouin* population of the Negev, which had not been censused since 1922 when it numbered around 65,000, was expelled in successive waves after 1948.[6]

The second and largest segment, roughly 1,000,000 (out of an estimated total in mid-1948 of 1,400,000 Palestinians overall) remained in, or moved into, those parts of Palestine that did not fall under Israeli control until the War of 1967. These became the 'Gaza Strip' and the 'West Bank', entities that did not correspond exactly with pre-war Palestinian districts. The Strip was a truncated version of pre-war Gaza; the West Bank was formed of the sub-districts of Nablus and Ramallah, plus large parts of Jenin, Tulkarm, Jerusalem and Hebron. The annexation of the West Bank of Palestine by Jordan and the placing of Gaza under Egyptian jurisdiction obscured the Palestinian character of these two remaining parts of the country.

Refugees in these two areas outnumbered the original residents: around 590,000 as against 500,000. The disproportion was particularly flagrant in the Gaza Strip, where 200,000 refugees piled in on top of a normal population of around 80,000. In the West Bank, residents exceeded refugees by a slight margin: around 425,000 as against 360,000. But, apart from the totally displaced refugees, there were also 80,000 residents of Gaza and 40,000 residents of the West Bank whom the War had deprived of their livelihood.

West Bank Palestinians were now offered Jordanian citizenship, in conformity with the Hashemite policy of absorbing into Jordan as much as possible of both the land of Palestine and its Arab population. Anyone who wished to travel, work in the public sector, register the births of children, or enter them in state schools, had no other option but this. As for Palestinians in Gaza, they were issued with special ID cards by the Egyptian authorities.

A third segment, around 300,000, fled beyond Palestine's borders altogether: some 104,000 into Lebanon, 110,000 into Transjordan, and

82,000 into Syria. Some 12,000 went even further afield: to Iraq, Egypt, Libya, Saudi Arabia, London (many who had worked with the Mandate Government had been given British passports). These never officially registered with U.N.R.W.A. as refugees, either for repatriation rights or for relief.

The core of the Palestinian *ghourba* was the camps of Lebanon, Jordan and Syria. Palestinians in Jordan, like those in the West Bank, became officially Jordanian; in Syria and Lebanon they were issued with special refugee ID cards, with rights and restrictions that were gradually defined in the years that followed.

Consequences of the Loss of Palestine

The most immediate political effect of the 'redistribution' of Palestinians, besides the effacement of their national identity, was that, through becoming minorities in several countries instead of being a majority in one, they became easier to control. The degree and forms of control varied with region and period, Syria being considered until recently the least repressive of the host countries, and Jordan the harshest. But the crucial point to mark is not the variation: dispersion itself constituted the primary instrument of suppression.

The constellation of the Palestinian diaspora reproduced the regional and class divisions that had existed in pre-1948 Palestine. The gulf between the educated urban middle class and the uneducated peasant, *bedouin* and proletarian classes was deepened: middle class Palestinians spread to all the cities of the Middle East, and beyond it, while the masses remained pinned down by poverty in the camps of the three host countries. Social inter-action between camp Palestinians and those outside was reduced to a minimum: the camps were the most obvious, concrete reminders of the humiliating defeat of 1948. Moreover, government surveillance discouraged visits to camps by Palestinians known to be 'active'.[7]

The annexation of the West Bank to Jordan reinforced the conservatism of this part of Palestine, where the political influence of the notables had always been strongest. In contrast Gaza, where no one could become rich except through contraband, became one of the most revolutionary parts of the diaspora, breeding successively an enthusiastic Nasserism, then Palestinianism. The peasants of Galilee and the proletariat of the coastal cities, that had together formed the backbone of the 1936-39 Rebellion, were mainly expelled into Lebanon and Syria where they responded to all the political currents set in motion by the defeat of 1948. But those who remained in Israel were largely quiescent until 1967, deprived of leadership, and harshly repressed by the Israeli regime. There was some movement into the Jewish dominated communist party, Rakah, but the first outward sign of revived national consciousness did not come until 1956, when the Al-'Ard group was formed,[8] to be suppressed almost immediately.

Dispersion had both centrifugal and centripetal effects upon Palestinian social structure and consciousness. By scattering them and exposing them to different political systems and influences, it increased their tendency to form small groups and factions. Yet at the same time, it constituted a condition that all suffered from, even if not equally, and against which most would ultimately rebel. It did not create unity, but it did create a pressure for unity as a means of changing a situation that was intrinsically threatening. In no region of the dispersion could a Palestinian feel completely secure or free. Nowhere could he enjoy full equality with nationals, except on terms of unconditional loyalty to the regime. The preservation of separate Palestinian purposes and identity became suspect, dangerous, involving penalties that ranged from loss of employment, to imprisonment and deportation.

Palestinians and Arab Politics

Even in the political movements that opposed the post-colonial regimes (e.g. Nasserism, Ba'thism, the Parti Populaire Syrien) Palestinians were conscious that Arab unity meant something different to people from each region and party. Adherence to the principle that 'Palestine is the first cause of all the Arabs' should have led to joint political and military struggle to regain Palestine. But it did not. All these movements were fuelled by Palestinian enthusiasm; none, in fact, put Palestine ahead of regional or party interests. It was the Palestinians' growing awareness of these divergent interests underlying the rhetoric of party slogans that constituted another uniting factor. When it emerged after 1967, Palestinianism would be both a reflection of this tendency towards the crystallization of sub-regional Arab interests, as well as a reaction against it.

Palestinians have been almost as harshly repressed in parts of the Arab diaspora as under Israeli occupation. But two vital distinctions must be made. First, it needs to be remembered that Israel was the origin of the Palestinian dispersion; it was their expulsion from Palestine/Israel that transformed the Palestinians into the 'Jews' of the Arab world, a 'people without a country', both victims and threat; their oppression followed logically from their situation as a highly politicized minority opposed to any stabilization of the *status quo*. Second, the Palestinians have been the target of attack by regimes, not by the Arab masses. More than the Jews in Europe, Palestinians in the Arab world have the possibility of joining with fellow Arabs in a struggle that remains predominantly Arab nationalist, anti-imperialist, and radical.

When the Palestinians have been hit, moreover, it has been for very different reasons from those that fed pogroms against Jews in Europe. One reason is that the Palestinian masses threaten the delicate coalition of minorities upon which the regimes of all three host countries (Jordan, Syria and Lebanon) have rested since independence.[9] This they do both because they are predominantly Sunni Muslim,[10] and because of their pressure for Arab unity, liberation and people's war. At the same time, the Palestinian masses also threaten (more by the logic of their situation than by their action) the Arab regimes' Western connections.

Their experience in the Arab *ghourba* has given Palestinians a particular stance towards 'Arabism'. Their faith in it is fuelled by the crucial dependence on Arab support, and by their understanding that Israel threatens Arab, not just Palestinian, interests. The entire future of the Arab world depends on the outcome of a struggle into which, so far, only a tiny fraction of Arab potential has been put. The capacity of the Arab masses for endurance has not been matched by effort at the level of the ruling classes. Arabism has remained insubstantial and unrealized, a mood of hope and confidence that has prevented any clear analysis of political realities.

If middle class Palestinians have greater faith in Arabism than working class Palestinians, it is because their experiences in the *ghourba* have been radically different. The Palestinian bourgeoisie has participated along with other Arab bourgeoisies in oil financed development; its professional skills have been well rewarded; it has only experienced hostility and discrimination in their mildest forms. But the Palestinian masses have felt the hard underside of post-colonial Arab societies. Along with the rest of the Arab masses they have had restricted access to employment, education, health care, and political influence. More than the Arab masses, working class Palestinians have suffered from police surveillance and harassment. Their poverty and ambiguous status (neither nationals nor foreigners) makes them victims of hostility and scapegoating in everyday encounters with officials and employers. More than the Palestinian bourgeoisie they have suffered from direct military attack — the camps are easy targets for Israeli and Arab armies alike — and, because of the difference between the classes in militancy, they have lost more sons in the liberation struggle. Nor can camp Palestinians easily forget that more *fedayeen* have been killed by Arabs than by Israelis. Because the bourgeoisie has hardly suffered in this way, it remains more tolerant of Arab anti-Palestinianism. While, increasingly, the large segment of the Palestinian bourgeoisie that feels its position in the Arab countries threatened by the Resistance Movement, tends to blame Arab attacks on the mistakes of the Resistance leaders, camp Palestinians see these attacks as following from the regimes' submission to U.S. influence. All these class contradictions underlie the Palestinians' political action in the *ghourba*.

The same social and political weaknesses that made the Arab states incapable of intervening effectively in Palestine in 1948 have made them unwilling to fully support the struggle to liberate Palestine since then, even though Israel's predominance also threatens their vital national interests. The reasons for failure in 1948 could well be labelled 'imperialist domination' and 'backwardness'; but if, after 30 years of independence and economic development, the Arab states are still militarily and technologically dependent on outside suppliers, it can only be because continuing dependence is profitable to the classes in power. National pride may have been hurt by the defeats of 1948 and 1967, and by the occupation of large parts of Egypt, Syria and Lebanon; but only the interests of the poor have been actually damaged: and they are merely peasants in peripheral areas who can easily be sacrificed to protect metropolitan centres of power. Thus, in a very real sense, militant Palestinians in the Arab world are still living the same struggle, over the same issues, and along the same lines of class polarization, that began in Palestine under the British occupation.

After 1948, a new phase of struggle opened for the Palestinian masses, marked by political suppression, social isolation and economic marginality. It is this phase that will be explored in this chapter. With 1965 a new era begins, characterized by open, ardent political activism and mass based armed struggle. This revolutionary phase (which is covered in Chapter 4) had its strongest roots in the expulsion from Palestine and in Israel's continued aggression. But it was not unconnected with camp Palestinians' experiences of political suppression and economic marginality in the *ghourba*. The passionate longing for return to Palestine was compounded of many elements, but one of them was disillusion with regimes and leaders which supported the Palestinian 'cause' whilst preventing Palestinians from active struggle. Ahmad al-Kodsy well describes the controlling function of the Arab regimes:

'Gradually a new *status quo* was established in the Arab East, a new "partition". The Russians dominated two or three states, while the Americans retained control of the economically important countries of the oil-bearing Arabian peninsula. Equilibrium was maintained by the *modus vivendi* between Israel and the Arab states: Israel, supported by Western imperialism, was to refrain from aggression, but in exchange the Arab states had to prevent the Palestinian people from challenging the Zionist colonization of their country.'[11]

On the whole, the Arab regimes were to keep to their side of the bargain better than the Israelis.

BRUTAL AWAKENING

Hijra and Humiliation

Even while still in Palestine, peasants who had taken refuge in safe villages near their own in the hope of returning as soon as the fighting was over, began to feel their new status. The Israelis issued them with ID cards stamped 'refugee' and in the course of time deported them. Once over the border there began the hassle with permits and papers that has been a basic

feature of Palestinian life ever since. The woman from Kweikat who, as a
girl, used to creep back through the Israeli lines to 'steal' flour for her
family,[12] recalls the next stage in their odyssey after their expulsion in
March 1949:

> 'We stayed in Nablus for fifteen days, then my father got us permits
> to go to Amman. The Jordanian police stopped us on Allenby Bridge,
> they said our papers weren't right. They made us sleep on the
> ground by the bridge, and if a woman hadn't got bread to feed her
> children, they'd die of hunger. My father went back to Nablus to fix
> the permits. Then we went on to Amman.'

This family was well off by peasant standards, since they could afford
to hire transport, unlike the vast mass of refugees who trudged the whole
hijra on foot. After staying for a week in a mosque in Amman, they hired
an uncovered truck, along with two or three other families who had been
driven out of Abu Sinan at the same time. Their plan was to reach Hawran
in Syria, but first they had to pass the police post on the Jordanian/Syrian
border. It was exceptionally wet and cold that winter:

> 'At Irbed crossroads it started raining. Then the police post at
> Ramtha wanted to send us back to Amman because they said our
> papers weren't right. I remember that one of the women who was
> with us jumped out of the truck, in the rain and the mud, and she
> cursed the police and all the Arabs. She was so mad that she got hold
> of her nine-month old grandson — his father was dead — and almost
> threw him at the police post, screaming, "You sons of pimps, are we
> Jews? We are Arabs!" '

There should have been a Tolstoy at hand to describe the *hijra*, a
leaderless trek of thousands of dazed and panic-stricken villagers, their
bundles of bedding dropping by the wayside, families separated, old
people dying of exhaustion, children carrying younger children, babies
dying of dehydration. Survivors remember eating grass and drinking their
own urine (it was high summer when the majority left). Settled peasants,
many of whom had never been outside their sub-district, they were
suddenly expelled into an alien world in which others would look upon
them as different, threatening, or even contemptible: 'refugees', 'displaced
persons', 'strangers'. As the man from Saffouriyeh who lost his daughter[13]
said: 'In twenty-four hours we were changed from (a state of) dignity to
humiliation.' It was particularly hard for self-respecting peasants to beg.
Accustomed to a high level of generosity, they were shocked at the
Lebanese selling them water: 'They even wanted to sell us the weeds in
their fields', said a woman who remembered how she had been refused a
glass of water for her five children because its price was 3p and she could
only offer 2½p. The man from Saffouriyeh had a similar story:

> 'We were walking on the road under Tibneen when the child began
> to get very thirsty, "Baba, I want water". I said, "Darling, take this
> penny", but no, she wanted water. We reached a village called
> Yehudieh. There was a girl sitting in a doorway. I asked her, "Lady,

please, a drink of water for this child." She said, "We don't have
water." I believed her because I thought that in that situation not
even an enemy would deprive a child of a drink of water. But then I
saw through the open door that there was a well in the house. I felt
crazy. I put my daughter down and I pointed my gun at her, "Give
me water, and if you don't let everyone drink, I'll shoot." My father
came and asked me, "Why are you standing there?" I said that I
wanted her to give us all water. He said, "Walk in front of me, *wila'*,
or I'll hit you." '[14]

Others remembered drinking from cattle pools, and buying water at one
Lebanese pound a gallon. Most of the villages of Southern Lebanon were
much poorer and more backward than those of Galilee; many refugees
spent one or two years in these villages, lodging with kin or paying rent,
before they finally moved into a camp. A man from Kweikat whose family
had brought their herd of goats and sheep with them into Lebanon (luckier
than the owners of land, their capital was movable), describes finding them
in a village called Yatha:

'They were in poor shape. Our herd had almost all died because of
the change in their pasturage; we had only thirty goats left. We had
no money, the goats weren't giving milk, so we had to live on
U.N.R.W.A. relief. I had just one pair of trousers and it had so many
patches that you couldn't see the original material. My mother was
seriously ill, and we couldn't look after her properly.
There were dirt and lice and bugs filling the village. In Palestine, if
we had parasites we'd find a way to get rid of them. But they were
used to it. Their clothes were filled with fleas and lice, but they
didn't notice them. We knew that they cause illnesses, but they
didn't know this. Their water was stagnant water from rain, and it
made people ill. So did their soap, which they made from tree bark
instead of from olives. To eat, there was only *burghul* — they had no
vegetables except tomatoes. Summer and winter they ate *burghul*.'

It was in the Shi'ite villages of the South that Palestinians had their first
contact with the concept of pollution. A family in flight who asked for
water remembers that only the adults were permitted to drink from the
jug because children cannot drink without touching the spout with their
lips. One of the earliest memories of a teacher in the camp of Bourj al-
Barajneh is, as a very small child in a Shi'ite village, putting his finger into
a pan of tomato paste and being cursed by the woman making it because
his touch obliged her to throw it away.

First Days in the Camps

However, the majority of refugees did not stop in the villages of South
Lebanon, but made straight for the cities of the coastal plain, mainly Tyre
and Sidon, where they would be more likely to meet others from their
village and hear news of missing family members. Conditions in the first,
improvised camps were at their worst, but the refugees, even then, resisted

arbitrary relocation, attempting to stay in large groups and as close as possible to Palestine. The man from Saffouriyeh remembered:

'We went on until we reached Tyre, and in Tyre started a life which none of us had imagined or dreamt of. There were three, four, five families to a tent. We had to go a long time without washing. Dirt increased. We lived a life that I am ashamed to describe, even if it's necessary.'

Another man who had been in Tyre commented:

'Abu Hussain is ashamed to say that we had lice, and he is ashamed to say that we used to live waiting for a sunny day so as to get rid of them. We lived like animals.'

A man whom the others addressed respectfully as *mrabbi*[15] gave a more elaborate version of the first year of living in a refugee camp:

'We gathered, not less than fifty or sixty villages, in a large mass at Bourj al-Shemali, east of Tyre. Life was difficult. As many as seven families to a tent, sometimes from different villages. Sharing a tent with strangers was painful for us because of our traditions. There weren't enough tents for everyone so some families had to live in caves. There was sickness and overcrowding. Many old people and children died because of the bad conditions.

'We spent the winter there, and then in the spring they forced us to leave. We tried to refuse because Bourj al-Shemali was close to Palestine, and we wanted to stay close to our country. Often four or five young men would risk death to go back over the border to our villages to get food.

'The Lebanese police came and told us we had to leave. They promised to settle us in better places, and said they would struggle with us so we could go back to our homes. But after our experience with the Jaysh al-Inqadh we knew it was all lies.

'We were people from sixty different villages and we insisted that we should all be moved together. But the distributed us, some to 'Ain Hilweh, some to North Beka', some to Anjar and Kar'oun. The sixty villages refused to be separated, so the police beat our old people and fired in the air to frighten us and force us to get into the trucks. They beat us with sticks and rifle butts.

'Our fate was to go to the barracks of Kar'oun. We found some of our kin from Saffouriyeh already settled there. They told us that many had died that winter because the snow there reached a metre or more. Provisions from Zahleh had been cut off. There had also been fighting between them and the neighbouring villages, when they'd gone out in the snow looking for a mouthful of bread.

'At the end of the summer we made a strike with the refugees in Anjar to force the authorities to let us leave the Beka' because of the hardness of the climate. This is something which we have to thank our parents for, that they forced them to allow us to leave Kar'oun. So they moved us to Nahr al-Bared camp.

'I remember that the day we arrived in Nahr al-Bared it was raining. There were women who had given birth to children in the trucks taking us from Kar'oun to Nahr. We found tents there, and they distributed us among them.'

Another man from this group in Nahr al-Bared had spent the winter of 1949 at Kar'oun:

> 'I had a younger brother who died aged seven in Kar'oun, at the beginning of winter. Many children died. They put us in barracks, 20 to 30 families to a section. I remember there was a child among us who went out to the toilet in the night and was found frozen stiff next morning.'

Police were also used to move refugees out of storage sheds in the port of Tripoli:

> 'We were staying in train compartments until winter came, then we transferred to storage sheds in the port. . . The Lebanese police came one day to evacuate the sheds because the merchants wanted to use them. Fine. But where are we going to live? They told us to get ourselves tents and go to Nahr al-Bared (twenty kilometres north of Tripoli). The people gathered to resist because some of them had managed to find jobs, or put their children in school. But the police attacked, and there was a fight which lasted several hours. The police even had to send for reinforcements.'

Apart from the harsh conditions of the first few years, there was the psychological trauma of separation from homes and property. The village — with its special arrangement of houses and orchards, its open meeting places, its burial ground, its collective identity — was built into the personality of each individual villager to a degree that made separation like an obliteration of the self. In describing their first years as refugees, camp Palestinians use metaphors like 'death', 'paralysis', 'burial', 'non-existence', 'we lost our way', 'we didn't know where to go, what to do', 'we were like sheep in a field'. Thirty years after the Uprooting, the older generation still mourns, still weeps as it recalls the past. The passion of their attachment is shown in the way old people make their children promise to re-bury their bodies in Palestine, after the return. The same word, *hajj*, is used for visits to Palestine/Israel as for the pilgrimage to Mecca.

For more than a year after the Armistice Agreements, the refugees went on believing that they would soon go home. A survivor remembers, 'We used to encourage one another by saying "Next month we'll be back".' Anxious to hide the depth of the defeat of 1948, the Arab governments kept issuing encouraging statements. As we saw when the Lebanese police moved refugees from Bourj al-Shemali to the Beka', the authorities had already adopted the practice of deflating Palestinian anger by promises of support for the struggle, or a speedy return. In addition there were the traditional peasant values of patience and acceptance of God's will which, along with a strong streak of healthy optimism and toughness, kept the mass of refugees from despair, however black their present situation and uncertain their future.

AMBIGUITIES OF BEING REFUGEES

The same question, bitter and ironical, that the woman screamed at the police post at Ramtha, 'Are we Jews? We're Arabs', recurs in most camp Palestinians' description of their situation as refugees. It arose from the ambiguity of Arab attitudes towards the Palestinian people and their struggle, in which theoretical support was often combined with unconcern in practice. It also arises from a fundamental difference of definition. To themselves, the Palestinians were a people who had struggled, and who would have resisted expulsion if they had not been starved of arms; at worst they were victims of an imperialist Zionist alliance too powerful for them, or any other Arab people, to defeat. But to many other Arabs, the refugees were a burden and a problem, as well as a reminder of national humiliation.

There was an immediate, spontaneous surge of sympathy for the refugees amongst large segments of the Arab public, but it was a sympathy that often did not have political staying power. Arab ignorance of what had happened in Palestine was widespread; and the fact that the elites and press of the Arab world were still, in spite of Arab nationalist sentiment, susceptible to European influence meant that the Zionist version of the Palestinians' flight, which passed unchallenged in the West, came also to be accepted by some segments of Arab public opinion. It was easier to believe that the turbulent, destitute refugees were themselves to blame for their situation — that they had sold their land, or fled in needless, cowardly fear instead of standing up to the Powers that protected Israel. Also, from the perspective of the host governments, the refugees were a threat to stability and order; the immediate need was to stabilize their presence through restricted areas of residence — the camps — and through special regulations controlling their actions.

When the host governments had opened their borders to the refugees, they assumed like everyone else that their stay would be temporary, and they were not prepared to assume the economic cost of supporting them. Unable to force Israel to repatriate them, the only course left to the Arab governments was to put every possible pressure upon the international community, represented by the United Nations, to shoulder responsibility for keeping the Palestinians alive. This was easier because of the internationalization of the 'Palestine problem' which had preceded the War of 1948. The U.N. was already heavily involved in Palestine, and the establishment of an Agency to aid the refugees, first U.N.R.P.R., then U.N.R.W.A.,[16] was merely a logical continuation of this involvement.

U.N.R.W.A.: the Contradictory Assumptions

From the outset, the states that made the largest contribution to U.N.R.W.A. (the very same states that supported Israel), intended that it should be used to phase out the 'refugee problem'. The Clapp Mission's report of 1949, which provided U.N.R.W.A.'s blueprint, made two major proposals: that the burden of supporting the refugees should be passed on as soon as possible to the host governments; and that U.N.R.W.A.'s funds should be mainly used to integrate the Palestinians into the host economies. Thus a three-cornered struggle developed: between U.N.R.W.A. and the host governments over the issue of responsibility for refugee support; and between U.N.R.W.A. and the refugees over the issue of 're-settlement'. The Arab governments succeeded in winning their argument that the refugees were an international, not an Arab, responsibility.[17] As for the refugees, one of the first struggles through which they manifested their continued existence as a people was their resistance to permanent resettlement outside Palestine. U.N.R.W.A. was forced to drop the projects that came to be known as *towteen* (implantation), and focus instead upon relief, education and health.

An activist from the Tripoli area recalls this early period:

> 'We felt that U.N.R.W.A. had a certain policy that aimed at settling us. They wanted us to forget Palestine, so they started work projects to give us employment. This was part of the recommendations of the Clapp Report. They used to give loans to people to set them up in small businesses such as shoe-mender or carpenter; then they'd take away their ration cards. More dangerous was the way they tried to encourage emigration to Australia or America. They'd give a man a ticket, and take away his ration card. We opposed all this, through publications and secret meetings, night visits and *diwans* — these weren't prohibited. Politically conscious people used to go to these gatherings, and take part in the conversation. We opposed these projects because we felt that, living in poverty, we would stay attached to our land.'

The camps set up to shelter and contain the mass of refugees epitomized the ambiguity of their situation. Politicized Palestinians saw the camps as part of the machinery of dismemberment and dispersion, separating them from each other and making them easier to control. At the same time, the camps offered rent-free housing and minimal services (garbage collection, water, health care, education). While registered refugees who qualified for relief and/or services[18] were not forced to live in camps, most preferred to stay close to the distribution centres. Moreover, whilst the camps made it easier for the authorities to control the refugees, they also made possible the continuation of Palestinian village relationships and values. They became foci both of oppression and of Palestinianism.

Although Palestinian national institutions had not been totally effaced by the Disaster,[19] they had no political force until 1964 when the Palestine Liberation Organization (P.L.O.) was set up. The Mufti and the Arab Higher Committee continued to have contacts with the people in the camps, shoring up the traditional leadership of family and village elders, and abstaining from contesting the authority of the host governments. In Lebanon, it is alleged the Mufti was used by the authorities to pacify refugee discontent. Possibly this function was a condition of his permit of residence.

The Refugees and the Host Countries

There was no attempt by any of the host governments to train the refugees for liberation struggle,[20] and strict control over the camps made it impossible for the refugees to initiate their own training. In any case, for the first decade, the masses were too crushed, by the struggle to survive, to have energy left for national struggle. For many, this appeared deliberate:

'U.N.R.W.A. and the host governments intended that we should be absorbed in seeking our daily bread and never have time to work seriously to regain our country (an ex-U.N.R.W.A. school teacher).'

To the militant minority who demanded a role in the struggle, the host authorities would say exactly what the Arab governments had said in 1948 to the Palestinians in Palestine: 'Leave it to the Arab armies.'

The political and economic systems in which the Palestinians now found themselves were those of neo-colonial states still tied by formal treaty or habit to the imperialist powers. The ruling classes were still composed predominantly of large landowners and merchants. Religious dignitaries still had great political influence. The experiments in democracy championed by the Westernizing upper and middle classes had become discredited. There were still no truly mass political parties whether rightist, leftist or liberal; indeed parties were little more than city based cliques of students and intellectuals. The merchant class, small and large, was still a political force, and the cities predominated as centres of power and resources over the neglected and impoverished rural hinterlands. Both government income and expenditure on public works were extremely low, but in all three host countries government was an important economic sector in itself, employing a high proportion of all employees. Everywhere the agricultural sector was stagnant and depressed. Industry was in its infancy.

Jordanization

The way each government defined the refugees varied with their policies towards the 'Palestine problem'. Jordan pursued an energetic policy of integration, with its newly acquired half of Jerusalem as the priceless asset in its tourism plan. Jordan refused to recognize a separate Palestinian identity; the authority of the West Bank notables was carefully preserved; and Palestinians were recruited in vast numbers into the Army and government services. But though Palestinian 'ultras' were well rewarded with ministerial posts, popular discontent was ruthlessly

suppressed and the camps kept under close surveillance. Someone who
attended a camp school between 1958 and 1967 remembers how armed
patrols would surround the camps on days commemorating national events:

> 'The camps are always more supervised on certain dates, for instance
> May 15 (the establishment of Israel). When we were children in
> school, before 1967, the tanks would surround the camps so that no
> demonstration could take place against the Uprooting. On those
> days they would make the school children walk in single file, three
> or four metres apart, and we were forbidden to talk together. When
> we reached our street each one of us had to go straight to his home
> and stay there. We weren't allowed to listen to the Voice of the
> Arabs from Cairo or to Damascus (Saudi Arabia, Amman and Israel
> were permitted). Soldiers filled the camp all the time and used to
> listen at the windows to hear which station we were listening to.
> People used to put blankets over their windows to stop the sound
> going out.'

Equal Rights in Syria

In Syria, the most Arab nationalist of the three host countries,
Palestinians were allowed equal rights with Syrian citizens, while keeping
their own identity. As in Lebanon (but not in Jordan) a Directorate of
Refugee Affairs was set up, directly linked to the Ministry of Interior and
to the Intelligence Services, and whose function was to issue Palestinians
with the papers needed to carry on normal life. Those who wanted to
travel were issued with a *laissez-passer*, renewable every two years. These
were harder to get than ordinary ID cards, and constituted a useful form
of pressure. Unlike in Lebanon, Palestinians in Syria could join the Army
and work in government service. Promotion opportunities and salaries may
have been lower for Palestinians than for nationals, but discrimination
seems to have been least in Syria. There was no need for work permits, and
Palestinian professional people could practise as freely as Syrians. Because
of their slightly higher level of education, Palestinians found city employment more easily than rural Syrians, many of whom had to migrate each
year to work in Lebanon.

Ambiguous Status in Lebanon

Lebanon differed from the other two main host countries in several
ways. Lebanon has a European as well as an Arab face; Palestinians were
placed in an indeterminate category, neither 'foreigners' nor 'nationals',
and were excluded from joining the Army or entering public service. The
authorities' stance towards the refugees was dictated by two fears: firstly,
that they would upset Lebanon's delicate sectarian equilibrium (in reality
its Maronite hegemony); this fear was particularly acute during the rise of
Nasserism in the Fifties. The second fear was of Israeli retaliation against
fedayeen action; this fear grew after the break-up of the U.A.R., and the

beginning of Resistance Movement operations inside Israel.

Because the Lebanese labour force was more highly skilled than that of Syria or Jordan, there was direct competition between Palestinian and local workers, taking place in a framework of lopsided development, chronic unemployment and gross inequality. As a result, Palestinians were excluded from all public and many kinds of private employment[21] as well as being forced to apply for work permits. A Palestinian lawyer describes the Palestinians' situation in Lebanon:

'The policy of the Lebanese authorities regarding ID and travel papers has always fluctuated, depending on the political situation at the time. The same was true of work permits. There have never been any specific texts applicable to Palestinians as regards travel, work, or residence.[22] There was never anything clearly defined in law. Granting any kind of permit depended on "discretionary powers" and was thus a form of pressure which had no control, and against which there was no appeal.

'To take a specific example: travel documents are issued by the Directorate of Refugee Affairs via the Surete Generale which issues passports to Lebanese, and which is a part of the Ministry of the Interior. According to the political interests of the moment, the Surete Generale would be helpful or difficult about issuing travel permits. At one time Palestinians wanting to go to Damascus would have to wait two or three weeks for a permit; at another time — which lasted several years — the Deuxieme Bureau also had to give its OK. If the D.B. said "No", there was nothing a Palestinian could do about it. This lasted through the regime of President Helou.[23] They never said to someone, "We forbid you to travel because you did such and such", it was simply a "No" without any reasons.

'Of course this kind of harassment was directed particularly against Palestinians who were active politically, but the number of suspects was always very high. The D.B. would keep lists of people who attended meetings in camps; such people would be considered suspects and their requests for travel permits refused.

'In regard to work, Palestinians were regarded as non-nationals and had to apply for a work permit from the Ministry of Social Affairs. Here, too, there was fluctuation. In periods of tension the number of permits would decrease, even though President Chehab once said in an official speech that Palestinians ought to be treated like Lebanese. But when we asked that this should be applied, or that there should be a law which would regulate employment of Palestinians, the authorities always refused to present a text to Parliament. They would tell us, "It's true that you are treated as foreigners, but you have *priority*". Palestinians were always able to get low-level jobs: masons, labourers, concierges. But if they tried to do something more ambitious it was very difficult to get a work permit.

'In 1966, when they established social security for sickness and accidents at work, they began to deduct contributions from the salaries of Palestinian workers just as from Lebanese — the law demanded it. But Palestinian workers got no benefits, on the grounds that they were foreigners. We asked the Social Security Department at least to compensate Palestinians who had work permits, or exempt them from contributing. After two years of waiting, Social Security said that they were going to request the advice of the Council of Consultation in the Ministry of Justice. Because this Council gave its opinion that the Palestinians ought to benefit from social security payments, the Ministry of Social Affairs chose to ignore it. And to justify their decision, they brought up the law of reciprocity, which means that a foreign worker employed in Lebanon gets the same security benefits that his government gives to Lebanese workers. Because the Palestinians have no state, you would expect this law could not be applied to them. But they went back to the laws of the Mandate, and when they found there was no mention of Lebanese workers being entitled to social security, they told us, "We're sorry, we cannot give you Palestinians the benefits of social security in Lebanon".'

In all three host countries there exists a solid core of 'legitimate' refugees, Palestinians who registered with U.N.R.W.A. when it was first set up, who had documentary proof of property in Palestine, and who were enumerated in early censuses. They had a certain minimum security: they could not be deported. But there was another category of refugee who belonged officially nowhere. Palestinians expelled from Israel *after* 1950 could not register with U.N.R.W.A. and had to find other ways to stabilize their existence. There were cases of people successively thrown out of Israel into Lebanon, from Lebanon into Syria, from Syria into Jordan, often to end in prison. Political crisis added to the number of second and third time refugees; after Black September in Jordan (1970),[24] a large number of Palestinians took refuge in Lebanon, but their residence there, though not forbidden, remained highly insecure, and they had no right to travel permits or ID cards.[25] Increasingly now, all the host countries are refusing entry to any but 'their own' Palestinians; for instance, entry into Syria now depends on having a relative inside to apply for a visa. The same is true of most of the Arab countries to which Palestinians migrate for work.

The never-ending hassle with permits that arises from their statelessness has been no small part of the oppression of Palestinians in the *ghourba*. The comment of a laundry worker in Bourj al-Barajneh camp is strikingly true: '*Everything* in our lives is struggle.'

ECONOMIC MARGINALITY

U.N.R.W.A. relief meant that the refugees could not starve, but it also created a false image of total dependence on international charity, concealing the fact that, through the destruction of an independent Palestinian economy, the Palestinian peasantry had been transformed into a pool of landless labour. Aid also formed an invisible subsidy to wages, this in countries where employment possibilities were so scarce that all have been exporters of labour over the last three decades. In fact U.N.R.W.A. support per capita never exceeded 20 U.S. cents a day. From the beginning it was hardly possible to survive without working[26] and the Palestinians' readiness to 'do any work at any wages' provided the Arab economies with a zealous labour force.

Poverty in the Early Years

Recollections of the early period of exile reveal the conditions of exploitation in which Palestinian refugees worked. The first three speakers are from Nahr al-Bared camp, in North Lebanon, where even today a large proportion of camp-dwellers work as agricultural day labourers. They belong to the generation that was adolescent in 1948:

'When we moved to Nahr al-Bared (from Anjar) I started working. First I worked moving sacks of onions for LL.¼ a day, though because I was a kid I didn't even get paid my salary. Then I worked in a sugar factory, walking seven or eight kilometres to work. In those days the best worker, the *qabady*, used to take from LL.1 to LL.1½ a day. At first it was just enough because people didn't want more than a mouthful of bread. If we ate meat once a year we thought it was great.'

'In 1948 I was twelve. From the time of the Partition Plan the schooling of my generation had been interrupted by the disturbances. When schools opened in Lebanon we were already too old, at 14 or 15, to attend. In any case, my family didn't have the means. I was the only son and I had to work. We weren't educated, we had no craft or skill, we couldn't write — so we had to work as labourers, at any wage, so as to be able to live. Most of us worked in agriculture because there's no industry near Nahr al-Bared. Agricultural work is seasonal, one month you work, the next you don't. There's more than one harvest, but there are also periods without any harvest. One day you work with the shovel, the next with the pruning knife. Changing jobs all the time, we had to work like donkeys to prove our worth to each new employer.'

Apart from agricultural labour there was construction work. A union organizer from the north remembers digging tunnels through the mountains in the Fifties:

'I remember the project of Kufr Halda, which cost LL.10 million in 1954-56. When they dug this tunnel, which was more than five kilometres long, our workers had only very primitive tools. Women and girls carried the rocks on their heads, and the men dragged loaded trucks with their bare hands. They worked day and night, as if they were in coal mines. The women got LL.3 a day, and the men LL.5 for a 12 hour day. They used to sleep in the open. There was no limit to the working hours, they were never less than twelve.'

In this early period, women found work more easily than men because they were paid less. Inspite of a strong dislike of women working outside the home, Palestinian women did enter the labour market, mainly in agriculture and domestic service. Families preferred women to work in factories because of its supervised, collective character, but this was only possible in the rare cases where factories were located near to camps. As for men of the *jeel Falasteen*, especially those who had never done anything but work their own land, the majority were unemployable. Only gradually, as a trickle of income began to flow into the camps, generated by the salaries of the first generation to go through school, did the small crafts, trades and services practised in the villages of Palestine reappear in the camps.

A study of the refugees carried out in 1951-52[27] gives a clear overall picture of their economic plight. The average annual per capita income of all refugees, including the middle classes, was $21.7, or £P8.9, compared with £P41 in Palestine in 1944. When it is remembered that the average was artificially heightened by large sums paid in pensions and indemnities by the British Government to ex-officials, as well as by the relatively high earnings of entrepreneurs and professionals, the destitution of refugees unable to find work can be imagined. Even those who could find casual labour, estimated as earning a yearly income of $15.2 in Jordan, $33.1 in Syria, and $39.8 in Lebanon, would have had difficulty in feeding their families. Since working class families were larger than middle class ones,[28] it can be seen how much lower than average were the actual per capita incomes of Palestinians in the camps.

The gap in income between urban middle class Palestinians and the unschooled masses in the camps can be gauged from the table below:[29]

INCOMES OF PALESTINIAN REFUGEES IN 1951

Source of Income	*Average Annual Income per Earner ($)*		
	Lebanon	*Syria*	*Jordan*
Private Business	2.000	1,500	840
Regular Employment	1,000	1,000	140
Employment with government or security forces	—	—	403
Casual Labour	60	75	37

Even casual labour was not readily available outside large cities, and conditions in camps like Nahr al-Bared, Wavell (near Ba'lbeck), Nabatiyeh and Tyre were so bad that it was painful for many to recall them. A woman whose father had been a prosperous farmer in Sohmata remembered their first years in Ba'lbeck. They had brought a little money with them from Palestine and were able at first to rent rooms in the town. But the second year they had to move into the camp:

> 'Each section of the barracks had six families. Separating us there was only a thread and a blanket. Everything took place in public, eating, washing, sleeping. Those who had six children wouldn't have place to spread their feet at night.
> 'My mother didn't want us to work, me and my brother, so she went to work in the fields with the other women so we wouldn't feel that our lives had changed.

'When I got married we had nothing. I went to live with my husband in Tripoli. He had seven brothers, three sisters, his father and mother. We all lived in one room, half the size of this one. He was the oldest, the only one working.

'In the old days it was the custom for every woman to have a chest, and I had one, with a mattress and a pillow. When we left his family, they gave me a quilt, an aluminium saucepan, and a baking pan. With this, we started our home.

'We moved back to Ba'lbeck where my husband was given a job as school director, at LL.125 (£25) a month. For a while we lived with my family, and we brought one of his sisters to live with us, to lighten the load on his family. We used to send them LL.25 (£5) a month, spend LL.50 (£10) on food, and every month we saved LL.50 (£10) to buy something for the house.'

The effect of such extreme poverty on children was indelible. Reactions would be varied, but some were propelled into political activism by the sight of their parents' suffering. A woman member of the Popular Front for the Liberation of Palestine (P.F.L.P.) in a camp near Beirut remembers her childhood in Ba'lbeck (youngest in a family of five, she was born in 1950):

'I remember that both my father and my mother used to go out to work and leave me with my elder sister at home. I began to ask questions, "Why do my parents both go out, why do we stay alone at home, why does my mother come home tired and then have to do all the housework?" The worst thing about it was that they used to work very long hours for very little money. My mother took LL.1½ and my father LL.1¾ to 2. And sometimes they worked 16 hours a day.'

The history of a man from Bourj al-Barajneh camp gives insight into the attraction of the camps near the capital for refugees in the rural areas. A boy of twelve at the time of the Uprooting, he spent the early years of exile in the south, working with his brothers on a large citrus plantation for a wage of LL.1½ a day. Married at sixteen to a girl from his village[30] he went, as custom prescribed, to pay his respects to her family in Bourj al-Barajneh. There, his wife's relatives told him he could earn more in Beirut than in the south, even in agricultural labour. So he moved to Beirut, where he bought a hut of flattened petrol cans for LL.16, and installed his girl-wife with their only possessions: a mattress, a quilt, and a primus.

Conditions in the Beirut camps were no easier at the beginning than anywhere else, but they did have the great advantage of being nearer to the centre of things. Beirut was the location of U.N.R.W.A.'s headquarters, employing some 2,000 Palestinians. It had large offices and banks, three universities, and numerous small private training establishments. Above all, it was a place for personal contacts, all important in the struggle to survive.

M.R. continued working in agriculture for some time, then got a job in U.N.R.W.A. at LL.50 a month, serving coffee in the canteen. His family opposed the change on the grounds that he could earn more by digging, but he convinced them that his chances of promotion would be better with U.N.R.W.A. He had never had the chance to continue schooling, but now he started attending English classes. He was promoted to clerk at LL.150 a month, then to the switchboard at LL.350 a month. Like so many eldest sons, he was the sole earner not only for his own family, but also for his parents and younger brothers and sisters who had by now left the south to join him. His description of his working day at the time gives some idea of Palestinian endurance and tenacity:

'I used to work at U.N.R.W.A. from 7 to 2p.m., I'd eat a sandwich on the way to the Institute. After the class, I'd go and work as an agent in a building in Ras Beirut, where I took LL.170, until 12p.m. at night. . . I never saw the children. I'd come at midnight and see them sleeping, and when I left in the morning they were still sleeping.'

Another glimpse into early economic conditions comes from a woman in Bourj al-Barajneh who, at the age of fifteen, married the only educated man from her village. At the time of their marriage in 1953, he was working with the hoe, like everyone else; but one day they happened to meet an old acquaintance from Palestine, a doctor. This encounter led to the husband getting a job as nightwatchman in a bank,[31] at LL.50 a month. It was not much for a man with two children, but Palestinians always understood the advantage of monthly as against daily wages. Ambitious and energetic, the wife looked for ways to supplement their income:

'As soon as he got employed with the bank we bought a cow. It gave 30 kilos of milk a day. It ate for LL.3, so we made LL.7. We sold a lot of milk and we bought another cow. . . I used to have to bring them water from the tank, I'd carry one jar on my head, one under my arm. I was six months pregnant. I used to feed them and clean them and someone else would come and milk them.'

One of the cows got sick and died, so they sold the other, and her husband bought her a sewing machine:

'I learnt to embroider and take the work to a shop. I'd make LL.20 to 25 a day though I'd never done that kind of work before. I learnt it from someone from Tarshiha. Then there was a Jew who had a workshop, making bras; my younger brother and sister used to work there. They'd bring me the pieces, about one dozen a day, and I'd do the machine work on them. I'd work from 8a.m. until midnight making bras and embroidery.'

Although the jobs that men of the generation of the Disaster could find remained marginal (unless they had M.R.'s exceptional capacity for self-education), schooling gradually began to improve the earning power of the young. The hunger of the peasant class in Palestine for schools for their children has already been described. In dispersion, the hunger was sharpened by the feeling that there was no other way to survive. Illiterate parents had no more urgent message for their sons than success in school. A self-employed carpenter remembers:

'I said to my sons, "We have lost everything, our land and property
is gone. You must go to school and get educated if you don't want
to do hard labour all your lives." So my sons worked hard, first to
secure their future, then to get back our country from the enemy.'

Education as a Way Out?

Fund-raising publicity for the refugees has often given the impression of
an 'educational miracle' through which the mass of refugees has been
transformed into technicians, teachers, doctors and engineers. Though
schooling has been the means to occupational change, there are two flaws
in this picture: one is that the education provided to camp Palestinians by
U.N.R.W.A. has always been limited in quantity, so that camp families
have to make sacrifices to keep children in school long enough to reach the
diplomas they need for well-paid jobs.[32] The second is the suggestion that
camp Palestinians' occupations and income levels have been drastically
improved through education. The purpose of what follows here is to give
some idea of the effort which camp Palestinians have themselves invested
in the struggle to become educated; and to point out the structural limits
to changes through educational improvement alone.

An extraordinary zeal was invested in education in the early period,
both by students and teachers (who were all Palestinian). Schools were
charged with a symbolic and emotional significance that went far beyond
their job creating potential. In the destitution and monotony of camp life,
schools were generators of hope, windows to a different future. They were
seen as the key to the improvement of the nation, to progress, science and
the recovery of the homeland. Teachers became the leaders and guides in
this community of exiles, consciously striving with small means to create a
'new generation'. Some idea of the conditions in which refugee children
got their schooling comes through in this early account from the Tripoli
area:

'I was among the first group of students from Nahr al-Bared school.
There were 70 to 80 of us in the first tent school. There weren't any
seats or school equipment — we'd sit on the sand or bring stones
from the shore to sit on. Twelve of us managed to pass the
Certificat[33] and were transferred to the House of Education[34] in
Tripoli. There we really felt the depth of the Disaster, from our
living conditions and the way they treated us. There we were, in torn
clothes, sitting next to sons of Tripoli who had different clothes for
every season,[35] and pocket money. They put us Palestinians in the
section for orphans, that way they got our rations from U.N.R.W.A.
as well as aid given by different charitable organizations that used to
help the refugees.[36] In spite of all this, we had faith that there was
no road but education. We used to go down into the street at night
to study under the street lamps.'

Any camp Palestinian from the *jeel al-nekba* who reached a diploma has
a similar story of struggle. There were organizations and individuals ready

to help, but the masses in the camps (particularly the rural camps) had no easy way to reach them. A thirty-year old teacher in Bourj al-Barajneh told how he had managed, the only surviving male in his family, with a mother and two sisters to look after, to reach a teachers' training certificate. Like many others of his generation and class, he partly worked his way through secondary school, in summer harvesting, selling encyclopedias, giving private lessons. His mother and sisters had taken in sewing. In his race for certification, every year of education was a year of lost wages for his family, and it was thus a severe setback when he was refused a permit to go to Syria to sit for an exam. His story here is typical of the frustrations camp Palestinians face in their struggle for survival:

'I needed a travel permit from the Lebanese Surete to go to Damascus to sit for the *towijihiyyeh*[37] without which I couldn't get further training to become a teacher. I went to the Surete on Saturday hoping my permit would be ready, for the exam was on Sunday. I waited until 1.30, and the Surete was about to close. I was desperate. I knocked on the Director-General's door, apologized for disturbing him, and pleaded with him to sign my permit. I told him, "Please Sir, one moment of your time can save a year of my life." He told me that if I wasn't careful I'd lose a year in prison. He didn't sign the permit, and I couldn't take the exam until the following year.'

It seems to have been very rare for families not to make every possible sacrifice to put their brightest children through school. But some had to struggle with their parents. M.R., the man whose parents married him off at sixteen, pleaded with them to give him the money they would invest in his bride (the *mahr*), so that he could get himself educated. They refused. One of U.N.R.W.A.'s most outstanding school directors had a similar struggle with his father, which he won:

'I made many attempts to persuade my father to let me go beyond the intermediate level. I even asked other people to intercede with him to help me continue my education. Sometimes I used to weep all night, begging him to pay my fees. Eventually he gave in.'

The difference in earning power between these two men, of roughly the same age and both from village families, shows the importance of certification. The gap between the educated and the uneducated that existed in Mandate Palestine not only deepened in exile, but also began to create class differences within the masses in the camps, discriminating not only in current earning power but, more seriously, in funds available for the education of children. A study of school records in Tel al-Za'ter camp found that children who stayed in school longest and got best results tended to be from villages that had had schools in Palestine. Educational difference tends to perpetuate itself: the man in Nahr al-Bared camp whose family did not have the means to put him in school in 1952, and was forced to work as an agricultural day labourer, today cannot afford to put his sons through secondary school. The Christian camp of Dbeyye was generously endowed with two secondary schools, one Catholic, the other Evangelical. As a result, it had a headstart for good jobs in the developing oil countries; by 1973, when I stayed there, a substantial proportion of the men were working outside Lebanon. By 1975, when the Lebanese Civil War started, many of them could afford to take their families out of the camp before it was overrun by the Lebanese Rightists.

It is true that Palestinians in general have an unusually high proportion of university graduates,[38] and that this reaching for higher education (which arises from the lack of their own independent economy) is also reflected in the camps, where as many as 0.2% in Lebanon had university degrees in 1970-71, and many more are engaged in sandwich courses at Arab and Lebanese universities. But these figures, though striking, tell little about the struggle for qualifications and jobs of the mass of camp Palestinians. A mother expressed a universal worry when she said: 'If I kiss a thousand hands I can't reach a job for my sons.' Every year the hurdle of qualifications gets higher, the competition with other Arabs who have prior rights as 'sons of a government' gets fiercer. Increasingly Palestinians have to go abroad (this is also true of Palestinians in Israel) to get training as well as jobs.

A look at U.N.R.W.A.'s educational statistics reveals some of the limitations of the 'educational miracle'. Enrollment (1970-71 figures) shows a marked fall-off at age 14:

6-11 years	88.4%
12-14 years	67.1%
15-17 years	37.3%
18-20 years	8.3%

The drop in school attendance from 67.1% of the potential school-going population to 37.3% is more serious because of the almost total absence of vocational training. U.N.R.W.A.'s technical and training college at Sibleen has a total intake of only 200 students and cannot be entered without first getting the difficult Baccalaureat.[39] Beirut's suburbs team with private establishments offering diplomas in everything from accountancy to aviation, but their fees are out of the reach of most camp Palestinians. This means that the mass of adolescent camp boys start working in repair shops, garages, small factories, with no hope of other training than learning on the job.[40]

Changing Class Structure

The narrow limits of the occupational transformation of camp Palestinians is revealed in a Manpower Survey carried out by the Lebanese Department of Statistics in 1971. One clear indicator of economic marginality is the fact that 58.4% of all employed camp workers are still paid on a daily basis; in contrast, only 8% have long-term contracts. Sectoral distribution is another key indicator: 21.1% are still employed in agriculture, with 13.6% in building and construction, 11.8% in industry,

2.4% in transport and corporation services, 14.4% in trade and hotels. But a massive 36.7% fall into categories which the Survey euphemizes as 'other services' and 'unspecified'. Only 40% of the working age population is employed.[41]

A recent study of Palestinians in Lebanon by Samir Ayoub[42] found that 62.9% had a monthly income of less than LL.500 (£100). Since the sample contained middle class as well as working class Palestinians, it can be taken that the proportion of working class families with less than LL.500 a month is around 80%. Ayoub also found that a high proportion of families had debts; most said that their income did not cover their needs and that they wanted to change their jobs because they needed more money. The study provided very clear evidence of a shift in the type of work done by Palestinians: whereas 68% of the respondents' grandfathers had worked in agriculture, only 17% of the sample now did and only 3% said that this was their desired occupation. On the other hand, where only 22% of grandfathers had worked in services, 74% of respondents were employed in this sector and 78% wanted to be. In contrast to the move into services, employment in industry showed less change (2% of grandfathers compared with 9% of respondents), reflecting the fact that industry in Lebanon is almost exclusively Lebanese.

Another significant change found by Ayoub's study is that whereas 76.4% of respondents' grandfathers and 59.4% of fathers, were self-employed, 79.0% of respondents were employed by others. A people of small farmers, artisans and traders has changed into a people of clerks, accountants and administrators — *muwazzefeen*.[43] Although no figures on occupational distribution are available for the Gulf, it seems likely that a larger proportion of Palestinians work in government service or big companies, than in construction and industry.

This mass move into services reflects a general Arab trend,[44] but it also stems from the fact that Palestinians depend for a livelihood on economies they do not control and can only indirectly influence. A finding indicating Palestinians' job insecurity was that most of the sample had more than one occupation. Economic hardship was evident in the fact that the majority had more than one job at the time of the survey, while around 75% expressed dissatisfaction with their current job, either on account of low pay, poor working conditions, or the employer's attitude towards them. One of the most interesting of Ayoub's findings was that 88% of his sample said they thought it impossible for the Palestinian individual to change his class position.

The occupational categories used by economists — industry, services, agriculture — give little idea of the class level at which a given population participates in these sectors. 'Services' in particular can mean anything from a cabinet minister to a nightwatchman. Hani Mundus's study of a single camp, Tel al-Za'ter,[45] is invaluable for its minute occupational breakdowns and concrete detail. Though one of the poorest of Palestinian camps in Lebanon, Tel al-Za'ter was unique in having a major proportion of its labour force (60%) employed in industry, because of its closeness to the industrial zone of Mkalles. But what does 'industry' mean in a country of underdeveloped capitalism? 80.4% of all industrial units in Lebanon employ less than ten workers. Only the larger ones offer modern working conditions and benefits such as paid sick leave, paid holidays, or compensation for accidents. Out of Tel al-Za'ter's 1,355 workers in the industrial sector, only 50 were in establishments of more than 50 workers, and these were mainly girls.[46] Although a Lebanese employer who gave work to a Palestinian without a work permit could be fined, a great many did so because the difficulty of getting permits enabled them to offer lower wages.[47]

Mundus's study points out the basic features of Palestinian employment in Lebanese industry: a high rate of periodic unemployment and job insecurity, low wages, no benefits, and no legal protection. In one respect, however, the situation of Palestinian workers in Lebanon is better than that of most ethnic proletariats in that the General Union of Palestinian Workers (G.U.P.W.) works closely with the progressive Lebanese workers' unions.

Dispersed through many small industrial units, Palestinian workers can only with difficulty be termed a proletariat. Mundus places only 7% of Tel al-Za'ter's work force in this category, designating 85% as 'sub-proletariat' and 3% 'lumpenproletariat' (e.g. lottery ticket sellers). The fragmentation of the Palestinian work force is clearly shown by the fact that Mundus lists 10 different main occupations, as well as 17 miscellaneous ones.[48] Further fragmentation arises from the small size of each unit (the same applies to agricultural labourers, employed on an individual rather than a collective basis, through long-term employer/worker relationships). The difficulty of organizing workers so dispersed is obvious. What gives them solidarity is less a developed class consciousness than their common insecurity as Palestinians, and the fact of living together in a camp. Their experience of exploitation seems to them to arise primarily from the fact of being Palestinian, only secondarily from the class structure of Arab society. Their difficulty in obtaining work permits[49] and their exclusion from social security benefits reinforce their sense of national rather than class oppression.

Discrimination, job insecurity and poor work conditions in Lebanon have propelled an unknown, but large, number of camp Palestinians into job migration, but Mundus's Tel al-Za'ter study proves that this is only a feasible solution at a high level of skill. Few who go can save enough to change their situation radically. The details that Mundus gives of the conditions of Palestinian workers in Germany (more than half of Tel al-Za'ter's 900 migrant workers were there), make it clear why few stay there permanently. In the first place, residence and work permits are issued through a special office in Zerndorf, established with American assistance to place political refugees from communist countries. If they refuse this channel (as most do), Palestinian workers must go to offices that specialize in finding work for people without permits, taking 50% of their wages. These kinds of jobs available to unskilled workers are: digging roads, building, cleaning, restaurant service, moving snow, and unskilled industrial work. That Palestinian workers are ready to migrate to Europe and put up with conditions like these, indicates the increasing difficulty of finding work in the oil producing Arab countries, most of which operate informal quotas restricting Palestinian entry, as well as demanding increasingly high professional qualifications.

From the data available it is clear that, in spite of education and occupational change, Palestinians in Lebanon suffer from economic as well as political insecurity, and that large pockets of extreme poverty continue to exist, particularly in the rural camps. If we take even a relatively prosperous camp like Bourj al-Barajneh, which has benefited from its closeness to Beirut, we find that while some families have improved their economic situation sufficiently to move out of the camp and rent apartments in the nearby suburb, the majority have no hope of doing so.

At the very bottom level of poverty are a number of families who have lost their chief male wage-earners, and who depend mainly on help from the Resistance Movement, U.N.R.W.A.'s 'special cases' programme, and the solidarity of kin and neighbours. The Civil War in Lebanon has greatly added to this category of family. Slightly better off than this 'most miserable' category come the bulk of families in the camp, those with one unskilled or semi-skilled wage earner, perhaps a nightwatchman or a concierge, earning around LL.300 a month, on whom as many as 10 children, a wife and two aged parents may well be depending. Some are self-employed artisans — carpenters, tile-fitters, plumbers — usually working under subcontract to larger building contractors, and highly vulnerable to economic fluctuations. Others are small traders in fish, fruit or vegetables, operating from barrows and bicycles. Slightly more prosperous, again, are the small shopkeepers — bakers, butchers, grocers — and the owners of laundries, TV and bicycle repair shops, or one room sewing factories. When a camp family has a small regular source of income and one or two adult sons working, it can be said to have reached the highest level of prosperity that the mass of camp families aspire to.

To be able to draw an accurate class map of Palestinians throughout the *ghourba*, or even in one region, we should need much more accurate information on occupation and income than now exists. But certain broad trends are obvious: the massive move into services at low and medium income levels; the only slight development of an industrial proletariat; the movement away from agriculture, even in a country like Syria where the potentiality for an expanded agricultural sector exists; the attraction of the intellectual professions, especially teaching; the increasing flow of skilled workers and professionals to the Gulf;[50] and the continuation of poverty amongst the families of unskilled workers.

Important as the acquisition of new skills has been, it is clear that there are structural limitations to further change. Those economic changes that have occurred do not seem to be great enough to eliminate Palestinian consciousness of their economic insecurity as an oppressed nation. Even the prosperous minority of professional people and entrepreneurs cannot wholly assimilate with the bourgeoisies of the Arab world because their political power does not match their economic position and therefore cannot protect it. For the less prosperous and the really poor, political oppression is matched by economic insecurity. National consciousness has been developed to the maximum by the present leadership of the Resistance Movement, capitalizing on the alienation of all classes of Palestinian in the *ghourba* and under Israeli occupation. Channelled into the goal of the Return, or of an independent Palestinian state on the West Bank, discontent is deflected away from existing Arab political and economic structures in the *ghourba*. Yet the inability of these structures to create the conditions for the Return (or even a truncated Palestinian state), ultimately must channel Palestinian discontent into attacking these structures too.

SOCIAL AND PSYCHOLOGICAL EFFECTS OF THE UPROOTING

In as far as Zionists took note of the possibility that Arab Palestinians might suffer from the establishment of Eretz Israel, they argued that Jewish rights must be given priority.[51] Zionists turned the ideology of Arab nationalism against Palestinians to argue that, because they were Arabs, they could be at home anywhere in the Arab world. Leaving aside the question of native-born Palestinians' *political right* to their country, the Zionist argument overlooked what as Jews they should have known, that a displaced people feels at home nowhere. It was true that urban Palestinians usually had connections of kinship or trade or even religion in other Arab cities, and it was thanks to these relationships that so many of the small bourgeoisie were able to keep out of the camps and build new lives after the Disaster. It was also true that a common Arabism did much to create sympathy and support for the refugees in the first years. But it was absolutely out of the question for the huge peasant class of Palestinians to forget its roots in the land, and settle elsewhere. The fact that they had been displaced by violence only increased their determination to return.

Social Isolation

In order to grasp fully the social isolation of the refugees in the Arab *ghourba*, we have to remember that Arabism is the ideology of the cities and the urban intelligentsias, whereas the rural masses, because of their exclusion from wealth and influence, have always been the basis for heresies and local loyalties. Peasants lived out their lives often without leaving their villages, preferred in-village marriage, and took their knowledge of the larger world from itinerant story-tellers and traders.

Barriers between Palestinian peasant refugees and the peoples of the host countries were partly due to cultural differences (e.g. of dialect, food preparation, and clothing), partly to their abnormality as 'displaced persons', victims of a catastrophe that few outside the newspaper reading minority in cities knew anything about. Their destitution made them objects of superstitious fear ('People turned us away because they feared we would bring them bad luck'), or of ridicule ('When we left the camp they used to follow us pointing and laughing. Often we would return weeping'). An early and extraordinary form of mockery was the shout, 'Where are your tails?'[52] Lebanese children are reported to have asked their parents to buy them a Palestinian to play with. The other side to Arab friendliness is a kind of barbed teasing that grows out of a rich vocabulary of insults.

Differences in food habits seem to have been much more of a barrier than one might suppose. An anecdote told by B.S., whose family spent a winter in Hawran (Syria), shows the close connection of diet to class status:

> 'They were kind to us, and the better-off families used to give us food. But can you eat *burghul* without vegetables? Mint and parsley they didn't have — they lived on grain, *semneh*, and *lebneh*, like the *bedouin*, though they were peasants. We were about to die of hunger. Once our father went to Damascus and brought us back a fish. The people of the village said, "Come and see these Palestinians eating *snakes*!" They'd never seen fish before. I don't know how they could live.'

For, destitute as they were, the refugees felt themselves to be less primitive than the villagers of Hawran or Southern Lebanon. They found Shi'ite lack of modern hygiene as backward as their ideas of ritual pollution. Their villages seemed even more lacking in education and medical care than the villages of Palestine.

A major factor in the early social isolation of the refugees was their own sense of loss and shame, which made them turn inward, shunning contact with non-Palestinians who at best did not share their abnormality and at worst would taunt them with having sold their country or fled in cowardice. And with the establishment of the camps, the 'otherness' of the Palestinians was concretized in a particularly humiliating way. Now they were marked out as 'different' by a special identity (refugee), special areas of residence (camps), special restrictions on movement, special schools, and — most humiliating of all — U.N.R.W.A. rations. Their ambiguous status as transients whose stay became ever more permanent, crystallized around the stereotype of 'refugee'. Gradually their abnormality came to be accepted as their special fate.[53]

A secondary basis for the isolation of the refugees from their fellow Arabs arose from an interesting difference in the class and religious character of Palestine on the one hand and the three host countries on the other. In Palestine, the peasantry was predominantly Sunni Muslim, with small Christian and Druze components. Unlike Jordan, it had few *bedouin*, and even these were partially settled. Jordan's peasants were mainly Sunni too, but they were outnumbered by the far more numerous tribesmen. As for Syria and Lebanon, the peasant class there was mainly formed out of minority sects: Shi'ite (Alawi), Druze, and Maronite Christian. Palestine had almost no Maronites, and so no familiarity with Lebanon's dominant minority. Thus the majority of the refugees found themselves cut off by religious differences from their fellow peasants. In the cities, of both Syria and Lebanon, the population was predominantly Sunni Muslim; but even here Palestinians were cut off from their fellow Sunnis by the still profound class barriers dividing peasants from city people. Very few refugees settled permanently in villages; their instinct was to get as close to the major cities as possible because of their greater employment and educational resources. To city Arabs, the refugees were still very much peasants (in Arabic as in English the term implies primitiveness). Apparently in the early Fifties, the people of Sidon (who were later to fight beside the Palestinians) used to call the nearby camp of 'Ain Hilweh 'the zoo'.

Loss of Respect

If the refugees were over-sensitive to jibes like this, the reason should not be sought in some psychological quirk of 'the Arab mind', but in culture. The Palestinian peasants' system of status and respect was part of a larger system of social relationships through which individual behaviour was controlled without an expensive apparatus of law enforcement. Through a carefully nurtured need for respect from others, each individual was made the censor of his own actions. At the same time, respect was closely linked to other values like loyalty, oath-keeping, honour, and the supremacy of social and moral obligations, all of which underwrote clan and village membership, patron/client ties, and ultimately social order.

While honour and respect were supposedly unrelated to material values,[54] peasants also attached great importance to the ownership of land and clan size. In theory, all (male) members of a village were equal in respect, and peasant etiquette was punctilious in honouring this theoretical equality. All this was brutally smashed by the Uprooting. The peasants remained culturally peasants, with their built-in need for the respect of others. But their new identity as refugees put them in a category similar to that of 'gypsy' or 'bastard' — a person of no known origin, and therefore of no respect, the lowest level of human being.[55] Like loss of land and property, their loss of respect had revolutionary implications, making them determined to recapture esteem through militant action.

While many of the abrasive encounters which brought home to camp Palestinians their 'fallen' status were essentially political in origin (part of a policy of control set up by the Lebanese authorities), a great many of them were experienced at the hands of the population at large. In this respect, Lebanon was very different from the other host countries, where Palestinians mostly found the people more friendly than their governments. Perhaps this was because Lebanon's peculiar combination of religious divisions and class polarization sharpens inter-group aggression far beyond that of any other Arab country.

Kinds of behaviour that camp Palestinians experienced in Lebanon included the following: exclusion from children's games; pointing, mocking, ridiculing; absence of normal politeness, for instance summoning a Palestinian by hand gesture instead of by name, not smiling in greeting, not responding to speech, avoiding normal expressions of welcome, 'cold looks';[56] scapegoating;[57] cursing;[58] cheating on deals. Camp Palestinians felt that the normal laws of reciprocity had been cancelled in their case: they followed the rules, and got punished; they worked hard, yet were badly paid; they treated others well, but others treated them badly.

Relatively few incidents of physical violence were reported, except in encounters with the police. But incidents of verbal aggression were so many, and had caused such strong reactions, that it was impossible not to see them as a factor leading to the Revolution of 1965. Apart from the loss of the *watan*, probably nothing contributed more to camp Palestinians' militancy than the stripping from them of the traditional systems of respect that had camouflaged their class subordination in Palestine. To regain respect, their own and others', they could only struggle to return to the place where their whole society was rooted.

Family Disruption

The Uprooting did not only tear peasants from their land, it also tore apart the natural groupings of clan and village. Although large fragments of these groupings were reassembled in the camps, making them continuations of Palestinian villages, this reassembling was by no means complete. There were those who died in the War of 1948 — perhaps 15,000 — mostly from the rural population. Certain others stayed behind.[59] The rest were scattered across an enormous area,[60] blocked from easy communication with one another by poverty and national frontiers. Permits for travel, as we have already seen, were always hard to obtain. Once refugees had been fixed in particular camps it was difficult to transfer their rights to rations and services to another. Even visiting other camps was difficult, at least in Lebanon.

Family ties are of immense importance to Arabs, and to poor Arabs in particular. The time and money they put into sustaining these ties cannot easily be imagined, and the fact that the dispersion separated kin groups did not prevent the contact from being kept up. Indeed, the difficulty of meeting probably stiffened Palestinian determination to maintain family ties, as a part of their cultural identity, apart from its practical benefits. It is significant that while the Uprooting scattered the Palestinians, splitting up their natural groupings, it did not erode the practice of family solidarity or family reproduction. All accounts of the early period show the refugees groping to re-establish family contacts and, in spite of the terrible conditions in the camps, neither the rate nor age of marriage fell. Underneath this continuation of family reproduction lies an almost indestructible mass of social relationships.

Whilst camp Palestinians reacted to dispersion by holding tightly to their family and village ties, the political forces that had expelled them from Palestine continued to press upon them in the *ghourba*. It is important to realize that the splitting up of families was not a once and for all explosion, but an ongoing process of 'redistribution' set up by Zionist domination in Palestine. This centrifugal pressure, which is both political and economic, splits up nuclear families as well as larger clans.

Israeli interests, as interpreted by all their leaders until now, have always demanded the minimum number of Palestinians in or near it. Beyond its boundaries at any one time, there lies a second zone where for security reasons Israel requires that Palestinians be under tight control, a condition long fulfilled in Jordan (except between March 1968 and September 1970), and now to some degree in Lebanon and even Syria. It is these two zones (the one occupied by Israeli forces, the other dominated by Israeli threat) which are the heart of the Palestinian dispersion, the area of greatest population concentration. It is here, where oppression and poverty are strongest, that Palestinian families are most likely to be split up for political reasons (e.g. imprisonment, deportation, death), and for economic ones (e.g. migration for work or education). The result is a continuous situation of domestic abnormality.

Of 10 families I got to know in Dbeyye camp, only two had their husband/father working in Lebanon. The distance of the countries of work migration and the high cost of air travel means that most men cannot visit their families more than once every two years. Because of the high wage levels of migrants from this camp, many have been able to transfer their families to the Gulf, at the risk of course of losing their rights to homes and services in the camp. But for the mass of camp Palestinians this is out of the question. For them, if they go abroad to work, there is no alternative to leaving their families behind in the camps.

In Bourj al-Barajneh camp there is a slightly different pattern of work migration, reflecting a slower development of skills. Of the 12 families I knew well there, only three father/husbands were working abroad, and it was clear that they were working at a much lower level of salary than the men from Dbeyye. Remittances to families are often hardly more than they could have earned in Lebanon; often there are long periods of unemployment or waiting for work permits; moreover the costs of rent, food and transport are much higher in the countries of work migration than in Lebanon, while the living conditions of unskilled workers are worse than the camps. In most cases the sacrifice of family life leads to no economic advantage.

While few of the older men in Bourj al-Barajneh are job migrants, a very high proportion of the children are working or studying abroad. No family I knew had no members abroad, and some had all their children above age 18 outside. While to Europeans it seems normal that grown-up children should leave home, to Palestinians of peasant origin this is a constant source of suffering, particularly for women. I have often seen them weep when they tell of sons working in Germany or Libya, even though they may be long past adolescence. They know that they will never be able to afford to visit these migrant sons, nor can their sons visit them more than once in a long while.

September, the month when students and workers who have been visiting their families return to their outposts in the *ghourba*, is a time of great sadness in the camps. Because of the inherent insecurity of Palestinians' lives, no one can be sure when or where they will next meet.

Because of the high rate of work migration from the urban camps in Lebanon, these now contain an abnormal proportion of women, children and old people. This is one reason why military attacks on them are even more atrocious than they seem, quite apart from their lack of adequate defence or shelters. For every family under siege in Tel al-Za'ter, there would have been husbands, fathers and sons working outside and unable to return.[61]

Any camp family picked at random will supply variations on the theme of disrupted family life. Every family has lost some of its members; some were almost wiped out during the Civil War (1975-76) in Lebanon. For a people as home-loving as the Palestinians, this continuing loss of normal family life has been one of the greatest causes of suffering although, because of the way they focus on the political aspects of their problem, it is not one they emphasize when talking to strangers. One finds two different reactions to this disruption: first, a clinging to vestiges of normality, particularly to family ties,[62] mingled with an emphatic nostalgia for the past. Every people has its idea of the Good Life, and for Palestinian refugees who lost it the idea is poignantly sharp and clear. One feels it in the voice of the woman who says: 'Every time I see a fruit tree I think that there must be one like it in my village in Palestine'; and in this: 'There we were all together, in one place'; and in this: 'My sons send me money, but it's *them* I want to see.' A retired carpenter of 60, when I asked him what made him feel conscious of being Palestinian, told me: 'When I see my Lebanese neighbour, content in his villa, with his grandchildren playing all around him.' Banal as the remark may sound to some, sentimental to others, it contains a great deal of the Palestinian tragedy.

A second reaction, almost an opposite one, has been to push to its utmost limits the sense of abnormality. This one finds amongst the young and the politicized. For them family bonds have been almost completely superseded by militancy. The Resistance Movement, the idea of the Return, have transformed a nostalgia for normality into a conscious assumption of the abnormality of struggle. In this spirit a young teacher told me of a current Israeli attack on Rashidiyyeh camp which might have killed one of his cousins, adding, 'But he is no different to me than any other Palestinian.'

POLITICAL OPPRESSION

Roots of Repression

The reality of the Palestinians' situation in the Arab *ghourba* was almost exactly the reverse of the picture presented by Israeli propaganda of the pre-1967 vintage. Israelis used to say that the Arab governments were using the refugees as pawns in their war against Israel. In fact — Arab rhetoric apart — none of the regimes had any serious intention of challenging Israeli military power, even though, as the October War of 1973 showed, they were capable of doing so for limited periods and purposes.

Oppression of the Palestinians arose directly from the inability of the Arab regimes to challenge the decision of the Great Powers that 'the Palestine Problem' must be solved by the transfer of populations. Palestinians would not accept their 'redistribution'; the Arab regimes would neither accept nor actively reject it. There was a deep difference in urgency between the Palestinians' and other Arabs' need for a solution. President Abdul Nasser used frequently to evoke the Crusades, but Palestinians in the camps did not want to wait four centuries before returning to their homes. They were patient, but they wanted signs of movement in the right direction. Though defeated and scattered, they remained a thorn in the Arabs' side, a 'fire under ashes', always reminding them that part of the Arab homeland had been transformed into a beachhead of Western domination.

Arab policy towards the Palestinians has always been a double one, dosing nationalism with caution. Action towards liberation has been encouraged at particular junctures, for particular purposes (those of regimes and parties competing for the support of the Arab masses); at the same time, while yielding to Palestinian and mass pressures just enough to gain popularity, the regimes all strove to keep Palestinian activism within very narrow limits.[63] In fact, only Syria out of the three host countries, and Egypt, Iraq and Algeria of those further away, actively encouraged the

Palestinians by giving them training facilities and arms. The other two, Lebanon and Jordan, suppressed all manifestations of Palestinianism, while supporting Palestinian rights verbally.

Something of the atmosphere of the earliest days in the camps comes through in this description by a militant from Nahr al-Bared, who was about eleven in 1948:

'I don't remember the reason, but in 1952 there was a demonstration in the camps and I was there, a boy, walking in the demonstration, and shouting "Syria, make us soldiers! We want to fight!" It was right in the middle of the camp, in the main street. It was suppressed by the Lebanese Army, not by the F.S.I.,[64] and they acted with great thoroughness. They gathered all the men in the camp, threw them into the barracks, and beat them. They wanted to crush the Palestinian voice and show that there's no more connection between us and our land. They beat us so that we would feel that it was dangerous to talk about Palestine.'

As always in colonial struggles, schools were a focus of national consciousness, not through policy, but because of the activism of the students:

'In 1954 there was a struggle against the projects of implantation.[65] We in school were demonstrating, and being suppressed. We had to struggle to get correct books on the geography and history of Palestine. For instance, there was one they gave us called *The History of My Country* — we demonstrated against it, and wrote down 25 reasons for rejecting it. I was chosen to explain to the U.N.R.W.A. inspector why we refused it. He was Palestinian, but he hit me in the face. He hit me, but they withdrew the book.'

Mechanisms of Control

The theory behind the Lebanese authorities' suppression of the Palestinians was expressed by the man who was head of the Palestinian section of the Deuxieme Bureau in the late Fifties and early Sixties, Joseph Kaylani, notorious among camp Palestinians for his harshness: 'The Palestinian is like a spring. If you step on him he stays quiet, but if you take your foot off, he'll hit you in the face.' Yet while the D.B. used force when they thought it necessary, there was nothing Prussian or systematic about their oppression. Kaylani used often to visit the camps and hold meetings with the inhabitants. Someone in Bourj al-Barajneh remembers him telling the people there not to put their faith in Nasser and the Voice of the Arabs, it was all simply lies to gain their support (a view that some of them would come to echo after 1967). At another time he gave a speech in Nahr al-Bared camp, and the militant quoted earlier offered a half-comic description of what ensued:

'Kaylani came to speak to the camp. All the old men, the *wujuha'*, were there, but they had to be diplomatic. At the end he said, "Does anyone want to ask any questions?" In those days I didn't wear spectacles, though I was already shortsighted, so I couldn't see his face clearly. If I'd seen him, definitely I wouldn't have spoken. I asked him something, and we had a bit of a discussion. The next day there was a summons for me to go to the D.B. office. I escaped to Beirut. But in 1961 when I wanted to go to Syria to sit the *muwwahhadi*[66] they refused me a permit.'

Much later a P.L.O. official went to President Chehab (1958-1964) to complain of police brutality to the refugees. Chehab said that he knew very well what was being done in the camps, but responsible Palestinians must understand his position:

'There are thousands of Palestinians, sitting in the camps, listening to the Cairo radio promising them that they will return to their homes. If I can't even control Joumblatt[67] and his Druzes, how am I to control the Palestinians?'

The methods used by the Lebanese authorities in their struggle to control the Palestinians give insights into traditional and neo-colonial Arab political behaviour. Although outright violence was not avoided, subtler techniques of persuasion and manipulation were also used. A typical example was the way soldiers sent to move the refugees at Bourj al-Shemali to Kar'oun told them that they would fight beside them to regain their homeland. Often the refugees were told: 'All you have to do is to eat and sleep. The Arab armies will get your country back for you.' Another technique was this:

'They used to throw a siege around anyone who worked in politics. For instance if they know Saleh is a friend of Walid and Walid works in politics, they'd tell Saleh to stay away from Walid. That way, they'd stop the "epidemic" from spreading.'

This speaker went on to say:

'If a teacher was a nationalist they'd have him lose his job. This was part of their work, also beating, shaving heads, and imprisonment. These were all daily problems for us.'

Although a few of the politicized knew what was going on in the camps, the majority of middle class Palestinians, absorbed in their normal lives, did not. In fact, they were not living in the same world. If a middle class Palestinian had a problem with travel papers or work permits, he could bribe or use high level friendships to get round it. If he got into trouble for political activity, again friendships could be mobilized. The case of a middle class activist, imprisoned as a student in the Fifties, illustrates the different fates of middle class and poor Palestinians in the *ghourba*: his father was a friend of the Mufti and invoked his help.[68] The Mufti sent one of his aides to tell the young man that he could get him set free if he would promise not to engage in politics. The boy refused, and was only finally freed because his father had Lebanese nationality,[69] which gave him the right not to be imprisoned without trial, or deported.

Isolating the camps was a part of the Lebanese authorities' control policy. To discourage activists from visiting them, they would harass any of the population who attended overtly Palestinian meetings. A P.L.O. official recalls going to Rashidiyeh to give a speech, and finding no one in the schoolyard except a few children. He took the loudspeaker and addressed the children, telling them that they were heroes and would be the generation to liberate Palestine. Within half an hour the schoolyard was full. But next day 12 people were in jail.

Suppression of the Palestinian Identity

In Lebanon as in Jordan, it was official policy to erase the Palestinians' sense of identity and connection with Palestine. 'To say the word "Palestinian" was a crime', said a schoolgirl who could only just remember the period before the Revolution. Though not under Palestinian control, U.N.R.W.A. schools were foci of national consciousness. There is some disagreement over the role of teachers; some remember them using memorial days to speak about Palestine, and teaching the children national songs; others say that most were too afraid of the Deuxieme Bureau to step outside the curriculum. But everyone agrees about the closeness of D.B. surveillance:

> 'They used to believe our school was behind political activity in our area. There was a period when they used to send two or three inspectors daily. Sometimes they'd take in young men for questioning, at midnight, simply to show they knew who was active. They counted every breath we took. Many times they stopped me[70] visiting the parents of my students in the camp — even this was against the law. Many of my colleagues were fired from their jobs to frighten others from political activities. Others were transferred from one area to another for the same reason.'

Unlike Jordan where repression was relatively systematic and unchanging,[71] in Lebanon it fluctuated according to the internal situation. In times of crisis, things always became worse:

> 'After the 1958 revolution against Chamoun they tried to put a curfew on all Palestinians. You had to have a permit to go from Sidon to Tyre, and another permit from Sidon to Beirut.
> 'In 1961, the year of the failed P.P.S. *coup*,[72] my sister's husband was staying with me. He had some relatives in the P.P.S. so the Deuxieme Bureau came and took him, and shot him, simply in retaliation. The only people involved in that *coup* who were killed were Palestinians. The (Lebanese) leaders were only imprisoned, and later they set them free.'

'It was really military government'

Control of the camps was maintained by setting up police and D.B. stations on their outskirts. In the early days, the mere presence of two armed policemen was enough to control a camp of several thousand people, but as secret organization spread, the forces of authority became more numerous and their methods more brutal:

'It was really military government, though it wasn't called that. Once the Army came at 4 a.m. and surrounded the camp and searched all the homes. There were two stations near the camp, one for the ordinary police, the other the D.B. — the two used to compete with each other to see which could arrest the largest number of people, so as to report this to their chiefs. Almost every day, and sometimes at night, they'd come to take people away. Once they came to our house to arrest my brother, and because he wasn't there they took me in his place.'

No one interviewed in this particular camp had not had painful encounters with the Lebanese authorities. These ranged from relatively simple types of harassment, to economic pressures, threats and finally violence. Permits were needed to visit another camp — even visiting neighbours after 9 p.m. could lead to trouble. Any kind of non-domestic meeting was totally banned; publishing and distributing pamphlets was prohibited. Inhabitants of the camps were constantly stopped in the streets and searched.

One of the earliest memories of a boy from this same camp was of the D.B. coming at night to take his father for interrogation. It happened many times; once they beat him on the head with a broken bottle. A girl of 17 had lost her father in the same reprisals for the failed *coup* that an earlier speaker's brother-in-law had been killed in. A woman whose husband had often been arrested and beaten for collecting money for the Resistance Movement told us how once the police came for him at midnight. He was in Sidon, so the police forced his old mother to dress and go immediately to bring him. On another occasion he was beaten so badly on his back (using water to intensify the welts) that he had to sleep on his stomach for more than a month.[73]

Although much of the brutality was random, aimed at general terrorization, it was more specifically directed at people suspected of being nuclei of political organization. Such men would be picked up, imprisoned, or beaten, over and over again. An Arab Nationalist Movement[74] member recalls being arrested while addressing a May Day workers' rally:

'We were holding this meeting when the D.B. came and arrested us. There were 70 or 80 workers, and even though they weren't trained in political struggle, they surrounded the police station where they were holding us; but they couldn't get us released. The D.B. took us to their main office in Badaro Street, then to the Helou Barracks. There we were beaten on our feet. They told us to take off our shoes. I wanted to be beaten first so I wouldn't have to see my brother beaten. They tied a rifle to my feet so that its teeth entered my flesh, and one of them began to beat my feet. When they untied me I thought they'd finished. They took me to a bowl of cold water, and while I was standing in it they started beating my brother. When they finished beating him, they brought him to the water and took me for another beating.

'I went back to my job, but the D.B. threatened me, saying that I was the only one working in my family, and if I went on with politics they'd get my employer to sack me. But we continued with

Extortion and Harassment

Although the main motive of oppression was political there was a great deal of harassment for purely private ends. Camp populations were sitting targets for extortion: a possibly exaggerated estimate of the monthly take of a police officer in charge of a camp was LL.5,000 (£1,000), around 10 times his normal pay. Apart from the continuous need for permits of every type, there was a long list of offences for which camp Palestinians could be fined: building without a permit; making any kind of small improvement or repair to homes (for instance putting rocks on to zinc roofs to stop them blowing off in winter storms); letting washing water trickle into the streets. This latter point was a sensitive one for several reasons: first, the camps had no covered drainage system and the only way washing water could be disposed of was by sweeping it out into open street drains; second, the lack of bathing facilities was in itself a form of oppression for Muslims, who have strict rules about personal hygiene, and (contrary to the European image) detest being dirty; third, the police often came water-spotting when they knew only women would be home, which came close to an offence against the Muslim laws of propriety. Another type of harassment is described by a woman from a camp in the South:

'The police would come into the camp and accuse people, or punish them without explaining why. If two neighbours quarrelled, one would accuse the other to the police. Some of them took bribes, others kept fines — they have to live! Sometimes they would visit homes and oblige us to provide them with an expensive meal, with whisky and 'arak. It could cost as much as LL.100 (£20) and a Palestinian hadn't even got LL.5.'

As camp Palestinians became more mobile through employment, the authorities attempted to control their movements outside the camps as well as their activities inside them. Military check-points were up on all the country's main roads, particularly those connecting the coastal cities. Certain zones were forbidden to Palestinians, and a teacher told a bitter anecdote of being allowed, with a group of Lebanese friends, to pass into one of these zones (near Tyre) because the soldier at the check-post thought from his American University notebook that he must be a foreigner: 'As a foreigner they let me through, though as a Palestinian they would have stopped me.' Ironically, it was the state of war with Israel that was always given by the D.B. as the pretext for its close watch on Palestinians' movements.

Two of the stories that circulate abour encounters between Palestinians and the Lebanese police at check-posts have that pungent Palestinian humour that converts painful experience into public entertainment. A Palestinian in a bus was ordered down at a police check-post. Asked to show his ID card he searches in all his pockets: 'I'm sorry sir, I must have left it at home in my other pair of trousers.' The policeman: 'What! A Palestinian with two pairs of trousers!'

The second story has a different flavour. A Lebanese policeman boards a bus at a check-post. 'Are there any Palestinian sons of whores on this bus?' Two Palestinians get up: 'Yes, sir, there's me and this brother.' 'Get down!' 'Yes, sir, but as a respected Lebanese, you should go ahead of us.' As the policeman turns to leave the bus, the Palestinians pounce and heave him into the gutter. The officer in charge of the check-post reprimands the policeman for using insulting language.[75]

Lessons of the Ghourba

Political oppression did not succeed in preventing the spread of Palestinian consciousness, or the growth of political organization. Nor could Palestinians in the camps be isolated from the Lebanese population around them. There, as in Syria and to a lesser extent in Jordan, political bonds were forged between Palestinians and fellow Arabs on the basis of a common understanding of Israel's role in the Middle East, and its ties with imperialism. Ordinary people outside the regimes also shared Palestinian scepticism about the real motives behind the speeches of their leaders: 'They speak about Palestine, but they speak only for themselves'; 'Any one who wants to become a *mukhtar* makes a speech about Palestine!'[76] Painful as it was, the refugee phase of the Palestinian struggle (from 1948 to 1965), was full of political lessons that perhaps could not have been learnt in any other way.

It was out of experiences and perceptions like these that the next phase of Palestinian revolutionary struggle was to arise. The strategy of the Palestinian Resistance Movement, as it took clear shape in the mid-Sixties, was mainly the product of small, clandestine groups outside the camps. But unlike the national leadership in Palestine before 1948, the new leaders were closely in touch with mass feeling, and their call for mass armed struggle was one to which camp Palestinians, young and old, responded fervently. Of those I interviewed none expressed this response, and its causes, better than this schoolgirl:

'Once there was a quarrel between Palestinian and Lebanese children, near our home. The parents joined in the quarrel — both families were our neighbours. Then the Lebanese neighbours said, "You Palestinians! Go and fight those who made you leave your country!" This incident upset me a lot. I was proud to be Palestinian, but others insulted us. It was because of such things that I was waiting for anyone to make a revolution, and, thank God, it came, and I can share in it.'

REFERENCES AND NOTES

1. T. Asad, 'Anthropological Texts and Ideological Problems; an Analysis of Cohen on Arab Villages in Israel', *Review of Middle East Studies*, No. 1, (1975).

2. A National Congress was convened by the Mufti, backed by the Arab League, in Gaza on October 1, 1948, and proclaimed a Government of All Palestine. An independent notable, Ahmad Hilmi Pasha, agreed to become Prime Minister, and continued to issue official statements from his residence in Cairo until the formation of the P.L.O.

3. King Abdullah countered the Mufti's initiative by convening his own Palestinian Congress in Amman, which denounced the Gaza Government. A second Congress held in Jerash on December 1, 1948, proclaimed him King of a united East and West Bank.

4. Private agricultural and industrial property of Palestinian Arabs (excluding public fixed assets and urban buildings), was estimated at £P757 million in 1945, Y. Sayigh, *The Israeli Economy*, (Cairo, 1963), Ch. 3. Based on detailed investigation, the historian Aref al-Aref estimated Palestinian loss of life during the war at 15,000. Aref al-Aref, *al-Nekba*, Vol. VI, (Al-Maktaba al-Asriyeh, 1958). Beyond this there was the loss of national identity and a national future in Palestine.

5. The first Israeli census of November 1948 gave a total for non-Jews of 120,000. 65,000 of these were *bedouin* in the Negev who had not been counted since 1922, which means that Arabs remaining in the rest of Israel would have been around 60,000. All the figures in this section are based on Janet Abu-Lughod, 'The Demographic Transformation of Palestine' in I. Abu-Lughod, ed., *The Transformation of Palestine*, (Northwestern University, Evanston, 1971); and on Y. Sayigh, *Implications of U.N.R.W.A. Operations in the Host Countries*, (1952).

6. See I. Shahak, *Israeli League for Human and Civil Rights*, N.E.E.B.I.I., (Beirut, undated), p.93-113 for a list of Arab villages destroyed and tribes expelled after 1948.

7. A Palestinian who used to visit the camps in Lebanon in the Fifties as a journalist was imprisoned and almost deported. Even after the official recognition of the P.L.O., its contacts with the camps were impeded, for instance by threatening camp Palestinians who attended meetings.

8. Al-'Ard (The Earth) was formed in 1956 mainly to defend the civil rights of Arabs in Israel, and to struggle against their subjection to military decrees, sequestration, deportation, etc. See Sabri Jiryis, *The Arabs in Israel*, (Monthly Review Press, New York, 1976).

9. The power base of the Jordanian regime lies in the *bedouin* and the

Army, with support from a merchant/entrepreneurial class largely composed of minorities. In Syria, the Alawites form the backbone of the Ba'ath Party and the Army. In Lebanon, a Maronite Christian hegemony rests on alliances with leaders of Shi'ite, Druze, Armenian and other communities.

10. The Sunni Muslim community — the majority in the Fertile Crescent — would have formed the natural social and political basis of an Arab nation if it had not been held in check by external support for internal minorities (Christian, Druze, Jewish, etc.).

11. A. al-Kodsy, 'Nationalism and Class Struggles in the Arab World' in Kodsy and Lobel, *The Arab World and Israel*, (Monthly Review Press, New York, 1970), p.49.

12. See Chapter 2, p.88, for B.S.'s recollections of the year of the War.

13. See Chapter 2, p.84-5.

14. The expression *wila'* is only used to a naughty child, showing the subordination of the peasant son to his father.

15. Literally 'one who brings up others', a community leader.

16. The first U.N. organization to work with the refugees was U.N.R.P.R. (United Nations Relief for Palestine Refugees), superseded at the end of 1950 by U.N.R.W.A. (United Nations Relief and Works Agency).

17. Winning the legal argument did not enable the Arab governments to put pressure on U.N.R.W.A. to improve, or even maintain, its level of services to the refugees. Since the Agency depended for its budget on voluntary contributions from member nations in the U.N., its income has not increased in proportion to the growth of the Palestinian population.

18. U.N.R.W.A. divides all registered refugees into three categories: (R), the smallest number, who qualify for rations as well as services; (S), who qualify only for educational and medical services; and (N), who are not eligible for any U.N.R.W.A. aid, or are only eligible for restricted aid. In Tel al-Za'ter, one of the poorest camps, out of a total population of around 12,000 in 1972, 3,540 were ration receivers, 1,000 got medical and educational services, and around 6,500 got only education.

19. The Arab Higher Committee continued to exist (see Note 2 above on the Gaza Government of All Palestine) acting as a focus for Palestinian nationalism, and publishing the magazine *Falasteen*. The Mufti continued to receive a small subvention from the Arab League until his death in 1974.

20. Palestinians in Jordan and Syria were encouraged to enlist in the national armies, and in Syria were subject to military conscription.

21. For example, unless they have Lebanese nationality, Palestinians are not allowed to work in banks, large foreign companies, hotels, or as taxi-drivers.

22. So great was the Lebanese dislike of committing anything to paper that in its 14 years of existence the P.L.O.'s Beirut office received only 10 official letters. All communication was by telephone.

23. President Helou's term ran from 1964 to 1970.

24. Black September: the name given by Palestinians to the most prolonged clash, in September 1970, between the Jordanian regime and the Palestine Resistance Movement.

25. Since the recent Civil War the Lebanese authorities have made it harder for Palestinians to obtain *laissez-passers*, insisting on documentary proof of registration with U.N.R.W.A.

26. So pervasive was the image of refugee dependence on U.N.R.W.A., that it influenced even Arab political analysts. For example the Lebanese Marxist Samir Franjieh, in 'How Revolutionary is the Palestinian Resistance?', *Journal of Palestine Studies*, (Winter 1972), wrote, 'the refugees, expelled in 1948 from the lands they tilled, have not since been integrated into any economic productive process and so know nothing of the economic exploitation to which a normal proletariat is subjected, and against which it ultimately rebels with the aim of establishing a new system of social relationships.' (p.53).

27. Y. Sayigh, *op. cit.*

28. An average family size of 5.5 persons was carried over from early Mandate village studies. From refugee families I have data on I think the figure is too low, even though infant mortality certainly rose sharply in the first years of dispersion. Probably it disregards the fact of the extended family.

29. Sayigh, *op. cit.*, Appendix C, Item V.

30. The story of this marriage gives insights into peasant attitudes at that time. The boy's parents forced his early marriage to a girl from the same village a) because her parents had a small plot of land; and b) because if he got caught in marriage by a Lebanese girl they would be obliged to give one of their daughters in exchange, and thus be forced to leave her behind when they returned to Palestine.

31. When a Lebanese Government decree made it illegal for Palestinians to work in banks, B.S.'s husband lost his nightwatchman job, though with typical Arab charity he was smuggled on to the payroll for several months after dismissal. The bank where he worked was almost entirely staffed by Palestinians, but none except him lost their jobs; all had Lebanese nationality.

32. U.N.R.W.A. schools do not take children before the age of six, nor beyond fourth secondary. Scholarships are given by U.N.R.W.A. and other bodies to the brightest children to continue their education, but these benefit perhaps less than 8% of camp children.

33. The *Certificat* is the lowest diploma in the Lebanese system, marking completion of the elementary levels only.

34. It is common for commercial establishments in Lebanon to give themselves high-sounding titles, using terms like 'national', 'institute' or 'centre'.

35. The importance of clothing in Arab/Muslim culture is very clear in this quotation. Refugees suffered far more from dirt and torn clothing than from hunger. Today, it is rare to see an adult camp Palestinian in clothes that are not clean and pressed.

36. It should not be forgotten that Arabs made large donations to the refugees via governments, religious institutions, and private charity. Sayigh, *op. cit.*, notes a donation of LS.8 million from the Syrian Government, of which LS.2 million were voluntary contributions from the population.

37. Because the Lebanese terminal exam, the *Baccalaureat*, is exceptionally hard, many Palestinian students sit the easier *towijihiyyeh* in Syria or Egypt.

38. See N. Shaath, 'Palestinian High Level Manpower', *Journal of Palestinian Studies*, (Winter 1972); and A.B. Zahlan 'Palestine's Arab Population', *J.P.S.*, (Summer 1974).

39. In order to restrict entry to the professional middle class, the Lebanese *Baccalaureat* is made so difficult that students only rarely pass it before 18 or 19 years old (thus also increasing the profitability of schools). Few professions, even technical and vocational ones such as nursing, can be entered upon without the *Bacc.*

40. In the last two years in Lebanon the Resistance Movement has opened numerous small training centres, teaching simple skills like sewing, nursing, pharmacy, laboratory work. Industrial trainees are increasingly being sent abroad on courses provided by friendly governments.

41. For a good overview of camp conditions in Lebanon, see B. Sirhan, 'Palestinian Refugee Life in Lebanon', *J.P.S.*, (Winter 1975).

42. S. Ayoub, *Class Structure of the Palestinians*, (in Arabic), M.A. thesis for the Arab University of Beirut, (1977).

43. The Arabic word *muwazzef* (employee) has a strong overtone of respectability. A *muwazzef* may not have power or a high salary, but his work is clean and relatively secure.

44. See G. Amin, *The Modernization of Poverty*, (E.J. Brill, Leiden, 1974), pp.24, 84.

45. H. Mundus, *Al-'Amal wa al-'Umal fi al-Mukhayam al-Falasteeni*, (Palestine Research Centre, Beirut, 1974).

46. Lebanese employers often mistakenly assumed that Palestinian women would be less politicized than men.

47. Out of an approximate total of 100,000 Palestinian workers in Lebanon in 1969, only 2,362 had work permits (Mundus, *op. cit.*).

48. Mundus lists the following occupations: carpentry (460); food processing (379); building (260); garage mechanics (200); domestic

servants (150, all female); iron workers and mechanics (173); textiles (125); agriculture (60); shop assistants, office and restaurant workers (50); plastic and rubber (30); soap and cosmetics (20); laundries (25); selling bric-a-brac (35); street vendors (25); lottery ticket sellers (22); plumbers (20); kerosene sellers (11); port workers (10).

49. Mundus's listing of the operations needed to get a work permit is a picture of oppression by bureaucracy: a) get a written statement from the employer (new permits must be got with each change of job); b) pay a fee of LL.15 (£3); c) get a medical certificate from a 'legal' doctor (LL.3-5); d) get two passport photos (LL.3.50 for six); e) get the signature of a notary public (LL.7-10), plus a fiscal stamp of LL.1 to take the record from the notary; f) LL.2 of fiscal stamps are needed on the permit; g) give up at least one day's work to take the papers to the Ministry of Social Affairs. Lateness in renewing permits is punishable by a fine of LL.105 (£21). Since the only place where permits are issued is in Beirut, workers in the provinces must lose further time and money in travel.

50. Zahlan, *op. cit.*, estimates there will be 1,000,000 foreign workers in the Gulf by 1980.

51. Jabotinsky made a statement in 1937 to a British investigatory commission that can be taken as representative of mainstream Zionism's stand towards Palestinian Arabs: '. . . Palestine on both sides of the Jordan should hold Arabs, their progeny and many millions of Jews. What I do not deny is that in that process the Arabs of Palestine will necessarily become a minority in the country of Palestine. What I do deny is that *that* is a hardship. It is quite understandable that the Arabs of Palestine would also prefer Palestine to be the Arab state No. 4, No. 5, or No. 6 — that I quite understand; but when the Arab claim is confronted with our Jewish demand to be saved, it is like the claims of appetite versus the claims of starvation.' J. Bowyer Bell, *Terror out of Zion*, (St. Martin's Press, New York, 1977), pp.29-30.

52. I didn't believe this story until I heard it confirmed by a Lebanese woman from Tripoli who had married a Palestinian. Doubtless a form of teasing, crudely associating poverty with animality.

53. A good example of this taking Palestinian abnormality for granted comes from a letter written by an indignant Lebanese citizen to the Beirut newspaper *L'Orient* when his home was destroyed by a rocket in the Lebanese Civil War: 'Am I a Palestinian refugee, waiting in a camp for the U.N. to repatriate me? No, I am a Lebanese citizen who put his life's savings into his home. . .' The implication is clear: it is natural for rockets to fall on Palestinians but not on Lebanese citizens; that is an affront to the moral order.

54. People often say in the camps, 'A man may have nothing but he still

has honour.' It is part of the ideology of honour that it is 'high', in opposition to 'low' material things, and its frequent expression doubtless springs directly from poverty. Honour is also used to establish claims, e.g. to others' support.

55. The image of animality constantly crops up in Palestinian descriptions of their situation, e.g. 'There are Arabs who treat us worse than animals.'

56. Arab culture attaches as much importance to facial expression as to verbal politeness, as part of the ideology of hospitality. The face must always express welcome and warmth.

57. People said, 'If anything goes wrong, it's always the Palestinian who gets blamed.' Some told stories of being falsely accused of stealing.

58. Curses are graded in power, the weakest being the direct curse, the most powerful those directed at the victim's religion, or the oldest members of his group ('Your elders are under our feet!'). A particularly wounding curse often used against Palestinians is 'Go to your country!'

59. Contacts between family segments inside Israel and those outside were especially difficult for the first two decades. Recently it has become possible for those who have relatives inside to make brief visits.

60. In a sample of twenty, I recorded the number of countries in which the respondents had relatives. The number was never less than three, and in two cases was eight.

61. Many students and workers did return to fight in Lebanon during the Civil War. But none could get into Tel al-Za'ter camp after its encirclement by the Christian Right and the Syrians.

62. To give an idea of the tenacity of camp family ties: a family I know suffered the loss of one of its young men during the Lebanese War; members came for mourning from Baghdad, Abu Dhabi and the U.S.S.R.

63. See F. Jabber, 'The Palestinian Resistance and Inter-Arab Politics' in Quandt, Jabber and Lesch, *The Politics of Palestinian Nationalism*, Rand Corp., (University of California Press, Berkeley, 1973).

64. Forces de Securite Interieure: a general term covering various branches of the Lebanese police force, including riot control.

65. These projects were initiated by U.N.R.W.A.

66. A higher level in the Syrian exam system than the *towijihiyyeh*.

67. Kamal Joumblatt, a leader of the Druze sect and of the Parti Populaire Socialiste, was assassinated soon after the end of the Lebanese Civil War, in March 1977.

68. See Chapter 2, p.77.

69. Palestine, Syria and Lebanon formed an area without internal boundaries under the Ottoman Empire, so that there is nothing strange in a Palestinian Arab having a parent or grandparent from

outside Palestine.

70. The speaker was a schoolteacher in Tel al-Za'ter camp.

71. Although Jordanian repression was more systematic than the Lebanese, yet the King could also be forgiving. A Palestinian from Amman said: 'The Jordanian regime is very intelligent. They deport a person for political activities, then, after a while, they tell him he can return, *ahlan wassahlan!* They give him a job, a salary, maybe a Ministry. That way they "burn" him before the masses, telling them, "This is the person you were betting on!" '

72. In January 1961, the P.P.S. party in Lebanon mounted a *coup* against the regime, which failed.

73. When telling me this story, his wife said: 'When I remember what they did to him it makes me feel that the *whole family must take arms and fight*. What did he do wrong? Just collecting money for the Movement!'

74. The Arab Nationalist Movement was the organization most persecuted by the authorities in Lebanon. It was also one of the best organized.

75. The woman who told me this story commented: 'There are some *good* Lebanese!'

76. Both these remarks were made by women, often much more pungent and direct in their criticisms of the Arab governments than men, who tend more often to endorse official positions.

4

THE PALESTINIAN REVOLUTION

'We have always believed and declared . . . that armed
struggle is not an end in itself. It is a means for a great
humanitarian aim. Since 1917 Palestine has been subjected
to wars, revolutions and bloody fighting. The time has
come for this land and its people to live in peace as other
human beings. We carry arms in order to achieve a truly
peaceful settlement of the problem, and not a false
settlement based on the imposition of aggression and
racism. Such peace cannot be achieved except within the
framework of a democratic state in Palestine.' (Abu 'Iyad)[1]

ROOTS OF THE REVOLUTION

The Six Day War

It is difficult to separate out the Palestinian Resistance Movement
(P.R.M.) from the historical moment and mood in which it first arose,
soon after the Six Day War, like a phoenix out of ashes, galvanizing a
whole nation humiliated by the collapse of the Arab armies. In this, its
first glamorous debut, the Resistance reaped a harvest of hero-worship
from a wide spectrum of Arab public opinion, salon nationalists going so
far as to call the *fedayeen* 'angels' and 'saviours'. This kind of support soon
showed its shallowness, but for a time it put pressure on the Arab regimes
to give the P.R.M. official backing. For the regimes, the Resistance
Movement (which they had tried to suppress before 1967) now had a
specific usefulness, in diverting public opinion from the defeat and giving
it new hope. The pre-War press ban on reporting guerrilla operations was
lifted, and the P.R.M. groups were allowed openly to recruit, train and
publicize their existence.

By 1967, many of the small groups formed in the early Sixties had
amalgamated, and Fateh had emerged as the most powerful, its strength
based on a combination of backing from the various Palestinian classes, a
broad national strategy, good relations with most Arab governments, and

popularity amongst the masses. Its leadership was strongly contested by other groups, especially the Popular Front for the Liberation of Palestine (P.F.L.P.),[2] but Fateh's decision in February 1969 to take over the Palestine Liberation Organization (P.L.O.), confirmed its character as, above all, a nationalist party. The P.L.O. underwent a degree of revolutionary transformation, with the National Assembly now representing the Resistance groups, rather than regions and social sectors as it had done earlier. The Executive Committee, elected by the National Assembly at its annual meetings, now also contained representatives of all the major Resistance groups,[3] as well as a few independents. Re-activated by the Resistance Movement, the P.L.O. became able to speak in the name of the Palestinian people.

For Fateh's leaders, the urgent need created by the 1967 defeat was to prevent the Arab governments from negotiating, from a position of weakness, an end to the Palestinian liberation struggle in return for Israeli withdrawal from the territories occupied in the June War. Their long-term hope was that Palestinian guerrilla operations would act as a spark to rekindle the broader Arab struggle against imperialist domination that had lost momentum in the narrow interests of neo-colonial regimes. Yet however compelling the logic of a broad coalition of Arab forces against an Israel that now occupied parts of Egypt, Syria and Jordan[4] (as well as all of Palestine) might seem to Fateh's leadership, there were more powerful interests that prevented such a coalition from solidifying. As the shame of the Six Day War receded into the past, the regimes still needed the Palestinian Resistance Movement to put pressure on Israel to negotiate, and as a weapon in their rivalries with one another. But none had any intention of being led into a popular war of liberation.

Thus, though the Six Day War temporarily discredited and weakened them, the regimes neither capitulated, nor took the road of popular mass struggle that the P.R.M. called for. Instead they continued the policy that had preceded the War, that of alternating military threat with political and diplomatic activity on the international scene. Revolutions like those that had been sparked off by the 1948 defeat did not follow the more crushing defeat two decades later.[5] Instead, what happened was a genuine, though partly aborted, revolution at the level of the Palestinian masses. For them, the call to action of the P.R.M. had a profound and lasting effect, for they sensed in it the first authentic answer to their crisis. It was 'the road to the Return', a way out of the limbo of the camps, a restoration of their humanity.

The P.R.M. appealed to the young, the oppressed, and the disinherited. For many Palestinians, armed struggle was a form of rebellion against those Arab civil and military bureaucracies that had exploited the Israeli threat in order to gain power for themselves, and that had then used Israel's military and political strength as a pretext for failure to confront it. For others, it was a way of rebelling against forms of oppression within Arab society that seemed to them to collaborate with Israeli and imperialist domination. For yet others, it was a way of discovering what was authentic in themselves, and in their culture.

National Liberation or Social Revolution?

Many will argue that the P.R.M. is not a revolution in the usual sense of the word, since it has overturned no regime; and in order not to overstate its claims some Palestinians now prefer to define it as a national liberation struggle. Yet when the Movement first emerged, Fateh leaders emphasized its revolutionary character, particularly in their discussions with Arab communists and leftists, whom they accused of supporting an oppressive reality through their failure to struggle against it.[6] A more compelling reason for keeping the term revolution is that it is so widely and constantly used by camp Palestinians that its subjective reality cannot be questioned. We need here to distinguish between the Palestinian Resistance Movement as an organizational structure that has grown and changed in response to successive crises, and the Revolution as a state of consciousness amongst the Palestinian masses. For them, the Revolution that was launched by Fateh in 1965 was an event of supreme importance, changing everything irreversibly. Two basic aspects of its revolutionary character were that it substituted mass struggle for passivity and speech-making, and that it brought back the Palestinians to the heart of the Arab/Israeli conflict. Even for those who say today that 'the Revolution has lost its meaning', this is only a way of disassociating the P.R.M.'s present leadership and policies from the mass revolutionary readiness which, as they see it, this leadership no longer embodies.

Study of the ways in which camp Palestinians use the word *thawra* in everyday speech shows it to contain multiple layers of meaning. It can mean the present P.R.M. and its cadres (as in 'So-and-so is working with the Revolution'), but more often it is used as a synonym for armed struggle, or the return to Palestine, or rejection of the *status quo*. Often it appears as a symbol of the life and destiny of the Palestinian people, reaching back into the past to cast new light on uprisings in Palestine, and pointing out a path into the future. Its resonances go far beyond the situation of the moment to a core of permanent identification, built around the ideas of fidelity to the land, to Arabism, to struggle, and to sacrifice: a powerful amalgam that requires little organization to sustain it, for its foundations lie in the collective experience of 50 years of oppression and betrayal. Were it not for the sense of organic relationship between the Palestinian struggle and the wider Arab struggle, one could see in this strong belief in their special destiny the seeds of a Chosen People myth. But their conscious adoption of a destiny of struggle is precisely what gives Palestinians a role and a message in the larger Arab world.

When did the Revolution Start?

Different dates are given for the Revolution's beginning. For Fateh, it is always dated from their first announced military operation inside Occupied Palestine, on January 1st 1965. A second key date is the Battle of Karameh, in March 1968, which opened Jordan as a base for guerrilla action. Whatever the achievements of the 1965 Revolution as a determinate organization, and whatever the dislocation between the masses and the structures of the P.R.M., crystallization of the Palestinians' sense of a 'struggle-identity' would not have been possible without the spark lit by Fateh in 1965. Nor, probably, would it have mobilized the masses on such a large scale without the vanguard work of activists like those of the Arab Nationalist Movement[7] during the refugee period.

In Lebanon, the Revolution did not come to the camps until the last months of 1969, but for all regions equally the War of 1967 was crucial in opening the eyes of the masses to the weakness of the 'progressive' Arab regimes on which, until then, they had pinned their hopes. At a single blow, the defeat of 1967 destroyed the regimes' prime argument for restraining the Palestinians, and, for a while, even their military and political power to do so. At the same time, it created a mass Palestinian readiness to respond to calls for mobilization.

But the roots of the Revolution can be traced back before 1967, or even 1965, to the first small operations carried out inside Occupied Palestine by different groups in the early Sixties; and before them to operations launched from Gaza in the Fifties; and on back to the War of 1948 and the whole history of Palestinian struggle, particularly the Great Revolt of 1936-39, and the uprising of Sheikh Izzideen al-Qassam that exploded it. Gaza played a particularly important role, between 1948 and 1967, as the only area where Palestinians could organize in relative freedom.

In discussing the origins of the 1965 Revolution, camp Palestinians always return to three fundamental sets of facts: first, the Zionist conquest of Palestine and the establishment of a racially exclusive state closely linked to U.S. imperialism, which by its nature threatens Arab independence and peaceful development. Second, as a consequence of the first, the dispersion of Arab Palestinians and their deprivation of both land and nationhood. This situation of dispersion and statelessness constitutes, for the mass of Palestinians, the primary compulsion to revolution because of its total unacceptability. To rebel is the only possible reaction. Third, they emphasize the subjective factor, their long history of struggle, constantly crushed or aborted, yet constantly resurgent. Like the genealogy of a clan, or a charter of membership, these three sets of facts are viewed in the same terms by all camp Palestinians, whatever their political affiliation, and form a solid basis for collective action.

Beyond these fundamental positions, however, lies the complicated

147

interaction of Palestinian and Arab politics. The Arab dimensions of the Palestinian problem have always been crucial, not only in the collusion of Arab leaders in aborting Palestinian resistance, as in 1939, 1948, 1970 and 1976,[8] but also in the radicalizing effect of the Palestinian struggle on the rest of the Arab world (the most obvious example being the revolutions in Syria, Egypt and Iraq during the Fifties); also in the participation of militants from all over the Arab world in the Rebellion of 1936, and again in the 1965 Resistance Movement. Final as the disappearance of Palestine seemed to be to outside observers in 1948, it was not final precisely because, even after the collapse of their own leadership, Palestinians could find support and a role in other revolutionary movements of the Fifties. While Israel revealed ever more clearly its aggressive and colonialist nature, Palestinians in exile were learning at first hand about the political structures and ideological currents of the neo-colonial Arab world.

Palestinian Disillusion with Arab Radicalism

Pinned down in the camps, the Palestinian masses in the *ghourba* were no longer able to react to events through uprisings as they had done in Palestine. All they could do was to scan the Arab scene for signs of movements towards, or away from, liberation. During the Fifties, they could feel that Palestine, though struck off the map, still existed through the appalling effects of its loss. But gradually, as time passed, faith became harder to maintain and the urge to independent Palestinian action stronger.

It would be wrong to see the Palestinian Resistance Movement *only* as a reassertion of Palestinianism since one of its fundamental aims was to give new impetus to the wider Arab struggle. Yet there can be no doubt that disillusion with the Arab regimes and movements contributed its share to the 1965 Revolution. Nor was this growing impatience limited to the P.R.M. leadership, with their closer view of the personal and party ambitions that underlay pledges of support to the Palestinian 'cause'. Palestinians in the camps may have kept their faith in the progressive Arab regimes longer than the middle class activists outside. But in addition to frustration at the lack of action towards liberation, the masses also had to bear the squalor and misery of camp life. All these experiences — the humiliation of being refugees, economic exploitation, but most of all the absence of concrete signs of progress towards liberation — combined to create a revolutionary readiness among Palestinians in the *ghourba* which only required a spark to set it off.

To the origins of the 1965 Revolution, then, we need to add the specific events of the early Sixties which made politically active Palestinians begin to turn away from the Arab parties they had joined or helped to form in the Fifties. In the period immediately after 1948, Palestinians had been strongly drawn to all those parties or movements that opposed, in whatever way, the *status quo*. These were mainly the Parti Populaire Syrien (P.P.S.), the Ba'th, the various Arab Communist parties,[9] the Muslim Brethren, Nasserism and the Arab Nationalist Movement. Because of the widespread belief that Arab unity must precede liberation, it was the pan-Arab movements that gained most from Palestinian support.

At least three distinct attitudes towards the political movements of the Fifties can be discerned amongst Palestinians in the camps. First, the majority of the older generation, the *jeel Falasteen*, remained fixed in their pre-1948 loyalties, whether to national or provincial leaders, and distrusting the new political parties as divisive, or anti-religious.[10] Second, a large number of the younger *jeel al-nekba* joined the opposition movements, following the principle that a younger teacher expressed when he said: 'We would have joined the Devil's party if it had put Palestine among its aims.' Third, a very small minority examined the positions of all the existing parties and decided that none of them had been able to provide a correct analysis of the Palestinian crisis, and thus that they were unlikely to provide a correct programme of action to solve it. In consequence, this group set out to form a new political movement that finally took the form of the Arab Nationalist Movement.

The mood of the Fifties — confidence in the progressive regimes in Egypt, Syria and Iraq — began to change in the early Sixties. Several events were crucial in crystallizing the new mood which Fateh was to express when it first emerged, that Palestinians must have an active and leading role in their own liberation. The first of these was the break-up of the union between Egypt and Syria and the subsequent failure to re-form the unity of the progressive camp. Another was the failure of the Arab summit meeting of 1964 to prevent Israel's diversion of the River Jordan. It was at this conference that President Nasser went on record as saying that he had no plan to liberate Palestine (unlike Syria's President Amin al-Hafez who was reported to have presented the summit with a plan to defeat Israel in 48 hours). Egypt's long drawn out and unsuccessful involvement in Yemen[11] was another source of concern to Palestinians. It began to look as if the Arab unity on which the mass of Palestinians had pinned their hopes of liberation was not coming closer, but rather moving further away. The fact that the Algerians had achieved their independence against superior force in 1962, with little Arab support, was a further spur to independent Palestinian action.

It was in this period that activist Palestinians became increasingly aware, through their experiences in the different pan-Arab movements, that, although they all put the Palestinian 'cause' in the forefront of their programmes, they were simply using it for local and sectional ambitions. As Palestinians, they began to realize that it was not only the regimes, but also the opposition movements, that had been influenced by the neo-colonial structures of the Arab world. Before 1967, such perceptions were confined to a small minority; the masses continued to believe that 'Abdul Nasser would give us Palestine on a plate'. But the new tendency towards independent Palestinian action did not only exist among a politicized minority outside the camps, it was also manifested inside them in a sudden proliferation of small, purely Palestinian cells calling for armed struggle.[12] These groups made no attempt at mass mobilization — the control of Lebanon's Deuxieme Bureau was too harsh for that — but they tried to create a new mass atmosphere through the distribution of leaflets, and a few began to undertake actual operations inside Occupied Palestine. The camps were full of informers and the militants of this period formed strict habits of secrecy. In a return to the patterns of peasant mobilization in Palestine, they recruited with extreme caution along existing ties of family, village, or party comradeship. And just as in 1936-39, when Arab support from outside Palestine had enabled local peasant leaders to gain some independence from a national leadership always too ready to negotiate with the British,[13] so, during the germination of the new Revolution, activists in the camps worked outside the control of the Palestine Liberation Organization (P.L.O.) which they distrusted because of its dependence on the Arab regimes.[14]

Growing Repression in Lebanon

Lebanese surveillance of the camps grew harsher in the Sixties, in direct proportion to the growth of Palestinian activism, each side responding in an opposite way to the same set of shifts on the Arab scene. But the harshness of repression added its own momentum to the building up of a revolutionary readiness amongst the Palestinian masses. In the Fifties, the Lebanese ruling class had feared that pan-Arab, pan-Muslim forces mobilized by Nasserism and Ba'thism would disrupt Lebanon's fragile sectarian balance. As this fear receded in the Sixties, a new one took its place: that Palestinian attacks on Israel from Lebanon would end by provoking Israeli retaliation, and that this in turn would create pressure for a larger army based on national conscription, instead of the existing, small, selectively recruited army through which the Maronites could maintain their hegemony.

The rise of the Deuxieme Bureau in Lebanon as a political power centre coincided with the opening of guerrilla training camps for Palestinians in Syria, Algeria, and, to a lesser extent, in Egypt. Despite being few in numbers, the trainees became a nucleus of new militant Palestinianism in the camps. This worried the Lebanese authorities so much that in 1962 a decree was passed forbidding any Palestinian who had left for military training from returning to Lebanon.

Gradually the mood in the camps changed from one of patience and suppressed anger to one of revolutionary readiness, which Lebanese oppression only made more explosive. The quotations below show clearly the inter-relationship between the beginnings of Palestinian armed struggle, militancy in the camps, and Lebanese oppression:

'When the U.A.R. was formed we began to train our youth in Syria, and a few went to Egypt. We believed in forming a military nucleus which would go to Occupied Palestine and start work there. Our aim was to increase these training courses, so that those who went outside to train would come back and train our scouts.'[15]

In 1964, the Arab Nationalist Movement lost their first fighter, Khaled Abu 'Aisheh, inside Israel. The news was not publicized -- such was the secrecy surrounding military operations that most A.N.M. members did not know the identity of their own fighters. The next year came Fateh's first publicized operation, which had an instant effect on the mass mood in the camps:

'Palestinians in the camps received this news with joy, and after it the situation in the camps changed. Everyone started talking about this new step, and their desire to participate -- especially the students and young workers.'

Lebanese oppression increased in intensity, and being suspected of membership in a Palestinian organization became increasingly dangerous. Even collecting funds could lead to beating or imprisonment. In 1966 Jalal Kha'wash, a Fateh member, was killed after torture, and his body thrown from a high building to make his death look like suicide. An A.N.M. organizer, Walid Kaddoura, was beaten 'to plaster' in front of the assembled inhabitants of Bourj al-Shemali camp.

Although oppression fell most harshly on members of organizations, the masses in the camps also suffered from the escalation of repression. Families of activists lived in a constant state of expectation that the police would appear.[16] Mothers whose sons were suspected of having gone for military training would be constantly interrogated. Often, if a wanted person was not at home, another member of the family would be arrested in his place. The overall atmosphere of repression encouraged random brutality, for instance the hitting of children in the streets with the *korbaj*.[17] Many young militants had their first experience of struggle through the D.B. coming at night to take their fathers away for interrogation.

Oppression in Lebanon did not lighten in the aftermath of the Six Day War, since the Lebanese Army had not been involved in the defeat. But the freeing of Jordan for guerrilla action after the Battle of Karameh (1968) had an effect on the situation in Lebanon, by increasing the flow of recruits for training. There were no arms in the camps in Lebanon, but the mass mood was growing steadily more defiant:

'We saw our young men eager to go to training camps in the Ghor, and take part in operations. They'd come back with stories of the war; so, instead of telling the old stories, people began to tell these new stories, about how our young men were fighting. The whole nature of talk changed, as if there had been a deep psychological change among our people. Because the Arab states were defeated, we Palestinians had a chance to be active, and we felt we had to use it to the ultimate extent.'[18]

Looking back on this period of mounting militancy and oppression, someone from Rashidiyyeh camp said:

> 'We can't say that the Revolution entered the camps at a precise time, on a precise day. We can say that it was the continuation of our growing political and military existence. The Palestinian masses in the camps were waiting for the armed revolution as a dry land thirsts for water.'

THE PLACE OF ARMED STRUGGLE IN THE RESISTANCE

The call to armed struggle issued by the leaders of the 1965 Revolution was not a product of a militaristic outlook or training on their part (most were middle class professionals turned revolutionaries, very like the leaders of the Cuban Revolution). The centrality of armed struggle in the Palestine Resistance Movement's programmes arose directly from the historical experience of the Palestinian people who, in every crisis, had been systematically disarmed. This had been their experience in Palestine under the British Mandate, particularly after the outbreak of the 1936 Rebellion. This also had been their experience in the *ghourba*: those of the fleeing villagers who still had their guns when they crossed the borders into the 'host' countries were forced to lay them down.[19] In the camps, there was no possibility of procuring or hiding arms. Thus, for the masses, their lack of weapons came to symbolize not just the loss of Palestine, but also the suppression of the liberation struggle by the Arab regimes.

There can be no doubt that, in the Arab context of the Sixties, the P.R.M.'s bid to mobilize the masses for armed struggle was a revolutionary act. The Arab regimes, progressive as well as reactionary, had demonstrated their susceptibility to Western pressures too often for doubt. The socialist and anti-imperialist elements in both Nasserism and Ba'thism had become submerged in state building, while the leftist movements had remained for the most part city based cliques composed mainly of students and intellectuals, too concerned about ideological warfare to work amongst the masses. Although the P.R.M. shared these tendencies with the other Arab movements, it reached the masses and related its action to its slogans to a degree that no other political movement in the contemporary Arab world had been able to do. By setting itself squarely in the framework of Third World struggle against U.S. economic and political domination, the P.R.M. revitalized radical elements in the Arab world and exposed the real character of the regimes.

The revolutionary nature of the call to mass based armed struggle in the Arab context arose also from the class related roots of militancy in Palestinian, as in Arab society generally. This characteristic class difference in militancy was clearly visible in Palestine under the Mandate, when the national leadership constantly vacillated between struggle and negotiation, using struggle in an attempt to increase its bargaining power, stopping struggle in response to imperialist or Arab pressures. The mercantile and bureaucratic middle class contributed very little to the uprisings in Palestine, and in the *ghourba* their non-militancy became even more marked. And more generally during the Sixties, the new national Arab armies were showing themselves to be instruments for the protection of ruling classes that did not spring from the peasants and workers, whatever their policies towards them.

The greater readiness for militancy amongst poor as against middle class Palestinians after 1948 needs little explanation. In part, it was a product of their oppressive situation in the camps which made the return to Palestine an urgent necessity, not a distant dream that could be postponed until 'the Arabs are ready'. Influenced by a traditional idealism, many Palestinians in the camps claim that their struggle arises purely from love of the homeland, not from 'material things'.[20] Others claim the camps are 'factories of men for the Revolution'. Economic exploitation has not been as important as political oppression in generating a positive mass response to the Resistance Movement, since the people see their situation as the result of national rather than class oppression.[21] Yet even if a sense of class oppression was secondary, it existed like a foetus in the womb of the more clearly defined nationalist programmes. This can be clearly seen in the radicalization of the Palestinian national movement after 1967, with the Arab Nationalist Movement moving into overtly Marxist-Leninist positions, and Fateh, the mainstream of the P.R.M., adopting the language and some of the practice of Third World revolutions, and synthesizing these with the masses' living memory of struggle in Palestine. The P.R.M. as a whole, not just its leftist currents, opened the Arab world to critical currents of thought which the progressive regimes, while interacting at a governmental level with the Communist bloc, had never allowed to reach their masses.

The primacy of armed struggle for camp Palestinians is clear from the fact that, even in the first years after the Disaster, when middle class Palestinians were preoccupied with hunting for jobs or sunk in individual trauma, we find that one of the first post-1948 organizations to be formed amongst the masses was called 'The Military Organization for the Liberation of Palestine'. Its militarism was a very distant dream, but underlying its formation was the same peasant obstinacy and toughness that had terraced Palestine's stony soil.

With the growth of education and political consciousness, the appeal of armed mass struggle to the Palestinian people grew as the only way to end both their national and their class oppression. It was young workers and students from the camps who became *fedayeen*, while middle class Palestinians who joined the P.R.M. moved mainly into 'white-collar' forms of struggle: organization, diplomacy, information. The idea of struggle mobilized them too, but not with the same readiness to sacrifice their lives that was shown by the masses in the camps.

In understanding the primary place of armed struggle in the consciousness of camp Palestinians, it is also necessary to recall how many times the camps had been targets for Israeli or Arab attack. When West Bank villages were hit by the Israelis before the Six Day War, they were neither defended by the Jordanian Army nor allowed to form their own defence militias. In Lebanon, later, the same situation was repeated. Even in Syria, the camps near Damascus came under both Israeli and Syrian attack. To camp Palestinians, the lesson to be drawn from these experiences could hardly be clearer. In this they shared a common perspective with the unarmed Arab inhabitants of the Jordan Valley, the Gholan Heights and Sinai, who had seen the national armies withdrawing to protect city based regimes in 1967, abandoning the border areas and the poor peasants who inhabited them.

Few peoples have been more systematically kept helpless in the face of attack than the Palestinians, and it is not surprising that the symbol of their resurgence after 1967 was the gun. To a people for whom dispersion had added new divisions to the older class and party divisions in Palestine, the gun was both a means to creating 'one mass for the return', and also a symbol of their regained identity as strugglers and Palestinians.

However, what Fateh militants have called 'the unity of the gun'[22] soon became fractured in the ideological conflicts that had marked the Resistance Movement from its gestation. Fateh was accused of mindless militarism: a charge it did not deserve, since its call to armed struggle was backed up by projects of social, cultural and economic development. In spite of its limited middle class origins and backing, Fateh expressed the pragmatism of the Palestinian masses, their longing for the reality of action as against the unreality of *felsefeh*. The words of a camp laundry worker who said, 'If a man tells me that he is going to fight, I don't believe him unless I see him take a gun and go', well express how, for the masses, the gun had become a touchstone of authenticity.

It was true, as the leftist groups point out, that the gun was not enough, that what was needed was a clear revolutionary ideology backed up by a programme of revolutionary mass mobilization. These never fully materialized, although their embryo is clearly visible in the short period of the P.R.M.'s freedom in Jordan from March 1968 to September 1970. To what extent the failure to realize its full revolutionary potential was due to the class origins of the P.R.M. leadership with their limited vision, or to Arab interference, is an argument hard to resolve because of the impossibility of drawing a clear line between the Palestinian Resistance and its Arab environment. But what differentiates all the Palestinian Resistance groups from most of the leftist parties in the rest of the Arab world is a much stronger commitment to mass armed struggle as a means to change the *status quo*. While awaiting a comprehensive study[23] of the ideologies of the different groups that compose the P.R.M., and their changes over time, it is useless to indulge in facile or partisan criticism, particularly as there are no clear class differences between their memberships.[24]

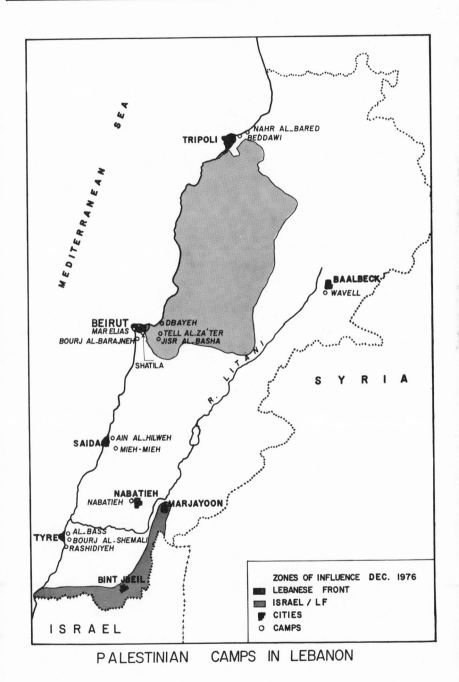

PALESTINIAN   CAMPS   IN   LEBANON

YEAR OF THE REVOLUTION

The Palestinian Revolution Comes to Lebanon

1969 was the year in which the Palestinian Revolution came to Lebanon, in a prolonged series of confrontations between the Lebanese regime and i) the *fedayeen* in the South, supported by part of the Lebanese rural population; ii) Palestinians in the camps; and iii) large segments of the Lebanese population of the coastal cities (national and progressive parties, students and the Muslim masses). Alliance between these different popular forces was based on a common opposition to Israel's role in the area, and forged through battles with the regime. With so many loci of protest to control, the regime's forces were spread thin and in constant danger of crumbling since their own internal divisions forbade their use in really ruthless repression. The course of the Revolution was thus quite different in Lebanon from Jordan, with a much higher degree of mass spontaneity, a closer alliance between Palestinian and local forces, and more lasting effects in terms of autonomy for the camps. The first *fedayeen* bases in South Lebanon were established in the winter of 1968-69, not far from the Syrian border, and began very soon after to attack Israeli settlements in Galilee.[25] With its mountains, caves and thick scrub, South Lebanon is a much better terrain for guerrilla warfare than Jordan or the West Bank. It is continuous with Galilee, the district in which around 60% of Israel's Arab minority lives and the two areas are linked by longstanding economic, social and political ties. Far from the capital, impoverished, neglected, predominantly Shi'ite,[26] the South also offered a promising socio-political basis for the Resistance Movement. The local elite were large landowners who willingly supported the Maronite hegemony, and had done nothing to improve conditions in their fiefdoms. Thus South Lebanon provided the Resistance Movement with some of the geographical and political conditions it needed.

Fedayeen Action in the South

Between 1968 and 1970 *fedayeen* action received deep popular support in the South. Not only this, but many of the younger, more politicized Lebanese southerners joined their ranks as fighters. The following account of one of these fighters is worth quoting at length because it shows the identity of experience and views between ordinary Lebanese and Palestinians:

> 'I come from the South, from a village on the border of occupied Palestine. Like the Palestinians, my family left our village in 1949 because the Zionists carried out a massacre in Hula, a village near ours, where they killed about 70 young men in a mosque. A great number of Lebanese from the border villages were forced to leave in this way, and they lived in Beirut in the same conditions as the

refugees. . .

'After the Palestinian Revolution, in 1968, we went back to our village, to live with the people there. There were daily *fedayeen* operations against the Zionist enemy's settlements. This created a revolutionary tide. The masses all supported the Revolution because they saw it was the only force able to stand up and say No after the defeat of 1967.

'At that time our material resources were few, and we had to rely on donations from the people. For a long time the masses were supplying all our needs, even clothes and food. On night patrol, we would knock on doors as we passed through the villages, and people would give us food and shelter. . .

'Before everything else, there must be an everyday political relationship with the masses, to look at their problems, and help them to solve them, especially through their own consciousness. . .

'In 1969 there were many battles between us and the Lebanese Army, and that is when we saw the villagers rise against the Army. I remember particularly Majdel Silm, where the Army put a force estimated at brigade size around the town to besiege a group of a hundred *fedayeen*. The population made a demonstration against the Army, protecting the *fedayeen* with their own bodies. This is the incident I consider the most expressive of fusion between us and the masses at that time.'

As in all Lebanon's rural regions, governmental services to the villages of the South were almost non-existent, so that supporting the Palestinian Revolution became a means of protesting against a corrupt and negligent regime.[27] Apart from one small hospital in Bint Jbeil, the only places where surgery or blood transfusion could be performed were the distant cities of Tyre and Sidon, and conditions there were such that most people preferred to reach Beirut if they could. The only schools in the villages were primary:

'They were hiring rooms to use as classrooms, scattered far from each other. The teachers were too few, and their qualifications and salaries were low. Most of them were sons of the village with no diploma higher than the Brevet.[28] Only a few of the bigger places had Intermediate classes. Our schools were not even attached to the Lebanese educational system.'

The Lebanese Army was not regarded by most southerners as a national army but as closer to an army of occupation:

'The percentage of southerners in the Army was very low, because it's always been difficult to get into the Army. It needed *waasta* and bribes. People in the South saw that the Army wasn't theirs. It illtreated them, and they saw how it was always withdrawing in the face of the enemy, and that it never defended them.'

Relations between the *fedayeen* and the Lebanese Army were never one of total confrontation, since it was not the clearly stated position of the government that guerrilla action in Lebanon was illegal, or that it must stop. Instead, limited action against the *fedayeen* was undertaken on legal pretexts, such as that they were carrying arms without a permit, or entering forbidden zones. The aim was to harass and deter the guerrillas, and raise segments of the people against them, rather than try to eliminate them entirely. The Army's ambiguous policy reflected its own internal divisions, similar to those of the regime:

> 'The Lebanese Army in the South wasn't unified. It had some people who wanted to defend their country, and others who were just puppets, henchmen, who wanted to deal with the Israelis. Others were only concerned to protect Maronite interests.[29] During battles between the *fedayeen* and the Israelis part of the Army would withdraw immediately, but part would stand and fight, even against orders from their headquarters. This happened many times. The Palestinian Revolution had relations with many men inside the Army, and they would let us through when we were passing checkpoints. Those who were pro-Israeli would stop us. One of their commanding officers used to pass all the information that the Army Intelligence office had on the *fedayeen* movements to the Israelis.'

The freedom of the *fedayeen* to carry on their action from the south was the issue that sparked off every demonstration in camp and city during the year of the Revolution. Support for the *fedayeen* spread far beyond the Palestinian masses to Lebanese schools and universities, and to the groups that made up the loose alliance of national and progressive forces. Students would taunt the soldiers sent to attack them with teargas and hoses: 'Why aren't you on the borders in the South?'

In spite of the relative freedom of the Lebanese press, the Army censorship code[30] was able to stop or delay news of the clashes occurring in the South from reaching Beirut. In April the Army threw a siege around Bint Jbeil to capture a group of *fedayeen* just returned from a mission. The people of the town refused to hand the *fedayeen* over to the Army, but after three days of siege and a threat of bombardment, the *fedayeen* gave themselves up to avoid bloodshed. News of their imprisonment in the barracks of Tyre leaked out, leading to the historic march of April 23rd, which weakened the regime, and prepared the way for the liberation of the camps later in the year.

The March of April 23

As news of the siege of Bint Jbeil spread, spontaneous demonstrations erupted in several camps, always the most responsive to interference with *fedayeen* action, and the Army put tanks around them. The *Yawmiyyat*[31] reports that four students were killed in Ain Hilweh camp, and twenty wounded: 'Similar demonstrations in other areas of Lebanon were suppressed by force and many people were killed, in Beirut, Mar Elias and elsewhere.' In Beirut a call for a march on the afternoon of April 23rd was put out jointly by The Gathering of National and Progressive Parties in Lebanon[32] and the Palestinian organizations. Leaflets explaining the situation in the South were distributed widely in schools and universities. The Minister of Interior refused an authorization for the march, and from the morning of the 23rd rumours began to spread that the authorities intended to use force, to deter people from participating. But the effect was the opposite. This eye-witness report from a participant describes both the mood of the masses (between ten and twelve thousand people are estimated to have taken part in the march) as well as the methods employed by the Lebanese authorities to suppress it:

'Around 3.30 to 4.00 p.m. people started gathering in the Makassad Square.[33] Groups came in from the North and the South in buses, from all the schools and universities of Beirut, and from all the Beirut camps except Bourj al-Barajneh, which was tightly encircled by the Army.

'We started to move at 4.00 a.m., and we had only moved about 25 metres when we came face to face with the Security Forces. They threw teargas bombs at us, and the fire brigade hosed us with hot water. This went on for about five minutes, as a warning to disperse. But the people regrouped and started to move again. The Security Forces had no choice but to carry out the orders they had received that morning, to shoot directly into the crowd, not to scare people, but to kill.'

What happened then was unprecedented in the long history of demonstrations in Lebanon: a battle lasting two hours between the armed Security Forces and the unarmed crowds. Instead of dissipating, or changing the course of the march, the demonstrators would spontaneously regroup after each confrontation, and try again to force their way along the road to the city centre which the Security Forces were blocking. With each re-starting of the march, the police would fire again into the crowd, killing or wounding several.

Many of those who participated in the march were students who had never encountered police violence before. A schoolgirl remembers seeing a man being carried away by comrades with blood streaming from his leg shouting '*Allahu akbar!*' Another participant remembers a group of demonstrators seizing a police transport lorry and distributing its load of helmets to the crowd. The eye-witness description continues:

'During all this time the people were shouting one slogan, "'*asifa, 'asifa!*"[34] Each time the march recommenced the police would shoot five or six people, then the marchers would regroup in the back streets and start again. The demonstrators had no weapons. The only thing we had were four or five wooden vegetable carts which some people used as shields, though the bullets went through them. The authorities wouldn't let ambulances into the area, we had to carry the wounded away ourselves. . .[35]

'No less than five times the crowd came back to attack, fully aware that the military force in front of them made it impossible for the march to go through. But the mass mood was at such a pitch that though people could have got to the city centre by other roads, they kept coming back to confront the police. . . The mass mood on that day was such that they were ready to confront tanks.'

In order to placate public opinion which was outraged by the fact that the police had aimed directly into the crowd instead of using more normal riot control methods, the authorities claimed that the police had been shot at first. However they were unable to produce a single bullet-wounded policeman, only a few slightly bruised by stones.

Forty-eight hours later, there was another confrontation with the Security Forces during the funeral march of one of those killed on April 23rd. The authorities tried to confine the march to one quarter, but it spread into small demonstrations all over the city. Student strikes went on for several days, until there was an agreement between the authorities and the Resistance Movement to free the *fedayeen* and calm things down.

It was discovered later that, instead of depending on the local quarter police, the authorities had brought in Army personnel from other areas and put them in F.S.I. uniforms. Police whose faces were familiar would be too afraid of retribution to shoot into the crowd.

The march of April 23rd was a turning point in many ways. It proved to an important segment of the Lebanese public what many had not believed before, that the authorities would use force against the *fedayeen* since they were ready to use it against their own people. The resignation of Prime Minister Karameh deprived the regime for many months of its normal Muslim cover. The Resistance Movement, which was not strong in Lebanon in terms of men and arms became, after April 23rd, a force that the authorities had to bargain with. Freedom of *fedayeen* action had shown itself to be a potentially revolutionary issue, and the Palestinian camps no longer faced Army tanks alone. In addition, it appears that, in the course of the confrontation, files containing the names of government secret agents fell into the hands of the demonstrators, thus weakening the State's information gathering apparatus.

Liberation of the Camps

April 23rd did not produce a sudden capitulation of the Lebanese regime. But, during the months that followed, changes in Lebanese mass consciousness were manifested in dynamite attacks on government instal-lations. Army tanks still encircled most of the camps, but there was a new feeling of hope and defiance. Nahr al-Bared, a large camp 20 kilometres north of Tripoli, was the first to gain its freedom.

On August 28, eleven policemen entered the camp with orders to pull down a Fateh office that they said had been built without a permit. The people of the camp refused and took the policemen hostage. Army rein-forcements were called up and threatened to enter the camp unless the hostages were surrendered. Someone who took part in the fighting that followed describes it:

'They brought tanks and the Army tried to enter the camps. That day, we can remember with pride, we brought out the few guns that we had — they were eleven. We did well at first, but then we ran out of ammunition. A rumour ran round the camp that the ammunition was finished and we tried to calm the people by telling them that rescue would come from the Resistance. But we didn't really know whether it would come. But what was amazing was that people returned to what they had been in 1948, preferring to die rather than to live in humiliation. Women were hollering because it was the first time a gun had been seen defending the camp. It was the first battle that we didn't lose. The children were between the fighters, collecting the empty cartridges although the bullets were like rain. It was the first time that people held knives and sticks and stood in front of their homes, ready to fight.'

Reinforcements did come during the night, and in subsequent negotiations the Army agreed to withdraw two kilometres from the camp, whilst the people of the camp agreed to release the 11 police hostages. Amongst the recollections of the man quoted above is that of a Deuxieme Bureau officer, 'a tool of oppression in the camp, impotently kissing our feet, and telling us that he had six daughters'. Someone else recollected seeing a man violently destroying an iron bed, to which he had once been tied with a stone on his chest, in the camp police station.

Although the Army continued to demand that the Fateh office in the camp should be pulled down, and 'troublemakers' in the camp handed over to the authorities, the situation in the country as a whole was too explosive for the launching of an all-out attack on the camp. Not only the Lebanese situation, but mounting Arab pressures limited Army action.

The next camps to contest Lebanese control were Rashidiyyeh and Bourj al-Shemali in the south. A militant from Rashidiyyeh describes what happened there:

'A week before the liberation of Nahr al-Bared a group of fighters entered Bourj al-Shemali camp and were welcomed by the supporting masses. But the political situation was still not mature enough to keep them in the camp. After negotiation between the P.L.O. and the Lebanese authorities, they found it necessary to retreat, and a group of people known not to be from the camp left it. A week after that the *fedayeen* entered Nahr al-Bared, and the Lebanese authorities tried to confront them. They fought for four days with very simple weapons and little ammunition, and the result was victory for the Revolution.

'The next camp was Rashidiyyeh, on September 10. After that the camps fell one after another, and the forces of oppression began to withdraw. . . They knew the people were waiting for the Revolution. They felt afraid because the people had started to confront them, and they didn't know from where the next blow would come.

'There was something in common between all the camps, that they provided people who prepared for the Revolution from within. Those who came from outside the camps were very few. In Rashidiyyeh there were 18 cells. We had few arms, but the authorities imagined that everyone in the camps carried a gun.'

The camps in Beirut were less easily surrounded than the more isolated rural camps, except for Bourj al-Barajneh which has sand dunes on three sides. Sabra, Shateela and Mar Elias melt into populous Lebanese (Muslim) areas, and could not easily be attacked. By the time of the September confrontations there were still very few arms in the camps, but the mood of both the Palestinians and the Lebanese masses had become much more confident.

'What helped the liberation of the camps was the state of mobilization of the Lebanese masses which prevented the authorities from hitting the camps fiercely. It wasn't the force inside the camps, or the quantity of arms, but the mood of the masses, and the continuous demonstrations, that paralysed the state. . . In Jordan there were arms, and in the South, but in the camps there were very few.

'Remember that at the entrance of Sabra camp there weren't more than four old Egyptian rifles, but every home had prepared "molotovs". It was incredible how many they made, every home had 10 to 15 of these bombs. But there were no other weapons. In Sabra there was only one "kalashnikov". . . But the authorities couldn't enter the camps because if they had, other areas would have exploded.'

It was during September that all the camps got rid of the police and D.B. offices that had oppressed them so long, although they continued to be besieged by Army tanks. In Beirut, Lebanese mass demonstrations reached a new intensity:

'I remember that there was a demonstration at Bourj Abu-Haidar, a Lebanese suburb, and some of us managed to get out of besieged Sabra to join it. The unarmed demonstrators entered a local police station and took their weapons and sent them to Sabra. Two other stations in Beirut were attacked by the masses and their arms taken.'

Some idea of the spontaneity of mass action at this stage is given by the anecdote of a P.L.O. official to whom an employee laconically reported one morning: 'We took over Shateela last night', upon which the official went off to put a new P.L.O. plaque on the old D.B. office. That there was any clear P.R.M. plan to replace Lebanese authority with revolutionary authority may be doubted. Unable to guarantee the security of their police in the camps, the Lebanese government in several cases requested the P.L.O. to intervene to protect them as they withdrew. Shortly afterwards a P.L.A. trained police force, the *kifah musellah*, was sent into the camps to reassure the authorities that law and order would be kept.

Although the mood of camp Palestinians had, by September, reached boiling point, it is impossible to establish that there was any over-all plan for the liberation of the camps. A veteran member of one of the Resistance groups describes how the Revolution came to Bourj al-Barajneh, almost accidentally, undirected even by a local command:

'I had worked that day in the city and as I left the camp I saw gatherings of students and workers demonstrating to kick out the police and D.B. from the camp. Among them I saw my father. . . An hour later I got a phone call telling me that my father had been killed. I returned to the camp and found that 16 had been wounded, and one killed. My father was one of the wounded and had been sent to a local hospital.'

As a known militant, the man could not risk staying with his wounded father in the hospital since the police would come to interrogate him. Later after interrogation, the old man was removed to a police station in a suburb near the camp. What happened next gives a fascinating glimpse of camp Palestinians in action:

'I bought medicine for my father and gave it to my wife, and told her to take some old women with her, and go to the police station and throw stones at it. So six or seven women went and surrounded the police station and demanded that they give up the wounded man. The police refused to give him up, so the women started throwing stones. The police got in touch with higher officials and finally they handed him over. As the women were bringing my father away a group of young men with arms surrounded the police station and this time the police and the D.B. did not shoot, but ran away, because now our people had weapons. . . Up to that moment there were very few arms in the camp, but within 24 hours of the police withdrawal, hundreds of arms were being carried.'

Clashes between the Lebanese Army and the *fedayeen* in the South continued throughout October, with growing Arab pressure on Lebanon to allow freedom of guerrilla action. During the siege of Mejdel Silm (October 18), in which there were many Lebanese civilian as well as *fedayeen* casualties,[36] Syria closed its border with Lebanon, Libya recalled its ambassador, Nasser sent a telegram to President Helou, and most Arab governments issued statements supporting the Resistance Movement. It was these pressures that led directly to the signing of the Cairo Agreement on November 2, by General Bustani for the Lebanese regime and Yasser Arafat for the Palestinians.

But the Cairo Agreement changed little. Only a few weeks later a clash took place between the Lebanese Army and *fedayeen* in the camp of Nabatiyeh in the South, during which an estimated 50 Palestinians were killed or wounded through long-range shelling. In their communique from Amman, the P.L.O. pointed to Saeka and the P.F.L.P. as having triggered off the clash. This was one of the early signs of splits within the Resistance Movement that were to vitiate guerrilla action in the South, and to some extent also the Revolution in the camps.

REVOLUTION IN THE CAMPS

The Palestinian Resistance has been criticized for the primitive level of its political training programme,[37] and for the *ad hoc* character of its work amongst the masses in the camps. Yet the absence in 1968-69 of a single, solid revolutionary Palestinian movement, with cadres trained in mass mobilization, should not surprise anyone. At that time the P.R.M. was a congerie of small, scattered clandestine groups which broke into the open before they had completed their merger attempts, in a bid to prevent the Arab regimes from submitting to an Israeli dictated peace after the Six Day War. It was a historic decision, taken prematurely from the point of view of the P.R.M.'s own development, yet necessary within the Arab context. Upon the new-born P.L.O. Resistance framework fell the weight of three sets of problems: sustaining armed struggle against Israel; maintaining a balance of forces within the Arab environment that would give the P.R.M. a minimum of independence; and becoming a government for the oppressed and neglected masses. Given the objective and subjective conditions within which the P.R.M. had to work if it was to exist at all, it can plausibly be argued that it did all that was possible. Others will argue that if the leadership had analysed the Arab scene more accurately they would not have gambled on spontaneous mass reactions, but would have put greater thought and effort into a plan of revolutionary mass organization. If they had done this, the weaknesses that showed up later in the P.R.M. might have been less serious.

The People's New Consciousness

If we ask camp Palestinians today how much the Revolution changed their lives, the answers are overwhelmingly positive. In a group discussion held in January 1978 in Bourj al-Barajneh camp, the changes most emphasized were these: first, the lifting of Lebanese oppression and the freedom to engage in political activity and struggle; then the restoration of the Palestinian identity; the defence of the camps; the normalization of ordinary life; the creation of new institutions — nurseries, workshops, training centres — and the revival of Palestinian traditions and folklore. It is noticeable that whatever a person's group affiliation the points emphasized hardly vary:

'The Palestinian felt after the Revolution that he's living like a normal person again after a life of humiliation. The camps now are like fortresses, where in the past people had nothing to do but die under these zinco roofs. . . A large number of the Revolution's leaders are from the camps, some in the first rank, such as Abu Maher, or Abu Ahmad Yunis — we needn't mention names, but they are a large number. . . Now we have new institutions which were forbidden before. Palestinian customs and arts have been revived. And there are many other changes. Palestinians now are like the Vietnamese and Chinese, moving in the same line.'

Someone who returned to his home in Tel al-Za'ter camp after the Revolution describes the changes that struck him most:

'The first moment I got down from the car I saw the Palestinian flag instead of the Lebanese flag, and a group of Palestinians in *fedayeen* clothes instead of the Lebanese police. As I moved through the camp I saw the happiness on people's faces, and in the schools there wasn't the frustration of before. The *sheikh* in the mosque now spoke clearly about the homeland — in the past he couldn't do this. There were many young men in the camp who have been outside, in Syria and Jordan, with the Revolution. . .

'Before, there had been a political and ideological siege around us, but now the camp radio played revolutionary songs and speeches. . . In the homes, mothers spoke clearly with their children about Palestine -- before this was only done in a whisper. In the past we used to listen to Sawt al Arab, but only in secret. Before the Revolution, meetings in the camps were limited to social problems; after it, discussion became political — the land, the nation, the Revolution. There were continual political meetings between the young people, the local Resistance group leaders and the old. There were many new projects which weren't there before: social activities, sports, meetings where people could say what they thought clearly, without censorship. . .'

A Palestinian sociologist who knows the camps well gives a similar view:
'The most important thing was that they felt liberated from the daily persecution of the D.B. They felt more able to defend themselves, and to participate more fully in the Revolution, and take part in the fighting. And they felt more pride. All that came to them from the Revolution was a matter of morale. . . The most important benefit of the Revolution was freedom of political activity, freedom to organize and to work. . .'

Naturally enough, the most vivid recollections of the first intense feelings of joy and liberation which surged through the camps with the ending of Deuxieme Bureau control, come from the people from the camps. A militant from Bourj al-Barajneh camp describes the atmosphere there:
'The people didn't sleep for weeks afterwards, from happiness at seeing their youth carrying arms to liberate the homeland. They were in total support of the *fedayeen*, and showed this by bringing them food, tea, coffee. Those were beautiful days in the camp, *like wedding days*,[38] after the uprising.'

A man from Rashidiyyeh said:
'It was impossible to find a person who didn't want to invite the *fedayeen* and offer his home as an office. It was felt to be shameful not to be the first to give the fighters food, water, shelter. The people were ready to sacrifice everything they had for the Revolution. When we said we needed money, the women would give their gold earrings, bracelets, watches.[39] And whatever they gave, they felt it was nothing.'

With the breaking of Lebanese control, camp Palestinians were free to organize themselves:
'The circle of fear was over, and now there was active movement in the camp. For the first time in our history women took their right role, and there was military training for girls as well as boys. We felt

we had regained our identity, not just as Palestinians, but as human beings.'[40]

An expression much used by people in the camps about the Revolution is 'It raised our heads', meaning that it restored their self-respect, crushed by expulsion from Palestine and oppression in the *ghourba*. Before it, they had been paralysed by the trauma of dispersion, and their sense of collective weakness.[41] After the Revolution, resignation and fear changed to self-confidence. Now the Palestinian masses could feel pride because the *fedayeen* were challenging an Israel that had just defeated three Arab armies equipped with modern weapons. Whether or not the new-found pride of the Palestinians verged on chauvinism is a point debated inside the P.R.M., but its mobilizing effect is undebatable. Before the Revolution 'two policemen controlled a camp of thousands'. After it, 'The policeman who used to curse us salutes us now!' The activism liberated by the restoration of camp Palestinians' self-respect set in motion changes in their relations with the Lebanese population around them, as well as in their own internal social relations.

Among the many differences that distinguished the *jeel al-thawra* from the *jeel Falasteen* was that, for the parent generation, identity was not a problem. Whatever their suffering in the *ghourba*, they knew where they belonged. For their children, who only knew Palestine from their parents' descriptions, uprootedness took on a deeper, more bitter dimension. All they had ever known was the camps. The parents could remember what it was like to be citizens in their own country; their children had only known what it was like to be 'strangers', 'refugees', 'different' in the countries of others. Childhood experiences of hostility from Lebanese neighbours had imprinted on many of them a sense of exclusion, almost of pariahdom. For camp Palestinians of this generation the Revolution brought a new identity which they eagerly grasped: Palestinian, struggler, revolutionary. As an 18-year old schoolboy phrased it: 'The Revolution gave me the answer to who I am.' Instead of being part of a despised, marginal group of 'displaced persons' Palestinians now adopted *en masse* the role of vanguard of the Arab revolution, strugglers against imperialism, closely linked with other Third World struggles. This conscious adoption of a 'struggle-identity' encompassed Palestinians of all ages in the camps, but was particularly strong in the *jeel al-thawra*:

> 'Before the Revolution I and all Palestinians wondered how we could return to Palestine. As a Palestinian I felt that I must have a role in the struggle. . . The Revolution was the most important event, not just in my life, but in the life of the Palestinian people. Our understanding, our talk, our thinking all changed. Before there was reactionary thinking, now there is revolutionary thinking.'[42]

Pride in being Palestinian is closely tied to the ability to struggle and to suffer: 'Maybe no other people could have borne such hardships.' This special capacity for suffering is seen as necessitated by the unique difficulty of carrying on a liberation struggle from 'countries that do not completely support us', against an enemy that is technologically and militarily superior, as well as being supported by the U.S. Another 17-year old girl shows the organic relationship between Palestinian identity and anti-imperialist struggle:

> 'I am proud of being Palestinian, especially among the Lebanese, because I feel I have a cause that will shake imperialism in the Middle East, and in the world.'

A boy of 18 from the same camp said:

> 'I feel proud to be Palestinian, one of a people that is revolutionary, struggling, and suffering. We were lied to many times, others tried to bury our existence as Palestinians. But with the Revolution we broke our handcuffs. Before I was living in a refugee camp, now I feel that it is a training camp.'

Because of their militancy, political consciousness and love of Palestine, hope for the future has become centred upon the *jeel al-thawra* who are seen as more educated than their parents, better equipped to challenge Israel's scientific and technological superiority, but no less courageous and patriotic. In defining their own distinct character, members of the *jeel al-thawra* tend to reproach their parents for leaving Palestine and express their own determination to protect the Revolution with their lives. *Nashat* — political activities — are the sign of the young, in contrast to what they see as the resignation and passivity of their parents in the refugee period.

Although there were differences in income between families in the camps, these were not rigidified into a class structure. Because everyone lacked possessions and shared the 'bad life' of the camps, all had an equal interest in radical change:

> 'If we look at the camps from a class point of view we find that all belong either to the very poor or to the small bourgeoisie. Most were ready to support the Revolution — this was clear from the way they welcomed it. For example, a man who had done twelve-hour guard duty would keep on clutching his gun after he was told to rest because he felt it was the symbol of his freedom, his hope for the future.'

Previous informers were treated gently:

> 'Everyone knew who they were, so the Revolution brought them out and tried to convince them that what they were doing was backward. We tried to correct them, and we weren't severe with them, because they lacked consciousness.'[43]

The only group in the camps who may have viewed the Revolution with misgiving (there is debate on this point), was the remnants of the peasants' own authority system, the old men, the family and village leaders. A camp school director describes their attitude:

'Most of the *wujaha* ' collaborated with the authorities and the informers, not because they were unnationalistic, but because they feared the new generation which was threatening their influence. These were the people on whom the Mufti depended — they worked together against the new current — they were both part of the leadership that had failed, and when the Revolution came to the camps its first conflict was with them. Everyone in the camps was with armed struggle except this group. They represented every traditional thing in our society and they held on to their position. Eventually they found it better to support the revolution, so as not to be isolated. Their time had gone.'[44]

Pride in the militancy of the young was certainly accompanied in some quarters by misgivings about the retaliation it would eventually provoke. But such worries were scarcely present in the first months of the Revolution. It is evident from all testimonies that the first relationship of the P.R.M. to the camps was one of complete identification. In all the 'answers' to the loss of Palestine produced by Arab leaders and parties, this was the first to weld itself into the consciousness of the masses as their own authentic answer. It combined their longing for Palestine, their rejection of expulsion and dispersion, their rebellion against oppression in the *ghourba*, and their insistence on struggling against external domination of the Arab area:

'The relationship between the people of the camps and the Revolution was very simple: it was one of.complete collaboration and fusion. Everyone said, "This is our Revolution".'

The Problem of Revolutionary Authority

In understanding what became of the Revolution in the camps after 1969, a key is the multiplicity of authority centres which made it impossible to produce a level of organization commensurate with the level of revolutionary consciousness. The *kifah al-musellah* which filled the interregnum between the authority of the Lebanese and the camps' own popular committees, the *lijan al-sha'biyyeh*, were not part of a new revolutionary authority structure, but took their orders from the P.L.O. Their specialized role is clear from the fact that they took no part in the new camp defence militias. For camp Palestinians they were a vast improvement on the Lebanese D.B., but they still occupied an ambiguous position somewhere between the old and the new order. A camp inhabitant comments:

'The *kifah al-musellah* sometimes make mistakes. Sometimes they intervene in social problems and make them more complicated because they have a military training, not a social one. But we don't look at them as we did at the Lebanese police or the D.B. We can tell them when they're wrong. If we'd done this with the Lebanese police they would have beaten us.'[45]

Almost as soon as the camps were liberated, popular committees were formed which harked back to those formed in Palestinian villages in the last years before 1948. Although their members were inhabitants of the camp, they were chosen by the Resistance groups rather than being elected by the quarters, thus creating a certain gap between the affiliated and the unaffiliated. They took on the important tasks of organizing defence, public hygiene, sports and cultural facilities, and facing day to day problems. With support from a united Resistance Movement, the *lijan al-sha'biyyeh* would have evolved into a strong tool of self-government and change.

Men chosen to work on the popular committees were those who had been outstanding during the refugee period as leaders and nationalists. Some were teachers who had refused the option of leaving the camps so as to remain close to the masses. Others were self-educated working men from the *jeel al-nekba*, the generation who had lost their schooling in the move from Palestine to Lebanon. Too young to fight in 1948, by the time of the 1965 Revolution they were too old. Tough and impressive people, their potentialities were not used as they should have been by a leadership which had no clear programme of mass organization outside the training for the *fedayeen*. Because they knew camp conditions and the problems of the masses intimately, from their own lives, they would have been a better bridge between the Revolution and the camps than the Resistance cadres, many of whom were young and inexperienced, though formally better educated.

At the beginning, building on the pent-up energies generated by Lebanese oppression, the popular committees were able to achieve a great deal without external support or direction. They collected money, dug wells, laid water pipes, set up quarter committees to keep the streets clean, started small libraries. That they were not able to do more was due to the same conditions that offset so many efforts in the camps: continual Palestinian/Lebanese crisis, competition between the Resistance organizations, confusion of authority, lack of funds, lack of an overall plan.

The real centres of power in the camps were the Resistance group offices, since they had arms and direct links with the leaders of the P.R.M. For the youth of the camp, they incarnated the armed struggle idea, and their appeal was irresistible. Stories are often told in the camps of children as young as four going on their own to the Resistance offices and demanding to be given a gun.

No one makes a secret of the fact that the primary purpose of the Resistance groups' offices in the camps was to recruit. Although most offered social benefits as part of their recruiting campaign, only three had social or training projects from which camp inhabitants as a whole, not just their members, could benefit.[46] Competition for recruits was bitter, and often inter-group conflict would be built on to family or quarter conflicts, occasionally leading to violence because of pent-up tension and the profusion of arms. There were no Resistance cadres with special training for work amongst the masses, although many acquired this with time.

Probably for most of them, the specialized role of fighting appeared enough in itself; only the most politically mature understood that the masses could not participate fully in struggle unless the Revolution came close to their lives and changed them. To gain the support of the masses, rather than to change their conditions, appears to have been the principal aim of all the groups at this stage.

The proliferation of groups within the Resistance Movement had characterized it from birth, and neither Fateh's mass popularity after the Battle of Karameh, nor its take-over of the P.L.O. in the National Assembly of February 1969, enabled it to construct a united national front. In the first months after liberation, the only organizations with a real presence in the camps were Fateh, the P.F.L.P., and the P.L.A. But soon others made their appearance, both those backed by Arab governments (such as Saeka and the A.L.F.), and splinter groups from the P.F.L.P. (P.D.F.L.P., Jibreel's General Command). Competition between the groups had many dangerous effects, not least, perhaps, an over-emphasis on ideological differences which were often irrelevant to the real problems faced by the Palestinian people. Another by-product was over-publicity for the military training programmes in the camps. A P.L.O. official comments:

'Definitely the Palestinians over-enjoyed their freedom in the camps, even if this was a reaction to be expected. We have to link this with the ambitions of the different groups who wanted to expand amongst the masses and so opened recruitment offices in the camps. That's when we began to get publicity about training. They'd hold a ceremony over the training of a few kids — it wasn't even real training — but it was the idea, the novelty, seeing a Palestinian in uniform, holding a gun, jumping over fire. Even the Lebanese bourgeois newspapers printed these pictures all over their front pages, simply as a thrill.'

Possibly the most serious effect of inter-group competition, comparable in gravity to the way it blocked the development of revolutionary organization in the camps, was the blow it dealt to morale. None of the attacks they faced ever disheartened the unaffiliated masses as much as the failure of the Resistance groups to achieve unity. Certainly there was a basis for group competition in the culture of the camps; and there were those who would argue that their number spread revolutionary consciousness more rapidly, and allowed more of the people to participate actively, than if there had only been one national front. But the feverish mass activism of the earlier years, during which everyone rushed to affiliate himself/herself in a group, gave way later to a dropping off of membership. To some extent this was inevitable and did not damage fundamental mass support for the Revolution as an idea. The camps remained a basic source of recruitment for the P.R.M.'s fighting wing and local political leadership. But disunity meant that, after all the demonstrations, marches, speeches, rallies and battles, and in spite of the heights to which revolutionary consciousness had reached, not enough remained in terms of revolutionary organization.

The camps were still, from an organizational point of view, as well as in terms of material conditions, areas of neglect.

The effect of the Resistance Movement on middle class Palestinians outside the camps, lies outside the scope of this book, but it is relevant to note that there existed a number of Palestinian organizations which were stimulated by the Revolution to try to carry out projects amongst the masses. The most important of these were the general Unions, particularly those of the Workers, Women, and Students, which had existed before the Revolution, albeit with a limited national/liberal role. With the Revolution, the Unions were freed from their earlier leadership and began to undertake mass-based projects. However, several problems (besides continual Palestinian/Lebanese crisis) hindered their work in the camps. One was that, outside their organizing committees, their membership remained largely passive, reflecting the lower level of politicization of middle class Palestinians in comparison with that of the masses. Another was that much of their energy was spent on internal conflict, reflecting differences among Resistance groups. Another was the socio-cultural gap which dispersion had deepened between middle class and camp Palestinians, and which was difficult to overcome in the short run, even between members of the same Resistance group.

Health and Education: New Fronts of Revolutionary Action

Although with education the economic situation of camp Palestinians improved between 1948 and 1969, the material conditions of the camps had changed very little. In certain respects they had even deteriorated, since living space and services had not increased in proportion to the population, and although the rise of a new, educated generation had created a trickle of emigration out of the camps, this was more than compensated for by the high birth rate. Other factors inhibiting migration were fear of losing precarious U.N.R.W.A. rights, insecurity of status in the countries of work migration,[47] and attachment to kin and neighbours. But living in the camps, as one ex-inhabitant said, was like living on a rubbish tip. Physical conditions which had been accepted stoically during the refugee period became increasingly unacceptable as Palestinians perceived the populations around them achieving a faster rate of progress than they, in spite of their diplomas and hard work.

In the first months after the Revolution under the leadership of the *lijan al-sha'biyyeh*, camp Palestinians began to attack some of their most urgent environmental problems. Students from outside the camps used to come to join the work groups digging wells, trenches and shelters. But for these projects to be completed on a mass scale would have required mass mobilization, or funds. Instead, aid came after crises that ought to have been foreseen and prepared for. An organizer from Tel al-Za'ter camp recalls:

> 'I remember that the first shelter in Tel al-Za'ter was built after the clashes of 1973,[48] and it was done by a group of young men from the camp and from outside. We started digging the shelters with our hands.'

He continued:

> 'Roads in the camps are bad. Health services are very poor though lots of money was put into this. Until now only about 10% of our children have kindergartens, the rest are on the streets. Social activities for young people and women are too few. Until now authority in the camps is not properly organized.'

A pressing problem to which all the Resistance groups gave their attention was health, in response to the obvious need for wider health care created by poverty, under-nourishment, overcrowding and tension. U.N.R.W.A.'s health services were underfunded to a point where they hardly existed for the masses. A camp of 16,000 people would be served by one clinic with a daily nurse, and a twice-weekly doctor. Admission to Lebanese hospitals was limited to a few cases a month in each district, so that it needed *waasta* to be admitted. In the rural camps, the situation was much worse because of the absence of alternative Lebanese medical services, private or public, outside the larger cities.

The importance attached by the Resistance Movement to health is evident in the fact that all the groups — even those which had no other type of social programme — opened clinics in the camps and distributed large quantities of free medicine. In addition, Fateh established a national health service, the *Hilal al-Ahmar* (Red Crescent). Originally formed to cope with emergencies arising from attacks on camps, its founders hoped to draw nationalist doctors from the middle classes to work as volunteers in the camps and bases. Some did, but they were not enough to expand the Red Crescent's services, and critics from the left blamed it for its bourgeois concept of health care, emphasizing hospitals and highly specialized doctors instead of attacking the health problems of the masses with new methods. What was needed was training programmes for health workers among camp Palestinians, prevented by the high qualification barriers[49] from entering the medical professions. Whilst the Resistance group clinics in the camps did give courses in First Aid, it was not until just before the Lebanese Civil War that regular training courses for nurses, lab assistants and pharmacists were set up in the Beirut area. In time, these will lessen the camps' dependency on expensive urban facilities and encourage the spread of basic medical knowledge among the masses.

The deficiencies in the quantity and quality of education available to camp Palestinians have already been discussed in Chapter Three. Of these defects, the one that the Resistance Movement was most conscious of, and set out most energetically to change, was the absence of any element of Palestinian nationalism in U.N.R.W.A.'s syllabus. In reaction, the P.R.M. strongly emphasized national political consciousness in its own training programmes for the *fedayeen* and *ashbal*. One of the first studies to be carried out by the Palestine Planning Centre (an offshoot of the P.L.O.) was a content analysis of history and geography textbooks used in the Arab educational systems, and by U.N.R.W.A.[50] They were found to be deficient, often inaccurate concerning Palestinian history, particularly in minimizing popular resistance to the British occupation and to Zionism. Pressure was also brought upon U.N.R.W.A. to adopt new textbooks; when I was living in a camp, one of these, consisting of photographs of Palestine, often used to be brought out to show me by children who were still not yet in school, like a family treasure. Admittedly, the new children's story-books published by Dar al-Fata had hardly begun to penetrate the camps by 1975, nor had the colourful wall magazines for children produced by the P.P.C. But parents in the camps who had lived through their country's severest crisis without knowing it as 'history' were impressed and happy to see these books in their children's hands. A laundry worker whose own schooling had been cut short in 1948 told me proudly: 'My sons will grow up knowing that they have a country, with a history and a civilization.'

Still along the lines of providing a more nationalist education was Fateh's *ashbal* children's training programme, first initiated in Jordan soon after Karameh, and conceived as supplementing normal schooling, not replacing it. It consists of basic military and physical training, with courses in Palestinian history and general political history (Zionism, the Arab world, imperialism and the Third World). Although at first the hostility of Western public opinion was roused by news photos of small children in uniform, carrying guns, Israeli attacks on the camps have provided more than enough justification for Palestinian militarism, which is increasingly viewed by world public opinion as legitimate defence. In spite of the restrictions placed on the P.R.M. in the host countries, *ashbal* training has not ceased, and every summer it brings together Palestinian children from different regions and classes. Another of its values has been its emphasis on the necessity of co-existing with Jews in a future Palestine.[51]

Until today, however, the Revolution has no general concept of an alternative educational system for the children whom they call the 'generation of liberation'. An independent Palestinian intellectual, I. Abu-Lughod, has raised the question of how suited conventional Arab education, with its strongly academic and clerical bias and its deeply ingrained elitism, is to a people engaged in a difficult liberation struggle.[52] Amongst a minority of radicalized camp Palestinians one finds an understanding that Arab education tends to make people middle class more than to liberate them, and such people are ready to say, 'We need a more revolutionary education'. But so far no Resistance group, from the most revolutionary to the most conservative, has sufficiently raised itself above day to day crises to consider this vital problem.

On the whole, the masses in the camps only want more schools, not a different system. They need schools, first and foremost, to improve their condition; but also they see education, along with political consciousness and armed struggle, as an enrichment of the Palestinian masses' human potentials and as a challenge to Israel's present technical and military superiority. Education is an integral part of the special role they see themselves as playing in the Arab world, as guides and path-finders, as modernizers and revolutionaries. Their longstanding class longing for education, combined with the crucial role it played in enabling them to survive the Disaster economically, makes it a part of their self-image, so that only with difficulty can they begin to view it critically or oppose its tendency to drain the camps of those with diplomas. Even the few who are aware of the way the educational system supports the class structure have hardly begun to draw the blueprint of an alternative. Yet people often say that education on its own is not enough; it has to be combined with political consciousness 'or we shan't succeed in liberating Palestine'. This is only one of many examples of the way 'ordinary' camp Palestinians often have a keener perception than the leaders and ideologists.

Thus to camp Palestinians, the deficiencies of U.N.R.W.A.'s medical and educational services persist, with the Revolution contributing mainly stopgap efforts here and there. There are more clinics and hospitals than before, but still no overall surveys of health needs, no mass health training programme, and only a few training courses for health workers. In education there has been a promising development in pre-school kindergartens,[53] by a group that recruits and trains its own teachers from the camps. But most supplementary education still depends on middle class volunteers, and therefore fluctuates with their availability: evening classes for Baccalaureat candidates have, for example, only been carried on in camps near enough to Beirut to attract volunteer teachers. The same is true of adult literacy classes for women, begun in some camps shortly before the Lebanese Civil War.

Another severe problem which has hardly begun to be tackled lies in the high drop-out rate of children at the end of intermediate school. There is need for mass work training programmes, designed to fill the manpower requirements of Palestinian and Arab economic development over the next decade, instead of leaving teenage boys to fill the basement factories, print shops, laundries and garages, so prolific in Lebanese city suburbs. Despite their limited scope, the work training courses which the Red Crescent and Samed[54] have recently initiated are valuable, not only because they develop Palestinians' manual and technical skills, but also because they carry political discussion and consciousness-raising into the work place, where as before there was a complete divorce between the two. In Samed's workshops a limited form of 'autogestion' is practised, with elected workers' committees, weekly discussion groups and seminars, training cycles and a magazine. The General Union of Palestinian Workers (G.U.P.W.) is making similar efforts for its members, and is gradually abandoning the traditional formula of inviting outside 'experts' to make speeches to a passive audience, in favour of seminars and discussion groups in which the workers themselves participate. One sign of evolution in the action of the Resistance Movement is the fact that a recent strike conducted by the Lebanese branch of the G.U.P.W., against employers in the port of Beirut who refused to indemnify Palestinian workers,[55] was turned into a two week training course in economic-political struggle. It is true that these organizational changes are limited to the Lebanese area, but their impact will certainly be felt by Palestinian workers in other areas.

An inhabitant of Tel al-Za'ter camp who works with the Revolution gave this evaluation of the P.R.M.'s achievements and failures, interesting because of the way it balances 'political and military victories' against lack of improvement in the life of the people:

'If we think of what was required of the Revolution to give to the camps we have to admit to being disappointed. . . The Revolution won political and military victories, but with all this we failed to satisfy the needs of our people.'

FIRST DECADE OF REVOLUTION: VICTORIES AND TASKS

Political Mobilization

In attempting to assess action of the Resistance Movement amongst the Palestinian masses, we can ask two questions: (1) To what extent has the first emotional identification of the masses with the P.R.M. been translated into organizational integration? (2) Has the P.R.M. radically changed internal social relations within the camps?

Perhaps we can begin to answer the first question by remarking that, although the 1965 Revolution's leadership saw the camps as 'factories of men for the Revolution', and regarded them as their primary mass support, they did not see them as its heart and centre. None of the groups ever set up its headquarters in a camp, though all maintained a 'presence' in them. The centres of the Revolution were not even the military bases, but were rather their offices in the capital cities. Amman, Damascus, Beirut: these were the areas of concentration for the P.R.M.'s cadres, close to the centres of communication and state power. Urbanization of the Revolution was already clear in Amman before the 1970 massacres,[56] and became even more pronounced later as armed struggle gradually yielded first place to diplomatic and informational action. This shift of emphasis inevitably increased the role of the middle classes at the expense of the masses.

At the same time, important changes have come about through the masses' belief that the P.R.M. is *their* Revolution. Most camp Palestinians below the age of forty have been active members in one or other of the Resistance groups, most have gone for periods of military training:

'For the Palestinian, being a member of an organization is a very natural thing, like his name, or his family. This is an important

> development. Of course it is also a danger because of the very big difference between the Palestinians' level of organization and that of all the other Arab masses.'[57]

Apart from full-time members, most camp Palestinians are affiliated to a Resistance group, giving part-time volunteer work or financial contributions. In times of crisis, women and children, as well as men, participate in camp defence. In addition, a significant number have become full-time, salaried cadres with the P.R.M., mainly at middle levels of leadership. As they gain experience, Palestinians from the masses will reach the higher levels of leadership which, until now, have been occupied mainly by revolutionary intellectuals. But such a shift in the class origins of the leadership is not likely to change the conditions of the masses, or the ideological direction of the Resistance Movement, unless at a certain moment the masses themselves, or their representatives, make a determined bid for control. What is more likely is that the P.R.M. leadership will show itself increasingly attentive to mass demands and needs, while steering them in broadly nationalist directions.

Even though a certain dislocation persists between the structures of the P.R.M. and the masses in the camps, it is striking to what extent the politicization of camp Palestinians is self-sustaining. Their material conditions have changed little, and many of the Resistance groups' early activities have lapsed through shortage of organizers. Yet there are still certain basic kinds of work that are carried on in the camps without much support or direction from outside — for instance defence, consciousness-raising, contacts with the Lebanese population around. There is a constant political alertness which keeps the sense of autonomous revolution alive. There is also a belief, expressed by old as well as young, that it is the situation of the Palestinians which is the primary creator of revolution, not a particular organization or leadership. One of the oldest people I interviewed, a veteran of the 1936 Rebellion, answered a question on organization in Palestinian villages by saying:

> 'Even if I feel that I have no power and no leader to direct me to rebel, I have another director which is suppression and subordination. Oppression creates in the human being the methods and ideology he needs to prepare the road of resistance against his persecutors.'

There is both continuity and difference between these words and those of a much younger man, a Fateh militant from an exceptionally poor family, who had nonetheless managed to become an engineering student:

> 'I thought of the things I must do to return to my country. I participated in all strikes and demonstrations on Palestinian issues. Finally, I joined one of the Resistance organizations, which represents for me the peak of my political consciousness. As an engineer, I feel there is a link between my specialization and the aims of the Revolution, so I am using my knowledge in a magazine for our fighters. There can be no separation between theory and action.'

For the younger man, an organization exists which he believes has an ideology and line of action which will ultimately lead to liberation. But in both, there is the same direct response, as human beings, to a situation that is unacceptable because it negates them.

Even those who believe that the Revolution has become bureaucratized, or say that it has 'lost its meaning', or accuse a particular leadership of betrayal, do not see this as the end of the story. The absence of hero-worship of the leaders of the Revolution is striking. The photos of *shuhada'* are much more visible on the street walls of camps than those of the Resistance leaders, and people praise the latter sparingly, saying, 'They live the lives of the people'. If one falls, another will take his place. It is the invincibility of the Palestinian people as a whole, not a given party or leadership, that people mean when they say, drinking coffee, 'Revolution until victory!'

Revolution and Social Relations: How Much Has Changed?

The second question, on the degree of revolutionary change in the camps, is not easy to answer. Definitely they are not foci of revolutionary ideology in the way that the guerrilla bases of South Yemen or the Sahara are. But nor are they areas of pure peasant conservatism, as the Lebanese Marxist Samir Franjieh once wrote.[58] We can begin by saying that the preservation of peasant values and social organization by Palestinians in the camps was itself a form of resistance and included struggle among its values. Certainly, traditional peasant culture contained many elements that were politically conservative, for instance deference to the advice of the old (who usually advised patience and submission), respect for 'leading families', loyalty to patrons. But it contained strong collectivist and egalitarian elements as well.

The impact of the Disaster upon this traditional peasant culture was not to destroy or erode it, but rather to build up counter-forces, particularly that of political organization, which affected traditional forms without attacking them directly. It is probable that the *idea* of the conservatism of the masses in camps was too deeply imprinted on the minds of the Resistance leaders for them to risk creating antagonism by encouraging 'premature' revolutionary practices. If correct, this may explain why none of the groups made any strong effort to change the situation of women.

Yet even before the Revolution of 1965 there had been signs of rebellion within the camps against the old order. A veteran militant describes this growth of generational conflict:

> 'When we left Palestine we brought with us our village customs and habits which were symbolized by respect for the oldest member of the family and the oldest man in the village. They had great influence. A few young men tried to confront these notables because they felt they held back the evolution of the people, but they couldn't achieve anything before the Revolution. Confrontation sometimes took a

violent form, for instance when the "infantile leftists" attacked religious values and feelings, which only had a negative effect. What had real influence was the slow growth of armed struggle. . .'

Given the strength of traditional peasant culture, and peasant distrust of 'foreign' ideologies, it was only in conjunction with national liberation struggle that revolutionary thinking could make any headway among the masses:

'Leftist thinking started to spread in the camps and in the Revolution itself, after 1967. Before that it had no chance to enter our very conservative society — the Communists tried after 1948, but they were accused of being atheists, and this was enough to end them then. After 1967, leftist thinking came to us through books, newspapers, organizations, and visits from European leftists. People began to say "It's the leftists who come to fight with us. . ."
'At the beginning of the Revolution, the leftists tended to oppose traditions, but with time this extreme leftism became modified and adapted to our reality. Through simplifying leftist ideas they have become more acceptable to our people. As a result, rightist thinking is much weaker than before. It still exists, but in the past it was the only ideology, whereas now leftist thinking is growing and is accepted.'

This quotation gives an accurate picture of the ideological flux in the camps which makes it difficult to distinguish a Fateh militant from one from the Jebha or the Democratiyeh. As for the Resistance groups, it is not evident that any one of them aimed first at changing social relations within the masses. Paradoxically, we find the largest Resistance group approaching the masses via the same leaders whom young camp militants had earlier challenged:

'The first thing I usually do when I start working in a camp is to have a meeting with the old people, the wujaha' and the heads of families. I say to them, "The camp belongs to you, it's up to you to solve the problems of marriage and neighbours' quarrels. We don't want to interfere in your affairs." I meet them regularly every week, in a different house, we drink coffee and talk. I ask them, "What do you want? You are asking for many things. To which do you give priority? To finishing the hospital? Or the sewage system? Or to distributing money?" Finally they decide to finish the hospital first, then dig wells for water, then make the sewage system, and not to distribute money. If I had come from above and imposed these decisions I would have been replacing one repression with another.'[59]

Before the 1965 Revolution, not only had religion and the wujaha' kept their dominant place in camp culture, but the peasant family had maintained its traditional control over the lives of the young. For centuries, family membership and solidarity had been closely tied in to the celebration of the great religious feasts. Fawaz Turki, from a social level somewhat above the camps, recalls his revolt against the convention of the feasts:

'. . . we shocked our parents by refusing to adhere to the social dictates that governed the observation of the Eid.[60] At a time of year when, traditionally, Palestinians go around dressed in their best attire and visit friends and relatives to celebrate the Eid, we opted to ostentatiously wear our grubbiest clothes, and head for the beaches.'[61]

For young camp Palestinians, revolt against the family took a less individualistic, more moderate form, compatible with cultural loyalism. A young man who went on a military training course in Syria sometime between 1967 and 1969 recalls:

'A teacher came to collect students who had left home without their parents' permission, and because there was going to be a feast. But we refused to go with him. We valued the feast, but we stayed in the camp. We forgot our families for the sake of our country.'

It is very clear here that national struggle was the *only* obligation strong enough to confront the moral authority of the peasant family. For the families, to let their sons go for military training was an immense sacrifice, since they represented their economic future, their only hope before the Resistance Movement of one day escaping the squalor of the camps. But after 1969 the mass belief that the P.R.M. was the beginning of the road back to Palestine made most families ready to let their sons go for training, and those whose parents refused them permission would go anyway. Daughters also began to claim a role in the struggle. From then on, camp families boasted of their children's participation in the Revolution and if they had anxieties, hid them.

Although the Resistance groups could count on the total support of the *jeel al-thawra*, they tried for the most part to prevent mass adolescent revolt, returning runaway children to their parents and trying to heal breaches in family solidarity. But the militancy of the sons definitely weakened the authority of the fathers,[62] already undermined by the loss of land which had been one of its main bases. Patriarchal authority was also reduced by the greater earning power of the new educated generation, giving daughters as well as sons relatively more weight in family decisions.

As family relationships changed, so did those between teacher and student:

'In schools before, there was absolute obedience to the teacher. If a student was absent from school for one day it took the whole family's pleading to get him readmitted. When the Revolution came, those who reacted to it most were students in the Intermediate classes -- they joined the Revolution, and supported it. The schools became training camps, and education took a smaller part, most time being given to mobilization and training. A teacher who was not with the Revolution would lose respect.'[63]

The Revolution not only changed teacher/student relationships, it changed the people's concept of the teacher's role. Whereas traditionally the job of teacher had been the means to middle class status and income, the Revolution honoured a new kind of teacher, one who not only preached struggle, but practised it. A trenchant criticism of teachers before the Revolution, reflecting on the entire middle class, is this, from a building labourer:

'Teachers told us something about Palestine, but they should have told us more. They should have participated in action, for example in demonstrations, but they hadn't the courage. Most were with the Deuxieme Bureau. . . They are good at making speeches, and arguing, but when the Revolution faces difficulties, they will not be there. Only when the difficulties are over, then you will see them, in the front.'

Today, most of the teachers who have remained in the camps are very far from the traditional *ustadh*, with his townsman's *tarboosh*, his *sibha*, and his cane. They are sons of the camp, close to the people, called on to fulfill political as well as cultural functions, interpreting political events to the masses, mediating new ideas.

While it is often claimed that, with the Revolution, 'woman took her right role for the first time in Palestinian history', if the subject is discussed more deeply, people admit that there are still deeply entrenched obstacles to the political activity of women:

'Up to now the Revolution hasn't given woman her authentic role. The Revolution still understands the role of the woman in a way that doesn't allow her to get free from her cage. . . The majority of our women up to now are not able to struggle against their families so as to share in political activity. . . I know people who are in responsible positions in the Revolution, and who claim that they are real revolutionaries, but who still do not allow their wives and daughters to take part in the Revolution.'

This comment comes from one of a minority of camp girls who succeeded in working in a Resistance group without defying her family. She, and other girls of her generation, had taken part in strikes and demonstrations at school, only to find at home that going out to meetings at night or joining a political organization were prohibited activities. A few have managed to persuade their families that their national feelings have the same right of expression as their brothers'. But the majority do not dare to undertake political activity against the families' wills, especially as they cannot feel confident of the respect of the male members of the organizations they join.

It has often been remarked that during crises the code of conduct preventing girls from taking an active role is dropped, only to be reinforced when the crisis is over. Most families argue that if girls want to help the Revolution, they must do it in traditionally female ways, such as sewing uniforms for combatants, nursing or teaching children. But — so they argue — the supreme form of woman's contribution to the Revolution (reinforcing her traditional role) is to bear sons and bring them up to be militants.

The diversity of ideological currents in the camps — from Maoism to

Muslim piety — is understandable if we remember that they are densely packed natural settlements, with three and sometimes four generations inhabiting the same household. Family consciousness is still very strong, and conservatism extends not merely over the sphere of religious ideas and deep cultural values like women's 'honour', but also shapes ideas of class and names the groups that can give rise to political action. 'The nation' and 'the Resistance Movement' have meaning in a way that 'the proletariat' and 'women's oppression' still do not. The struggle of segments of the people against internal oppression are at present subsumed in the struggle of the whole, to exist as a nation in Palestine.

Thus, the radicalization of mass Palestinian thinking that accompanied the rise of the Resistance Movement appears to have been mainly limited to: 1) understanding of the links between Israel, U.S. imperialism and Arab reaction; 2) the placing of the Palestinian struggle in a Third World context, with the alliances and antagonisms that this implies; and 3) the decision to struggle. But this, in the Arab context, is already a great deal. A sympathizer who knows the camps well, comments:

'For me, the most important thing is their extraordinary ability to bear loss, especially personal loss. It's something incredible. . . The masses are still giving, much more than the intelligentsia. I think this change was caused by the sense of belonging to a country, Palestine, which the Revolution expressed. The masses are attached to the Revolution as an expression of the homeland, consequently they are ready to sacrifice for it, simply, without pretensions. I have seen with my own eyes people dying every hour, in Baddawi and Tel al-Za'ter. Their capacity for sacrifice is something extraordinary.'

What is the political significance of this unusual capacity to bear loss and to recover from attacks? We can say without rhetoric that the determination to carry on their struggle, shown by the Palestinian masses since the rise of the Resistance Movement, has a political importance that goes beyond any 'diplomatic victories' gained on the international scene, and beyond any immediate concessions that may be squeezed out of the Israelis by Arab/American pressures.

First, it has political effects upon the Palestinians themselves, strengthening the identity that unites them in spite of conflict within the Resistance Movement and geographic dispersion. However costly, each phase of active struggle deepens the foundations of this unity. The immediate effects can be seen in the renewal of resistance inside Israel, and the refusal of West Bankers to be wooed away from the P.L.O. If this trend continues, it will become increasingly difficult for Israel — even in partnership with Jordan — to carve the Palestinians up into easily controlled cantons. One does not have to be a visionary to predict that the effort required of Israel to suppress the Palestinians will eventually weaken the structures of the Zionist state, and lead to their transformation.

A second gain from mass Palestinian resistance is that it has made it much harder to separate 'the problem' from the people, or to reach a settlement through handpicked politicians making minor adjustments to frontiers. As a result of mass struggle, Palestinians have become expert at seeing through attempts to deceive them and efforts to present failures as victories. Both their voices and their actions will surely prevent from becoming permanent any settlement that legitimates Israel's presence as an extension of America in the Arab world.

A third gain from the experience of struggle over the last decade has been an understanding of how long and difficult it still must be. For the first five years after the rise of the Resistance Movement many Palestinians believed that liberation was at hand. This over-optimism has now disappeared, giving place to a much more realistic appraisal of the difficulties to be faced.

A fourth gain has been the experience of mass organization, on a scale hardly paralleled in the Arab world. From this has come a clearer understanding of the objective and subjective conditions within which mass organization must progress to reach greater effectiveness.

The effects of mass Palestinian struggle on the Arab scene will be slower to reveal their shape, because of the complex interplay between revolutionary and counter-revolutionary forces. As the Palestinian scholar Walid Khalidi has argued,[64] a Palestinian state in the West Bank would tend to stabilize the present regimes and *status quo*. A mini-Palestine hemmed in by Israel on one side and Jordan on the other would have little scope for playing the role of 'fire under ashes' which Palestinian militants have seen as theirs since 1948. This would be a solution that would leave Israel's nature as a militaristic and racist state unchanged, and all the arguments that Khalidi puts forward to convince Americans of the proposed state's harmlessness are ones that make it unattractive for the masses. No Palestinian state could afford to become, as Jordan is, an instrument for suppressing the liberation struggle. And even if a West Bank state emerges, it will not be able to accommodate the majority of Palestinians. The dispersion will continue to exist, with all the pressures it generates towards changing the *status quo*.

In Lebanon, hostility to the idea of a West Bank state has been strong amongst camp Palestinians from the time of its first launching in 1973. They mostly come from Galilee and the coastal cities, and have no homes to return to in the West Bank. Many do not regard the West Bank state as a serious proposal, but rather as a means to divide the Resistance Movement; their opposition to it comes through pungently in comments like these:

> 'There is not one of our people who has not sacrificed, and is not willing to sacrifice. But we must see our leadership announcing revolutionary programmes instead of flying to meet this king and that president, and working towards concessions that will humiliate our people.'
> 'We have a Revolution and the Arab states are offering us a state. A people's war doesn't last ten years only, it goes on until it achieves something.'

These remarks reflect the attitude of the P.F.L.P. towards the P.R.M. leadership's adoption, since 1973, of a moderate, compromising stance towards a settlement. While there are indications that Fateh's leaders believed in the genuineness of the West Bank state proposal when it was first put out, it is not likely that they are as ready to sell out the Revolution as the Rejection Front[65] claims. There will have to be clear political gains from negotiation, or, as a camp mother said, 'All our sons' blood will have been shed in vain.' Not only the Rejection Front, but the mass of Fateh's following expect the leadership to reject submissive solutions, even if the alternative is to return once more to clandestinity and struggle.

REFERENCES AND NOTES

1. Abu 'Iyad, a Fateh leader, in an interview with Lutfi Khouli, Egyptian socialist and editor of *al-Tali'ah*, (published in June 1969). Translated into English in L. Kadi's *Basic Political Documents of the Armed Palestinian Resistance Movement*, (Palestine Research Centre, Beirut, 1969).

2. The P.F.L.P. joined the Executive Committee between 1971 and 1974, but for most of the history of the P.R.M. it has opposed Fateh's policies, blaming it for the 1970 massacre of Palestinians in Jordan, incorrect analysis of the present Arab regimes, etc.

3. The groups that have been associated with Fateh in the Executive Committee since its formation are: Sa'iqa (controlled by the Syrian Ba'th), the Arab Liberation Front (controlled by the Iraqi Ba'th), the P.D.F.L.P., and Jibreel's P.F.L.P.-General Command.

4. From a Jordanian point of view the West Bank is Jordanian territory, though it forms part of historical Palestine.

5. The Free Officers' Revolution in Egypt took place in 1952; the Kassem Revolution in Iraq in 1958; in Syria the first Ba'thist takeover came in 1958 (with the formation of the United Arab Republic with Egypt), and the second in 1963.

6. Abu 'Iyad, in the *al-Tali'ah* interview: 'Al-Fateh, which has not declared that it is a Marxist-Leninist movement, was the first to undertake armed struggle, offered martyrs and opened the way for a war of liberation. Uttering words is not enough. Action is the determining factor. We say that al-Fateh's actions are related to progressive thought more than those who merely declare their support for such thought. The important thing in any revolutionary movement is not propagating an ideology but actual action. Ideology alone is meaningless unless put to the test.' (L. Kadi, *op. cit.* p.69).

7. One of the founders of the A.N.M. describes its evolution: 'Our basic

idea was that Palestine could not be liberated except by force and that Arab power lies in unity. At first we had three slogans: unity, liberation, and vengeance. Then we changed vengeance to the restoration of Palestine because we felt that vengeance was a fascist slogan. After 1967 we changed restoration to socialism. We stood for unity of the Arabs, liberation of the Arab area from political and economic imperialism, and then the battle for Palestine.'

8. 1970 was the year of Black September, when the P.R.M. was crushed in Jordan. 1976 was the year of Syrian intervention in Lebanon, with adverse effects for the Palestinian/Lebanese progressive alliance.

9. The Arab communist parties are organized on a sub-Arab national basis, i.e. within neo-colonial boundaries, and have relatively less connection with each other than with Moscow.

10. An A.N.M. veteran who worked with Lebanese Communists in 1949, attributes their only slight appeal for the Palestinian masses partly to the religious factor, but more to the Communists' stand on the U.N. Partition Plan of 1947: 'In 1949 we started recruiting for an organization we called The Conference of the Dispersed. Its members came mainly from the Communist Party and it formed branches in most of the camps in Lebanon. It only lasted until 1950 because the authorities started pursuing the Communists. But it wasn't just what the authorities did that finished it, it was the stand they had taken on Partition.'

11. Egyptian military involvement in Yemen, which began soon after the revolution which deposed the Imam in 1962, was met with Saudi supported counter-revolution. The war in Yemen lasted until 1967, ending in a compromise that papered over the failure of Egyptian intervention.

12. One authority on the P.R.M. says that the number of Palestinian groups in the early Sixties reached 44. Another says not more than 14. Fateh initiated merger negotiations, but these had not produced results by 1967.

13. See G. Kanafani, *The 1936-39 Revolt in Palestine* (Committee for Democratic Palestine, Washington, 1978), p.26.

14. A P.R.M. militant said of the P.L.O.: 'We tried to co-operate at the beginning with Ahmad Shukairy and the P.L.O., although we knew that it was only an empty form, and that Shukairy didn't believe in revolution or armed struggle. We supported it because it represented the Palestinians and was speaking in our names. In 1964 Shukairy opposed military operations against Israel, saying that they would push Israel to attack the Arab states before they were ready. But the Arab states knew that the Palestinians would carry on this embryonic work, and that if the P.L.O. went on opposing it, it would lose Palestinian support.'

15. An A.N.M. member from North Lebanon.

16. The wife of a well-known political organizer used to keep a suitcase permanently packed for her husband's spells in prison.
17. The short leather whip sometimes carried by the Lebanese police in the camps, a relic of Turkish rule.
18. A P.R.M. member from a camp near Beirut.
19. As a boy of twelve, fleeing with his family from Acre, Ghassan Kanafani saw men putting down their arms at the frontier post between Palestine and Lebanon. Later he wrote about this scene, as a formative moment in his life as an activist, in a letter to his son: K. Kanafani, *The Story of Ghassan Kanafani*, (Palestine Research Centre, Beirut, 1973).
20. This idealization of patriotism certainly goes back to the nationalist struggle inside Palestine, but may also reflect more recent campaigns against Communism amongst the masses.
21. Most camp Palestinians tend to see all those who exploit or oppress them as 'sons of a government', attributing their own vulnerability to statelessness. Only a minority see the oppressors as members or agents of a ruling class.
22. This phrase implies more than the unity brought about through armed struggle, it refers also to the self-discipline required of the modern *fedai* as compared with the *mujahideen* of earlier uprisings.
23. Studies to date, like that of Chaliand, have been insubstantial. Even in Arabic no comprehensive or analytical study has appeared so far.
24. Fateh has both upper middle, middle class and mass backing, but the leadership of all the Resistance groups comes from much the same social background, i.e. the educated, small and middle bourgeoisie. At the camp level, there is no evidence that socio-economic level plays any role in affiliation. One finds families with members in different groups, others who appear solidly pro-Fateh or pro-Jebha, while some families and quarters appear unaffiliated.
25. An important strand in the revolutionary character of the P.R.M. was its refusal to recognize the borders between Occupied Palestine, Jordan, Syria and Lebanon as anything more than the legacy of colonialism.
26. The early sectarian consciousness which had acted as a barrier between Lebanese Shi'ite peasants and Palestinian Sunni peasants in 1948-49 had been modified by 1968 through education and the growth of anti-sectarian political parties in Lebanon.
27. One of the effects of Israeli attacks on South Lebanon was the formation of government sponsored committees to 'rehabilitate' southern refugees, who would otherwise swell the slums of Beirut.
28. The Brevet is roughly equivalent to one year before the British 'O' levels, and marks the drop-out point for non-professional workers.
29. During the Lebanese Civil War of 1975-76, Maronite militias were set up in the South by some officers in the Lebanese Army,

collaborating with the Israeli Army against the Palestinian/Lebanese progressive forces.

30. The Lebanese Army has been protected from the press by a censorship code since the time of President Chebab.

31. The *Yawmiyyat Falastiniyeh* is a daily diary of Palestinian events compiled from press reports and official statements, and published by the P.R.C. (Beirut).

32. This was a loose alliance of groups linked by their opposition to Israel and to Maronite ascendancy in Lebanon. Led by Joumblat's P.P.S., it included radical Muslim and neo-Nasserist groups, as well as non-political formations like the Alumni of the Makassad (an Islamic cultural foundation).

33. It was planned that the demonstration would gather in a solidly Muslim area, near the Makassad Hospital, and proceed down the main street to the city centre.

34. 'Asifa, the Storm, was the name first given to Fateh's fighting wing.

35. Newspaper estimates put the dead and seriously wounded at around seventy. Eyewitnesses say that five or six marchers were killed every time the police fired into the crowd.

36. The *Yawmiyyat* reported nine Lebanese civilians and 14 Palestinians killed in the first round of fighting.

37. See for instance G. Chaliand, *The Palestinian Resistance* (Penguin, Harmondsworth, 1972).

38. This metaphor linking the coming of the Revolution to the camps with marriage celebrations, has a profound significance given the centrality of marriage/fertility in Palestinian peasant culture.

39. Jewellery is a common form of women's property among peasant and bedouin Arabs, a security against widowhood or divorce, and only parted with under extreme pressure.

40. A militant from Nahr al-Bared camp.

41. 'I thought about our rations, this small quantity of flour we needed so as not to die of hunger. *This* was the Palestinian, a refugee, a person without respect, whom others summoned by gesture instead of by name, whom others portrayed as cowardly though the truth was the opposite' (30-year old teacher in Bourj al-Barajneh camp).

42. Schoolgirl, 18 years, Bourj al-Barajneh camp.

43. A P.R.M. militant from Rashidiyyeh camp.

44. A teacher from Bourj al-Barajneh camp.

45. An inhabitant of Bourj al-Barajneh camp.

46. Fateh's social programme initially emphasized support for the families of the *shuhada'* (just as the Algerian F.L.N. had done). Its social philosophy is clear in its basic aims: 'to raise the status of the Palestinian family'; and to 'prepare for a stable society in Palestine'. In contrast, both the P.F.L.P. and the P.D.F.L.P. aimed at revolutionary mass change. See G. Khoursheed, 'The Palestinian Resistance

Movement and Social Work' (in Arabic), *Shu'oon Falastiniyyeh*, No. 6.

47. Salaries for Palestinians with qualifications are high in the Gulf, Saudi Arabia, Libya, etc, but their future remains precarious. Even those willing to take local nationality, buy land, or start a business, cannot easily do so. Residence and work permits generally depend on political inactivity.

48. A serious round of fighting between the Lebanese Army and the P.R.M. broke out in May 1973, with artillery and aerial bombardment of the camps.

49. Even candidates for nursing school have to pass the difficult Baccalaureat exam before entering. Students from the camps have almost no possibility of entering any of the medical professions because of the high cost of training.

50. U.N.R.W.A. schools normally follow the syllabus of the country in which they are situated.

51. See T. Farah, 'Political Socialization of Palestinian Children in Kuwait', *J.P.S.*, (Summer 1977).

52. I. Abu-Lughod, 'Educating a Community in Exile', *J.P.S.*, (Spring 1973).

53. The Ghassan Kanafani Cultural Foundation directs these kindergartens, which continued to operate during the Lebanese Civil War, and are now being extended to the outlying camps.

54. See Political Glossary.

55. Many Palestinian workers in the port of Beirut had been longshoremen in Jaffa before 1948. Their recent strike was a reaction to dismissal without compensation, due to the fact that the port lies within the Kataeb Party's area of control.

56. In Amman (as again in Beirut), all the offices of the Resistance groups are clustered in the same area.

57. A Fateh organizer.

58. S. Franjieh, 'How Revolutionary is the Palestinian Resistance Movement?', *J.P.S.*, (Winter 1972).

59. A Fateh organizer.

60. *Eid* = feast (see Glossary under *'eed*).

61. F. Turki, *The Disinherited*, (Monthly Review Press, New York, 1972), p.155.

62. B. Sirhan, in his study of camp children (see Bibliography) notes that boys whose fathers are not militants tend to take *fedayeen* kin or leaders as their models.

63. A school director in Bourj al-Barajneh camp.

64. W. Khalidi, 'Thinking the Unthinkable: A Sovereign Palestine State', *Foreign Affairs*, (June 1978).

65. The Rejection Front (*Jebha al-Rafed*) is made up principally of the P.F.L.P. and the A.L.F.

EPILOGUE

All stereotypes — the images we have of other people — are political to the extent that they justify positions and roles in a hierarchy. We can see this as clearly at the level of the family as in the so-called pluralist societies, and in the division of the world into 'advanced' and 'backward' peoples. Today, long-established stereotypes are being gradually eroded as people become more conscious of their oppressive function, but some groups still remain their victims. Amongst these, until recently, were the Jews; and still today, the Palestinians. Indeed Palestinian history from the beginning of this century has been a case-study in the political use of images.

By early Zionists, Jewish and Christian, the people of Palestine were hardly perceived at all. In this extreme type of settler colonialism, focus was so firmly fixed upon the habitat that it automatically excluded the inhabitants: Nordau's famous slogan was 'A land without a people for a people without a land'. This fantastic notion of Palestinian non-existence paved the way for another, that of British imperialism; from Lord Balfour onwards, the British defined Palestine's indigenous population as the 'non-Jewish communities'. They were recognized merely as resident in Palestine, possessing minimal civic and religious rights as Muslims, Christians and Druzes, but not as a people. In this definition, both their Arabism and their Palestinianism were denied to suit Britain's imperial interests.

In Palestine as in other Third World areas, the 'backwardness' of the indigenous people was used by the settlers to justify their displacement. Arab Palestinians were represented in Zionist and pro-Zionist writing as primitive, uneducated, uncivilized and fanatical. There was no disinterested effort to understand their culture and social organization. If at all, they were viewed as decadent descendants of earlier civilizations. The comment of T.E.Lawrence, on a student walking tour through Galilee in 1909, is typical: 'The sooner the Jews farm it all, the better; their colonies are bright spots in the desert.'[1] Blind belief in the superiority of Europe prevented British imperialist and Zionist colonizer alike from seeing that the poverty of Palestine's peasants was politically caused, and that their agricultural methods and social relationships together formed an admirable mechanism for survival in a harsh environment. Medieval religious intolerance also played its role: Christian missionaries were at one with Zionist Jews in both despising and fearing Islam.

After 1948 the stereotype constructed around Palestinians changed again. Now the world saw them as 'Arab refugees', holding out tin plates for U.N.R.W.A. rations. Linked to an older European image of all Arabs as nomads, the 'refugee' stereotype effectively obscured their rootedness in Palestine and deepened the idea of their poverty. The media relied on a few over-worked adjectives in describing the refugee camps: 'seething with bitterness', 'squalid', 'desolate', 'soul-destroying idleness'. Palestinian children were described as 'nurtured on hatred'. Few journalists ever penetrated beyond the sample camp home selected by the local U.N.R.W.A. representative. None stayed. Yet to remain alive and sane, year after year, in conditions like these, required qualities of endurance that deserved to be celebrated, not ignored.

The rise of the Resistance Movement after 1967 gave birth to a new stereotype: instead of 'refugees', Palestinians now became 'terrorists'. Few newspaper readers remembered that Palestinians were themselves the victims of terrorism. Few could imagine the conditions (political and material) out of which the Resistance arose. Even fewer rejected the false distinction between state terrorism ('military action') and revolutionary terrorism. Palestinian violence was, and continues to be, condemned by the same media that draw a veil over the past of men like Begin, Allon, or Lahis; and seldom cover in depth the deportation of Palestinians from Israeli-occupied territory, or their treatment in Israeli prisons, or their exploitation on Israeli farms and factories. If ever it is mentioned, Israeli violence is subtly excused by setting it in a framework of the persecution of Jews in Europe. The Holocaust is irrelevant to Palestine; yet Palestinian violence, which is a direct reaction to expulsion from Palestine, is seldom correctly analysed by reference to its local roots.

Politically, the new Palestinian image as 'terrorists' has been exploited by all parties interested in reinforcing the *status quo* in the Middle East to justify their refusal to recognize the rights of the Palestinians as a people, in the land of their origin. Israel offers them no choice except between non-existence or struggle. Their lack of militancy between 1948 and 1967 brought them no nearer peaceful repatriation; now their militancy is used by Israel to justify its own continuing aggression. The cycle is a familiar one in settler societies; and only when Israel is correctly analysed as a settler society will Palestinian violence be correctly understood. And only then will progress be made towards breaking the cycle.

For the 'terrorist' image is as false as those used against Jews by anti-Semites. Like the Jews before Zionism, Palestinians are not a warlike people, and history records no aggression on their part. On the contrary, all descriptions of them before the British/Zionist occupation show them as peaceful, warm-hearted, hospitable to strangers. Even now, in spite of

the extreme degree of their victimization by the Zionist state, there is no
deep hatred of the Jewish people among camp Palestinians. It was a
laundry worker, whose education was cut short at the age of twelve by the
Uprooting, who said these words, so much more humane and civilized
than any so far uttered by Israel's leaders:

> 'We know that Israel exists, we don't want to throw the Jews into
> the sea. We don't want to die, we want to live. We want to live, and
> we want others (i.e. Israelis) to live. But we don't want others to
> live, and us to die.'

NOTE

1.   D. Stewart, *T.E. Lawrence*, (Hamish Hamilton, London, 1977), p.48.

GLOSSARY OF ARABIC WORDS

Note on transliteration: Arabic uses sounds not easily conveyed in English script, except through cumbersome hieroglyphs recognizable only to Arabists. I have adopted a simplified system, in which both the guttural *'ayn* and the glottal stop *hamzeh* are represented by ', and listed under the vowel that follows them. I have made no attempt to distinguish between Arabic's dual forms of d, h, s, and t.

s = singular; p = plural; m = masculine; f = feminine.

'aataba: a form of singing usual in villages.
ahlan wissahlan: words used in welcoming visitors to the home. A contraction whose literal meaning is, 'You have come to your folk and tread on level (i.e. easy) ground.'
'a'ileh: the most common word for 'family'. Though *bedouin* and anthropologists distinguish several different levels of family organization (e.g. *hamuleh*, *qabila*, *'ashireh*) the only one of these in force among peasant Palestinians is the *hamuleh*. Camp Palestinians generally use *'a'ileh* both for the household based family and the larger network of kin.
Allahu akbar: 'God is greatest', the opening words of the Call to Prayer.
'arak: an alcoholic drink made from grapes, flavoured with aniseed, like absinthe.
arakeesh: a kind of pizza eaten in Palestinian and Lebanese villages.
'atwi: formal reconciliation, reached through arbitration, between feuding groups or families.
a'yan: the upper class, privileged through titles, landed estates and traditional offices, in certain cases possessing genealogies going back to the Arab Conquest.

bamieh: okra.
bedawi (s), *bedouin* (p): nomads, distinguished from peasants by their pastoral economic basis, and somewhat different social organization and

culture.

bedouin: see *bedawi* above.

beit: house, home, often used as a synonym for family.

bseesi: a kind of cake made in Palestinian villages.

burghul: a wheat product much used by Arab peasants living in wheat-growing areas. The grain is boiled, then dried and ground to various degrees of fineness.

dar: house, home (like *beit*, often used for the family who inhabits it).

debkeh: a village dance performed by groups of men or women, strongly associated with weddings.

diwan: originally a 'place for sitting', it came to mean a meeting, social or political in purpose. In Palestinian village/camp life it means the informal gatherings of neighbours and kin which take place daily, usually after work.

dunum: four *dunums* = 1 acre; 10 *dunums* = 1 hectare.

'eed (s), *'iyad* (p): feast(s).

fareeki: green wheat grains, lightly roasted.

faz'a: the collective village response to external threat (derived from *faza'a*, to rush).

fedai (s), *fedayeen* (p): those who sacrifice themselves for a cause.

fellah (s), *fellaheen* (p): peasant(s).

felsifeh: literally 'philosophy', but used in everyday speech to satirize those who show off by using long words.

ghareeb (s), *ghuraba'* or *gharaeb* (p): stranger(s). Villagers used to use the word for anyone not from their village, but this usage is fading with the growth of Palestinian nationalism.

ghourba: a state of exile and alienation (related to *ghareeb*). The Palestinian equivalent of the Jewish diaspora.

hajj (m), *hajji* (f): one who has made the pilgrimage to Mecca that all Muslims are supposed to make at least once in their lifetime. *Hajj* is also used for the pilgrimage itself and Palestinians have adopted it for visits to Occupied Palestine.

hamuleh: the patrilineal descent group, males related to the fifth degree by descent from a common ancestor, bound by ties of mutual solidarity.

hara: quarter of a village or a camp, composed of families linked either by blood or marriage.

harrat: ploughman.

hijra: literally 'emigration', used by camp Palestinians in reference to the flight from Palestine. Also used of the Prophet's flight from Mecca to Medina.

imam: an unofficial Muslim prayer leader.

jebel (s), *jibal* (p): mountain(s).
jeel: see Chapter 1, Note 5.
jihad: holy war. Originally a war of Muslims against non-Muslims, the term was appropiated by anti-imperialist Arab nationalist struggles, like those of the Palestinians and the Algerians.

khameesa: the code through which members of a *hamuleh* to the fifth degree of relationship (*khamsa* = five) were obliged to avenge, or pay blood money, on behalf of one of their number.
khan: a room in a village where travellers stay overnight.
khirbeh: literally 'ruins', in Palestine a ruined or deserted village in the plains re-colonized by villages in the hills.
korbaj: a short leather whip sometimes carried by Lebanese police in the camps. A Turkish survival, like beating on the feet.
kussa: a raised part of a village's central square.
kuttab: Koranic school.

lebneh: a cream cheese made from *leban* (yoghurt), widely eaten for breakfast throughout the Arab world.

mahr: the brideprice, a sum decided at the time of contracting a marriage and written into the official document of engagement. Traditionally paid to the father of the bride, the *mahr* today is either overlooked, or given to the bride to furnish her home.
mahwa: a public space, or square, where villagers gather.
makhateer: see *mukhtar*.
maku awamer: Iraqi dialect for 'There are no orders'. There were many Iraqis in the A.L.A., which may be why the villagers recall the A.L.A.'s usual response to requests for help in this form.
mallak (s), *mallaakeen* (p): landowner(s).
masha': an ancient form of village land tenure. There were different forms of *masha'*, some more egalitarian than others. Either village land would be reapportioned periodically among its families in relation to the size of their holdings. Or non-cultivatable land would be open to all villagers for grazing, wool-gathering, etc.
meyjana: a type of song sung in Palestinian villages.
miri: state land.
mudafeh: guest-house. Each *hamuleh* would maintain at least one *mudafeh*, often more. They were open to members of the village as well as travellers and official missions. The size of gatherings would indicate the popularity of the family head.
mudeni (s), *mudeniyeen* (p): city-dweller(s).
mufti: highest level of Muslim religious dignitary, interpreter of Koranic

law and ethics, with political as well as religious influence.

mujahid (s), *mujahideen* (p): related to *jihad*, this was the term given to guerrilla fighters both in Palestine and in Algeria. Most of the *mujahideen* were peasants.

mukhtar (s), *makhateer* (p): village headman, the lowest level of administrative official, unpaid. Most villages had more than one *mukhtar*, who would be chosen to represent sects and clans present in the village.

musakhkhen: a dish of baked chicken covered with sliced onions, olive oil and spices and cooked in special mud ovens.

muwwahadi: a stage in the Arab educational system, higher than the *towijihiyyeh*.

muwazzef (s), *muwazzefeen* (p): employee, minor official.

nashat: activity. The adjective *nasheet* is much used by camp Palestinians in praise of those who undertake any form of political or social action.

(q)abady: s strong man (in politics, a ward boss or politician's henchman).

qadi: judge.

qaimaqam: district officer. (Many administrative forms set up by the Turks are still used in the Arab countries.)

qareeb (s), *qaraeb* (p): a relation, someone who is near.

(q)ursa: a kind of cake eaten in Palestinian villages.

rujuliyyeh: manliness, courage.

sahel (s), *suhool* (p): plain(s).

sahja: the ceremony of leading a bridegroom round a village, literally 'clapping'.

sanjak: see Chapter 1, Note 15.

semneh: butter, made from sheep's milk, much used in Arabic cooking.

shaheed (s), *shuhada'* (p): one who witnesses, a martyr for a cause.

shebb (s), *shebab* (p): young man/men, usually unmarried, the category on which villages depended for defence.

sheikh (s), *shuyookh* (p): old man/men, a local leader, or someone who gives religious instruction A term of respect.

Shi'ite: member of a sect of Islam who believe that the Caliphate should have descended on the principle of heredity, not, as it did, on the principle of group consensus. In most parts of the Arab world, Shi'ites are a minority, excluded from power and wealth, often peasants, thus potentially anti-*status quo*.

shuyookh: see *sheikh*.

sibha: Muslim prayer beads.

simsar: an agent or go-between (usually pejorative).

suhoor: the pre-dawn breakfast taken during the month of the fast of Ramadan.

Sunni: The mainstream sect of Islam, more powerful politically than Shi'ism in most parts of the Arab world, generally the orthodoxy of city dwellers and itself divided into different doctrinal schools.

taboon: the mud oven used in villages for cooking meat dishes like *musakhkhen*.

tarboosh: the red felt hat with a black tassel, a vestige of Turkish rule, now dying out. It is worn by city dwellers, in contrast to the peasant and *bedouin keffiyeh* (headscarf) which has become the symbol of the Palestinian Resistance Movement.

tfaddal: an Arab meeting any acquaintance near his home always uses this word to invite the acquaintance to enter. Not to do so is unfriendly and impolite.

towijihiyyeh: an examination roughly equivalent to British 'O' levels, used in Egypt, Syria, Iraq and other Arab countries, but not in Lebanon.

towteen: implantation, used of plans to settle Palestinians outside Palestine.

'umma: the (Arab) nation.

ustadh: title of respect, usually used of teachers.

waasta: a mediator, someone who can procure favours from those in authority.

wajih (s), *wujaha'* (p): notable, leading member of a family.

wali: the governor of a province in the Ottoman system, now in disuse. The *wilayat* was the area of the *wali*'s authority.

waqf: land donated to, and administered by, the Muslim community through its local institutions. Under one kind of arrangement *waqf* land continued to be cultivated by the donor family and could not be alienated from it. In another, *dhurri*, its proceeds belonged to the Muslim establishment.

watan: the homeland. A patriot is described as *watani*.

wujaha': see *wajih*.

zalabi: a kind of cake made in Palestinian villages.

POLITICAL GLOSSARY

A.H.C.: Arab Higher Committee, formed in April 1936, a few days after the beginning of the General Strike, representing the five 'legal' national parties. Like the earlier Arab Executive Committee, the A.H.C. aimed at unifying and controlling the national movement. The Mufti (Hajj Amin Hussaini) headed the A.H.C. from its establishment, on into exile; both continued to be viewed by the Arab League and Arab Governments as the legitimate representative of the Palestinians. Official statements and documents continued to be issued by the A.H.C. until the formation of the P.L.O. in 1964.

A.L.A.: Arab Liberation Army, a pan-Arab force recruited to fight in Palestine in 1947-48, led by a professional soldier of Lebanese origin, Fawzi Qawukji.

A.L.F.: Arab Liberation Front, a Palestinian resistance group backed by the Iraqi Ba'thist Government.

A.N.M.: Arab Nationalist Movement. Springing directly from the 1948 defeat, the A.N.M.'s first cell was formed in Lebanon by Palestinians, and spread rapidly to other parts of the eastern Arab area. Its founders were students and intellectuals from the middle and lower middle classes, but it gained members in the camps, even though overshadowed by Nasserism, to which it remained close until the early Sixties. After 1967 the A.N.M. diverged radically from the broad stream of Arab nationalism (which was becoming more conservative), with Palestinians forming their own separate branch, the P.F.L.P. (see below), or *al-Jebha al-Sha'biyyeh*, led by George Habash. Divorce from Nasserism crystallized around armed struggle, and the P.F.L.P.'s conversion to a Marxist-Leninist position on class conflict.

Ashbal (plural of *shibl*): literally 'lion cubs', the Fateh-directed out-of-school training programme for children, part military, part political, with an emphasis on nationalist elements lacking in the official school programme. Girls also participate.

'Asifa: the Storm, Fateh's military wing.

Ba'th: A pan-Arab nationalist movement, with socialist elements, originating in Damascus in the early Forties. After the 1948 defeat it steadily gained adherents, particularly amongst students and the new intelligentsia. Gaining power in Syria and Iraq with the support of Nasserists and Communists, Ba'thists succeeded in suppressing their radical rivals in both countries, but split into two factions: the Regional Command taking control of Syria in 1970, under the leadership of Hafez al-Asad, while the National (pan-Arab) Command remained in power in Iraq. Like most Arab political movements, the Ba'th is not working class or peasant in its origins and leadership, but has a strong social and economic development programme as part of its 'renaissance' ethos (*ba'th* = resurgence, renewal).

Dar al-Fata: A publishing house linked to the P.L.O. that specializes in books for children.

Democratiyyeh: Sometimes used for the P.D.F.L.P. (see below).

D.B.: Deuxieme Bureau, the Intelligence section of the Lebanese Army, created by President Chehab as a control instrument after the civil war of 1958. The D.B. was directed as much against powerful Lebanese politicians as against dissident groups, but it was particularly harsh with the Parti Populaire Syrien, Communists and active Palestinians.

Fateh: An acronym formed from the initials of Harakat al-Tahreer al-Watani al-Falasteeni (H.T.F.), the Movement of Palestinian National Liberation, the largest group within the Palestinian Resistance Movement (P.R.M. — see below), combining a wide range of ideological currents united round the belief in armed struggle. A national liberation movement first and foremost, Fateh preaches the postponement of class (or any other internal) conflict until after liberation. Relatively discreet in its criticisms of the Arab governments.

F.S.I.: Forces de Securite Interieure, the Lebanese police force, comprising several different sections.

Futuwwa: A youth movement, founded by the political leader Jamal Hussaini (related to the Mufti) to counteract the Najjadat, a youth movement linked to the pro-British, pro-Hashemite Nassashibi faction. Both were a reaction to the Zionist Movement's mobilization of youth in paramilitary organizations, as well as reflecting the ardent political activism of Palestinian youth which made political leaders eager to recruit them.

G.U.P.S.: General Union of Palestinian Students. Like the General Union for Palestinian Women, G.U.P.S. has been more active in the political and informational field than in work amongst the masses.

G.U.P.W.[1]: General Union of Palestinian Workers. A descendant of the Arab Palestinian League of Workers, it was founded in Haifa in 1925, re-established secretly in Lebanon in the Fifties, and enabled to organize openly after the Revolution of 1969. It has offices in most Arab countries except those, like Saudi Arabia, that do not tolerate workers' unions. It also has branches in Australia, West Germany, and Scandinavia.

G.U.P.W.[2]: General Union of Palestinian Women. Before the Revolution this Union conducted small handicraft projects to aid the refugees. Since 1967 it has been active in representing Palestinians in the International Women's Movement. Its activities in the camps have been limited by the lack of an active mass membership.

(al-)Hillal al-Ahmar: the Red Crescent, the Arab equivalent of the Red Cross. The Palestinian Red Crescent was set up by the Resistance Movement as a national medical organization.

I.P.S.: Institute for Palestine Studies, (Beirut).

Jaysh al-Inqadh: sometimes translated Arab Liberation Army (A.L.A.), sometimes Rescue Army. **Jaysh al-Rikad,** the army that runs away, was the satiric name given to the A.L.A. by the Palestinian peasants.

Jaysh al-Jihad al-Muqaddes: The Army of Holy Struggle, the only purely Palestinian military force in Palestine in 1948, led by Abdul Qader Hussaini.

Jebha: Front (often used for the P.F.L.P.).

J.P.S.: Journal of Palestine Studies (Beirut).

(al-)Kifah al-musellah: armed struggle, also used for the Palestinian police force that moved into the camps in Lebanon after the Revolution of 1969.

(al-)Lijan al-sha'biyyeh: Popular (or People's) Committees set up in the camps to integrate the Resistance groups with the population. They also existed in Palestinian villages in the last years of the Mandate.

Mashreq: One of the five main regions of the Arabic-speaking area, it comprises Palestine, Lebanon, Syria, Jordan and Iraq. It is often referred to by English writers as the Fertile Crescent.

Mejlisiyeen: The colloquial term for the Mufti's followers, from *mejlis*, 'council'.

Mo'arideen: Colloquial term for the Nassashibi Defence Party, literally 'opposition'.

Najjadat: See **Futuwwa** above.

P.D.F.L.P.: Popular Democratic Front for the Liberation of Palestine. Led by Naef Hawatmeh, this is a splinter group that broke away from the P.F.L.P. in February 1969. While the P.D.F.L.P. advocated cutting relations with all the Arab regimes and basing armed struggle only on the masses, it subsequently allied itself closely with Fateh, and followed a pro-Moscow line.

P.F.L.P.: Popular Front for the Liberation of Palestine (or Jebha). Originating from the Palestinian branch of the A.N.M., the P.F.L.P., led by George Habash, has a strong mass base in Lebanon and rivals Fateh for leadership of the Resistance Movement, basing its claim less on mass following, than on a clear revolutionary ideology. Unlike the P.D.F.L.P., Jebha maintains relations with some Arab states (e.g. Libya and Iraq), which enables it to remain outside the main Fateh-P.L.O. framework.

P.L.A.: Palestine Liberation Army, established in 1964 soon after the setting up of the P.L.O. A regular army organized along the same lines as other Arab armies, with its own commando unit. Stationed mainly in Syria, Egypt and Iraq, it has seldom been able to play an effective role because of the greater popularity of the Resistance groups.

P.L.O.: Palestine Liberation Organization, founded in 1964, according to a decision taken by the Arab summit conference of January 1964 which failed to produce a plan to prevent Israel from diverting part of the River Jordan. This followed an earlier decision by the Arab League Council in September 1963, appointing Ahmad Shukairy as Palestinian representative at the Arab League. In May 1964, a Palestine National Congress, the first since 1948, elected Shukairy as Chairman of the Executive Committee of the P.L.O. The first Congress was held in

Jerusalem, under the patronage of King Hussain, but relations between Shukairy and Hussain quickly deteriorated, so that most later National Assemblies have been held either in Cairo or Damascus.

P.P.C.: Palestine Planning Centre, a subsidiary of the P.L.O.

P.P.S.[1]: Parti Populaire Syrien. In existence since the mid Thirties, this Party has always advocated unity of the Fertile Crescent area under Syrian leadership, ostensibly as a stage on the way to Arab unity, but in fact as a counter-weight to Egyptian predominance. Banned in Syria since the rise of the Ba'th party, its main stronghold has been in Lebanon since the mid Fifties. Noted for its emphasis on discipline, and admiration for the West, the P.P.S. has always been vulnerable to charges of incipient fascism. But since 1967 it has moved leftwards, and it took a prominent part in the Lebanese Civil War, contesting the Kataeb (right wing Christian) Party in areas of Christian predominance.

P.P.S[2]: Parti Progressiste Socialiste, a Lebanese leftist party formerly under the leadership of Kamal Joumblat, and directed by his son since his assassination in 1977.

P.R.C.: Palestine Research Centre (Beirut), a research and publishing organization funded by the P.L.O.

P.R.M.: Palestine Resistance Movement, not an organization but a general term that includes all the groups.

Sa'iqa: Set up by the Syrian Ba'thist regime, Sa'iqa (Thunderbolt) is militarily stronger than any Resistance group except Fateh, but has little mass following among Palestinians, and no mass mobilization or social/political training programmes. It is led by Zuhayr Mohsen and takes most of its recruits from amongst Palestinians living in Syria.

Samed: Essentially an attempt to compensate for Palestinians' lack of an independent economy, Samed is a mixture of capitalist financing and populist work organization. Re-established in Lebanon after the ending of P.R.M. action in Jordan, Samed now has 27 workshops in Lebanon, employing 2,400 workers, more than half of whom are women. Training courses for Samed workers are provided by friendly governments. Products include: uniforms for the *fedayeen*, civilian clothing, shoes, toys, Palestinian folklore items. It publishes a magazine for its workers, and conducts seminars and study cycles.

Sawt al-Arab: Voice of the Arabs, an Egyptian radio programme much listened to by Palestinians before their own *Sawt al-Falasteen* was set up, also in Cairo. *Sawt al-Arab* was strongly anti-imperialist and Arab nationalist in its presentation.

thawra: Means revolution. Used by Palestinians to mean their Resistance Movement.

BIBLIOGRAPHY

Abu-Lughod, I. (ed.) *The Transformation of Palestine*, (Northwestern University Press, Evanston, 1970).

Abu-Lughod, I. and Abu-Laban, B. (eds.) *Settler Regimes in Africa and the Arab World: the Illusion of Endurance*, (Medina Press, Wilmette, 1974).

Abu-Lughod, I. 'Educating a Community in Exile: the Palestinian Experience', *Journal of Palestine Studies (J.P.S.)*, (Spring 1973).

Abu-Lughod, I. 'Palestine Arabs in Israel' (a review article), *Middle East Research and Information Project*, *(MERIP)* No. 58, (1977).

Abu-Lughod, I. 'The Demographic Transformation of Palestine' in Abu-Lughod, (ed.), *op. cit.*

Aruri, N. (ed.) *The Palestinian Resistance to Israeli Occupation*, (Medina Press, Wilmette, 1970).

Asad, T. 'Anthropological Texts and Ideological Problems: an Analysis of Cohen on Arab Villages in Israel', *Review of Middle Eastern Studies*, No. 1, (Ithaca Press, London, 1975).

Asad, T. 'Class Transformation under the Mandate', *MERIP* No. 53, (1976).

Asfour, E. 'The Economic Framework of the Palestine Problem' in Polk, W., Stamler, D., and Asfour, E. *Backdrop to Tragedy*, (Beacon Press, Boston, 1957).

al-Asmar, F. *To be an Arab in Israel*, (Frances Pinter, London, 1975).

Aswad, B. 'The Involvement of Peasants in Social Movements and its Relation to the Palestinian Revolution', in Aruri, (ed.) *op. cit.*

Barboor, N. *Nisi Dominus, A Survey of the Palestine Controversy*, (Institute of Palestine Studies (I.P.S.), Beirut, 1969).

Beinen, J. 'The Palestine Communist Party 1919-1948' in *MERIP* No. 55, (March 1977).

Bell, J.Bowyer. *Terror out of Zion: Irgun Zvai Leumi, LEHI and the Palestine Underground, 1929-1949*, (St Martins Press, New York, 1977).

Canaan, T. 'The Palestine Arab House', *Journal of the Palestine Oriental Society*, Vols. xii, xiii.

Carre, O. *L'ideologie palestinienne de resistance* (analyse des textes 1964-1970), (Colin, Paris, 1972).

Chaliand, G. *The Palestinian Resistance*, (Penguin, Harmondsworth, 1972).

Chomsky, N. *Peace in the Middle East?*, (Vintage Books, New York, 1974).

Cooley, J. *Green March, Black September: the Story of the Palestinian Arabs*, (Cass, London, 1973).

Coudroy, R. *J'ai vecu la resistance palestinienne*, (Palestine Research Centre (P.R.C.), Beirut, 1969).

Davis, U. Mack, A. and Yural-Davis, N. (eds.) *Israel and the Palestinians*, (Ithaca Press, London, 1975).

Davis, U. *Israel: Utopia Incorporated?*, (Zed Press, London, 1977).

Dodd, P. and Barakat, H. *River without Bridges: a Study of the Exodus of the 1967 Palestinian Arab Refugees*, (I.P.S., Beirut, 1968).

Finn, E.A. *The Palestinian Peasantry: Notes on their Clans, Customs, Religions and Wars*, (Marshall, London, 1923). (Her notes were published by Mrs. Finn's pro-Zionist son long after her death.)

Firestone, Y. 'Crop-Sharing Economics in Mandatory Palestine, Parts 1 and 2', *Middle Eastern Studies*, Vol. ii, 1 and 2.

Francos, A. *Les Palestiniens*, (Juillard, Paris, 1968).

Granott, A. *The Land System in Palestine*, (Eyre and Spottiswoode, London, 1952).

Granqvist, H. *Marriage Conditions in a Palestinian Village*, (Societas Scientiarum Fennica, Helsinki, 1931-35).

Granqvist, H. *Birth and Childhood among the Arabs: Studies in a Muhammadan Village in Palestine*, (Soderstrom, Helsinki, 1947).

Granqvist, H. *Child Problems among the Arabs*, (Soderstrom, Helsinki, 1950).

Granqvist, H. *Muslim Death and Burial*, (Soc. Sci. Fenn,, Helsinki, 1965).

Grant, E. *The People of Palestine*, (Hyperion Press, Westport, 1976) (originally published 1921).

Hirst, D. *The Gun and the Olive Branch*, (Faber, London, 1977).

Jabber, F. 'The Palestinian Resistance and Arab Politics' in W. Quandt, F. Jabber, and A. Lesch, *The Politics of Palestinian Nationalism*, Rand Corp., University of California, 1973).

Jiryis, S. *The Arabs in Israel*, (Monthly Review Press, New York, 1976) (first published in English by the I.P.S., Beirut).

Kadi, L. *Basic Political Documents of the Armed Palestinian Resistance Movement*, (P.R.C., Beirut, 1969).

Kanafani, G. *The 1936-39 Revolt in Palestine*, (Committee for Democratic Palestine, Washington, 1978) (translated from Arabic).

Kanafani, G. *Men in the Sun* (a novel), (Heinemann, London, 1978).

Kayyali, A-W. *Palestinian Arab Reactions to Zionism and the British Mandate 1917-1939*, (PhD thesis, University of London, 1970; forthcoming with Croom and Helm, London, under the title *Palestine: A Modern History*).

Kenaana, S. 'Survival Strategies of Arabs in Israel', *MERIP* No. 41, (1975).

Khalidi, W., (ed.) *From Haven to Conquest: the Origins and Development of the Palestine Problem 1897-1948*, (I.P.S., Beirut, 1971).

Khalidi, W. and Khadduri, J. (eds.) *Palestine and the Arab-Israeli Conflict: an Annotated Bibliography*, (I.P.S., Beirut, 1974).

Khalidi, W. 'Plan Dalet: the Zionist Masterplan for the Conquest of Palestine, 1948', *Middle East Forum*, (Nov. 1961).

Kuroda, Y. 'Young Palestinian Commandos in Political Socialization Perspective', *Middle East Journal*, (Summer 1972).

Lees, G.R. *Village Life in Palestine; a Description of the Religion, Home Life, Manners, Customs, Characteristics and Superstitions of the Peasants of the Holy Land*, (Longmans/Green, New York, 1905).

Lesch, A. 'Palestinian Nationalism under the British Mandate' in Quandt, Jabber and Lesch, *op. cit.*

Mallison, T.W. and S.V. *An International Law Appraisal of the Juridical Characteristics of the Resistance of the People of Palestine*, (P.R.C., Beirut, 1973).

Mason, H. (ed.) *Reflections on the Palestine Crisis*, (Mouton, The Hague, 1970).

Ministry of Culture and Guidance, Iraq, *Poetry of Resistance in Occupied Palestine*, translated by Sulafa Hijjawi, (Baghdad, 1968).

Nakleh, K. 'Cultural Determinants of Palestinian Collective Identity; the Case of the Arabs in Israel', *New Outlook*, (Oct.-Nov. 1975).

Nazzal, N. *1948: the Palestinian Exodus from Galilee*, (PhD thesis, Georgetown University; in publication with the I.P.S., Beirut).

Nazzal, N. 'The Zionist Occupation of Western Galilee, 1948', *J.P.S.*, (Spring 1974).

Palestine Research Centre, *Village Statistics 1945: A Classification of Land and Area Ownership in Palestine* with notes by Sami Hadawi (a reprint of an official publication of the Government of Palestine), (P.R.C., Beirut, 1970).

Polk, W., Stamler, D. and Asfour, E. *Backdrop to Tragedy*, (Beacon Press, Boston, 1957).

Quandt, W., Jabber, F. and Lesch, A.M. *The Politics of Palestinian Nationalism*, (Rand Corporation, University of California, 1973).

Rodinson, M. *Israel and the Arabs*, (Penguin, Harmondsworth, 1968).

Samed, A. 'The Proletarianization of Palestinian Women in Israel, *MERIP* No. 50, (1976).

Sayigh, Y. 'The Scarcity of Land: the Fact and the Problem' a report prepared as part of the Arab case for the Anglo-American Commission of Inquiry, (Feb. 1947).

Sayigh, Y. *Implications of U.N.R.W.A. Operations*, (MA thesis, the American University of Beirut, 1952: later published by the Pakistan Institute for International Affairs, Karachi).

Schleiffer, A. *The Fall of Jerusalem*, (Monthly Review Press,

New York, 1972).

Seoudi, Mona, (ed.) *In Time of War: Children Testify* (Drawings by Palestinian children), (Mawakef Press, Beirut, 1970).

Shahak, I. *The Israeli League of Human and Civil Rights* (the Shahak Papers), (NEEBII, Beirut, undated).

Shammout, I. *Palestine: an Illustrated Political History*, (Information section, Palestine Liberation Organization, Beirut, 1972).

Sharabi, H. *Palestine and Israel: the Lethal Dilemma*, (Pegasus, New York, 1969).

Sharabi, H. *Palestine Guerrillas: Their Credibility and Effectiveness*, (I.P.S., Beirut, 1970).

Shoufani, E. 'The Fall of a Village', *J.P.S.* (Summer 1972).

Sirhan, B. *Palestinian Children: the Generation of Liberation*, (P.R.C., Beirut, 1970).

Sirhan, B. 'Palestinian Refugee Life in Lebanon', *J.P.S.*, (Winter 1975).

Stetler, R. (ed,) *Palestine; The Arab-Israeli Conflict*, (A Reader) (Ramparts Press, San Francisco, 1972).

Trabulsi, F. 'The Palestine Problem; Zionism and Imperialism in the Middle East', *New Left Review*, No. 57.

Turki, F. *The Disinherited; Journal of a Palestinian Exile*, (Monthly Review Press, New York, 1972).

Waines, D. *A Sentence of Exile; the Palestine/Israel Conflict 1897-1977*, (Medina Press, Wilmette, 1977).

Zahlan, A. and Hagopian, E. 'Palestine's Arab Population', *J.P.S.*, (Summer 1974).

Zureik, E. *The Palestinians in Israel, a Study in Internal Colonialism* (forthcoming, Routledge and Kegan Paul, London).

Zureik, E. 'Transformation of Class Structure among the Arabs in Israel', *J.P.S.*, (Autumn 1976).

RECOMMENDED SOURCES

In Arabic: *Shu'oon Falastiniyyeh* (Palestinian Affairs), published monthly by the Palestine Research Centre, carries the best documented and most scholarly articles, with strong emphasis on the Resistance Movement.
Al-'Ard, published monthly in Damascus, carries research articles mainly based on press reports, with particular emphasis on Occupied Palestine.

In English: *The Journal for Palestine Studies*, published quarterly by the I.P.S., Beirut, has established itself firmly as a source of information about Palestinians, with useful sections on the Hebrew Press, documents and source material, the Arab press, reprints from the foreign press, and book/periodical reviews and listings.

Middle East Research and Information Project (*MERIP*), published from Washington by a radical collective, has maintained a high standard of research articles from a Marxist standpoint.

The Unified Palestinian Information Office in Beirut publishes *al-Thawra* (daily, Arabic) and *Palestine* (bi-monthly, English).

USEFUL ADDRESSES

Al-Thawra/Palestine: P.O. Box 145168, Beirut, Lebanon.
Journal of Palestine Studies: P.O. Box 19449, Washington D.C. 20036, U.S.A.
MERIP: P.O. Box 3122, Washington D.C. 20010, U.S.A.
Shu'oon Falastiniyyeh: P.O. Box 1691, Beirut, Lebanon.